SAINT CATHERINE OF SIENA

SAINT CATHERINE OF SIENA

BY

ALICE CURTAYNE

TAN BOOKS AND PUBLISHERS, INC.
Rockford, Illinois 61105

Nihil Obstat
THOMAS McLAUGHLIN, S.T.D.
CENSOR DEPUTATUS

Imprimatur
EDM: CAN: SURMONT
VIC. GEN.

WESTMONASTERII,
12 *Martii* 1929

Originally published in 1929 by Sheed & Ward, Ltd., London. Reprinted by Sheed & Ward, Ltd. twice in 1929, twice in 1931, 1932, 1934, 1938 and 1942.

Library of Congress Catalog Card Number: 80-53745

ISBN: 0-89555-162-4

Printed and bound in the United States of America

TAN BOOKS AND PUBLISHERS, INC.
P. O. BOX 424
Rockford, Illinois 61105

1980

CONTENTS

PREFACE

IN THIS sixth centenary of St. Catherine of Siena's death, it is a joy to welcome this new edition of Alice Curtayne's splendid biography. In 1939 a copy of the seventh edition came into my hands, and I remember how profoundly it moved me, and how it deepened my appreciation of the nature and meaning of the spiritual life.

Catherine, the twenty-fourth of the twenty-five children whom Lapa Benincasa bore to her husband, lived only thirty-three years, but she changed the course of world history, and will be loved and admired until the end of time for her wisdom and sanctity.

Her life easily divides into two periods. God favoured her from early childhood with special intimacy and high mystical graces. When she was about nineteen He admitted her to the mystical espousals, giving her a ring in the presence of the Blessed Virgin and many angels and saints. This was the climax of the first period.

Soon after, the Saviour asked her to emerge from the solitary and strictly contemplative life in which, under His direction, she had lived until then. Being a tertiary of St. Dominic, Catherine therefore began to devote much of her time to tending the sick in the hospitals, as well as to other works of charity.

The manifest operation of the Gifts of the Holy Spirit in Catherine, and especially the public ecstasies and levitations which began at this time, produced a phenomenal effect among the populace. It also brought a measure of persecution, slander, charges of hysteria and hypocrisy, but she serenely triumphed over all, and a band of faithful disciples gathered around her. Not a few learned and saintly men were among them, such as Blessed Raymond of Capua, who served as her confessor-director, and eventually became Master General of the Dominican Order.

When, some time later, a terrible plague struck Siena, Catherine lavished loving care on the sick and the dying, and buried the dead with her own hands. This and other things endeared her so much to her fellow citizens that they have preserved her father's house in good condition until the present day. There one may visit the tiny room which was her cell during the contemplative period.

In her active life she soon became famous as a peacemaker among warring Italian families. This in turn led to gradual involvement in the problems of the Church, especially those which arose from the incessant wars and intrigues of the Italian city-states. Before long she was in direct contact with the Pope, and with cardinals, bishops and secular princes. Although many of her astute political efforts and eloquent letters failed of their immediate aim (and there is a spiritual lesson here), she rendered the Church an immense service by persuading the Pope to move back to Rome from Avignon, where for two generations the papacy had been under the dominance of the French monarchy.

At all times and wherever she went grace flowed from Catherine's person like rivers of living water, drawing souls back to God or closer to Him. Three Dominicans had to be appointed to go wherever she travelled in order to shrive the streams of sinners who wanted to confess. When she went to Pisa in 1375, her very presence brought about a religious revival in that city. She is a perfect example of the spiritual power and radiation which attach to a soul totally immersed in God and responsive to the most delicate movements of the Holy Spirit. Catherine bore the stigmata during life (they became visible after her death), and all her immense labours, journeys and sufferings were supported in a frail, weak body. During her last years she lived principally from the Holy Eucharist. Other food made her ill.

This new edition of Alice Curtayne's sensitive life is timely for many reasons other than the centenary of Catherine's death: it contains lessons and warnings for certain groups and movements of our time.

For example, the "charismatic movement". Catherine is a concrete illustration of the never-to-be-forgotten truth that the Holy Spirit breathes *only* where He wills (cf. John 3:8-9), and that no one can attain high development of the gifts of the Holy Spirit without first passing through rigorous purifications in the furnace of suffering, humiliation and self-denial. No one can by-pass Calvary on the way to a glorious resurrection.

Today we hear prominent "theologians" and Scripture scholars claiming to be "Catholic", but who openly deny the infallibility of the Pope or other defined dogmas, and at the same time implicitly claim infallibility for themselves. They base this stance on their supposed "expertise" or learned "research". Such as these will find in Catherine a stunning lesson if they reflect that she who never had any formal education, could not read or write, never did any "research" or published a thesis — a woman, who died so young, has been proclaimed Doctor of the Church. We know that her sublime *Dialogue,* dictated in ecstasy as Alice Curtayne so vividly describes in this book, will be read until the end of time with great profit to souls.

Today we have the phenomenon of some women clamouring for "liberation" from the natural law and the role in human life manifestly imposed on them by God's will. These can learn from Catherine that *ubi Spiritus Dei, ibi libertas* (2 Cor. 3:17). Where the Spirit of God is, only *there* is true liberty. The same Spirit says: "This thought of yours is perverse; as if the clay should say against the potter . . . 'You did not make me'. Or the thing framed should say to him that fashioned it: 'You do not understand' (Is. 29:16). Does the object moulded say to him who moulded it: 'Why have you made me thus?' " (Rom. 9:20).

Then today we have the social activists, who twist the Gospel into a call for revolution, no weapons barred, and an all-out effort to establish a man-centred utopia on earth. These can learn from Catherine's example that only a person whose own heart is over-flowing with true justice, truth, peace and love can spread these benefits among their fellowmen. They will learn that right counsels, just works and true peace can only come from God.

Priests of good will, distraught, anxious, harassed, fearful because of the disorders in the Church and world — these can learn from the *Dialogue* how to build in their souls a refuge where the Master is always ready to counsel, strengthen and console them; a refuge where they can dwell peacefully in spite of tribulation, persecution or distress of any kind.

Finally, we can all learn from Catherine the supreme truth which her Master stressed as the foundation of all: "I am He who is, and thou art she who is not", The whole spiritual life, in a sense, consists in a continual growth in the realization of what this means and implies, and, at the same time, *loving* it. It is the truth which the Saviour taught Paul: " 'My grace is sufficient for you, for strength is made perfect in weakness.' Glady therefore" — and Catherine would echo it — "gladly will I glory in my infirmities, that the power of Christ may dwell in me." (2 Cor. 12:9). And then there is that other passage which can so aptly be applied to Catherine: "Consider your own call, brethren, that there were not many wise according to the flesh, not many mighty, not many noble. But the foolish things of the world has God chosen to put to shame the wise, and the weak things of the world has God chosen to put to shame the strong; and . . . the despised has God chosen, and the things that are not, in order to bring to naught the things that are — lest any flesh should glory in His sight." (1 Cor. 1:26-29).

Father Urban Snyder
Feast of the Assumption of Our Lady, 1980.

HISTORICAL INTRODUCTION

CATHERINE BENINCASA's lifetime (1347 to 1380) covers that interval of change, during which the true and splendid Middle Ages merged into the definite period of their decline and decay.

Before she was a year old, a cataclysm swept over Europe in the form of a monstrous epidemic. Under the high, dappled sky of January 1348, three trading vessels from Caffa, on the Crimea, sailed into Genoa. They had fled before the plague, but brought it with them : something more sinister on board than a dead albatross. When it was discovered, they were chased out of port again, but not before they had thoroughly infected the city. Six-sevenths of the population were swept away, almost wiping out that great maritime republic. The stricken ships sailed out of the Gulf and at least one of them put in later at Marseilles, thus providing Europe with another source of death. Venice, too, harboured suspect ships about the same time. All Italy was ravaged by the disease. Then the malignant tongue of infection forked, darting across the Adriatic, to Hungary, Austria, Germany, Poland, and striking north into Switzerland. By the Spring, Spain too was full of the poison. Sicily, Sardinia, Corsica and the Balearic Islands were devastated. From Marseilles, the pestilence raced up the Rhone valley, through the Languedoc, to Flanders and Holland. It was in England by July, devouring London, almost depopulating Oxford and Cambridge. When the Scots heard of it, they thought it a convenient judgment of God on their enemies and invented a new oath : " *Be the foul deth of Engelond.*" But it swept over the Border too, bringing ruin to Scotland, Denmark, Norway and Sweden.

The effects of this catastrophe came slowly of course. The immediate survivors did not perceive any great change in the

world about them.   It was at least a quarter of a century before
the results began to tell.   They were, therefore, becoming
obvious when Catherine Benincasa was grown up.   Change was
then apparent everywhere.   After the Black Death, the feudal
system was no more ;   the vernacular languages sprang up
(England emerged from it, speaking English).   Dante and
Boccaccio illustrate the transition :   on one side of the bridge
of death, Dante almost apologizes for using the vernacular ;
he has to defend the novelty.   But in Catherine's day, Boccaccio
takes such use for granted.   The Renaissance began to stir,
making tense this epoch of transition.   Doubt disturbed the
serene faith of the true Middle Ages and spoke through every
medium of expression :   the more realistic painting, the complex
and ornate architecture, the thousand foppish fashions.

   The effect on the Church concerns us most.   The Black Death
shook it at a moment when it was ill-prepared.   The Papacy
had already lost prestige.   The dissolvent of plague completed
the evil begun by Philip IV of France.   This monarch, whose
cold, empty stare used to unnerve his courtiers, had been
absorbed all through his reign in his quarrel with Pope Boniface
VIII.   Without entering into the details of this historical
struggle, it is certain that the closing scene of it had a profoundly depressing effect on the Christian world.   Emissaries of
Philip (this queer grandson of St. Louis), one William de
Nogaret and Sciarra Colonna, with a mob of hired soldiers,
invaded the Papal palace of Anagni where the Pope was residing.
The somewhat intransigent Boniface bore himself with great
dignity.   A Florentine chronicler tells us that he waited im-
passively for the intruders, wearing all the Pontifical insignia and
seated on his throne.   Colonna burst in first and is said to have
struck the Pope with his mailed hand.   Dismayed despite himself
by the tiara, keys and cross, De Nogaret restrained his companion.   Boniface was kept a close prisoner for three days.   He
was then permitted to return to Rome, where he died a month
later of high fever brought on by the outrage.   Philip may be
said to have won.   Boniface's successor, Benedict XI, died

within a year and then the French king succeeded in having elected a friend of his own, Bertrand de Got, who was crowned at Lyons in 1305 and took up his residence at Avignon under the name of Clement V. The Papacy then became and remained for seventy years more or less an instrument in French hands, a fact which continued to exasperate the rest of Christendom. This Philip the Fair was extraordinarily tenacious in his hates. It is remarkable how he pursued the dead Pope beyond the grave. He pestered Clement for *six* years to have Boniface condemned as a heretic and an immoral priest, and to have his body exhumed and burned. Clement, so compliant in all else, resisted this stubbornly enough. But Philip did not cease until angry mutters began to rise against him throughout Europe and three Catalonian knights made a general challenge that they would defend the name of Boniface with their swords.

When the residence of the Popes in Avignon had become an established fact, the Black Death further injured the Church, by making impossible the continuance of its best traditions. In order to exist, monasteries and religious communities everywhere had to make up their numbers hastily by curtailing their usual careful training and selection of religious. The evil effects of this were lasting. Most of these groups never again recovered their former numbers and a great part of the new members, hurriedly gathered in, proved unsuitable and thus sapped discipline and impaired the perfection of community life. The same happened in the ranks of the secular clergy. In order that public worship might continue, very young and often uneducated clerics had to be ordained. At the same time, the old Church revenues were kept in force and this brought about a great growth in the already existing abuse of pluralities. Priestly prestige was lowered through this forced abandonment of the traditional standards and through irritation over the question of revenues.

The weakening of the Holy See's independence and the harm wrought in the Church by the Black Death, explain— sufficiently for our purpose—the state of ecclesiastical affairs which provoked the action of this story.

Catherine Benincasa, when hardly more than a girl, set out on the amazing venture of trying to restore to the Church some part of what it had lost. Before she died, she had become one of the most-discussed women of her day. All the crowned heads of Europe knew her. It was debated whether she was a fanatic, a witch, an impostor, or a saint. She contrasted sharply with all the women of her epoch who had provoked anything like the same general discussion. Therefore, to seize the rare novelty of her position, one must visualize these contemporary women who had won fame or notoriety, and see them grouped on the stage of history behind her.

The only one who the least resembled her in type and action was Saint Bridget of Sweden. It would be impertinent, as well as invidious, to attempt a comparison in sanctity, but one may point out the material difference in the position of the two women. Saint Bridget worked in a far more restricted sphere and not until she was of mature age, the mother of a large family. Further, she had the advantages of great rank and means and, as her marriage was most happy, she was helped by her husband. In her case, there was none of the sheer audacity, the harebrainedness which distinguished Catherine, who fought alone, with no weapons, save the spiritual.

There was no other woman whose name could be coupled with hers. Occasionally an ordinary woman distinguished herself by prowess in war : in a siege, or some such extremity, rising to physical heroism. Of course under the influence of the troubadours, of the first poets of the Renaissance, and in imitation of Dante's idealization of Beatrice, there was a large group of women famous as the Inspirers of Great Love, like Laura, Fiammetta, Becchina and the rest.

Last in the scale were the notorious for immorality. *Their* number was legion, but three principally were of European fame.

Philip IV of France had a daughter, Isabella, who inherited all his ruthless vindictiveness. She became the protagonist in the most odious episode in English history. She was married to Edward II before she was sixteen, and her hatred of her husband was remarkable. One of the King's rebellious nobles, Roger de Mortimer, was her lover. He had been imprisoned in the Tower by Edward, but escaped to France, where the Queen joined him. This pair returned to England as invaders in 1326. Edward fled with his favourite, but he was caught and asked to surrender the throne. He refused. He was, therefore, moved about from prison to prison, at his wife's pleasure, for nine months, exposed to every manner of hardship. His health withstanding the treatment, he was finally murdered. When Isabella's son attained his majority, he had his mother imprisoned. She was still alive in her manor in England, when Catherine Benincasa, at the age of fifteen, was already mapping out her course.

This Isabella had a young relative in Naples, Queen Joanna, who was a kind of twin soul. (It was a bad strain of blood.) She was beautiful. All these women were, more or less. Since they devoted their lives to the cult of the body, it would be odd if they had not succeeded in *that*. This Queen of Naples was particularly seductive and had the distinction of shocking the European courts, which were not easily scandalized. She, too, had been married at sixteen to her cousin, Andrew of Hungary. She detested him. One of her most notable intrigues was with Louis of Tarente, another cousin. The affair was made abominable by the fact that the mother of this Louis fostered it to the extent of her power, thinking it a good idea to get Andrew out of the way and make her own son King of Naples. This was done. One night, Andrew was strangled by one of his courtiers. Joanna thereupon married Louis and was later publicly (though never popularly) absolved from complicity in her first husband's murder. She had four husbands before her career was ended and no children. Finally, she was killed by her nephew, Charles ; smothered in a feather bed, it was said. She was at the height of her notoriety when Catherine was already famous. Their action conflicted and they resisted each other in a prolonged and formidable struggle.

Spain provided a similar example in Doña Leonora, the

mistress of Alfonso XI. People whispered about the awful
patience of his wife, Queen Maria of Portugal.   Not an inspiring
patience though, but repellent, like that of an animal, who
squats and waits. Unfortunately for Leonora, Alfonso died
first and then the Queen swooped on her rival. She got her
son to murder her. The hatred of these two lived on in their
children. It was the motive of the wars waged by Peter the
Cruel, who was ultimately assassinated by his step-brother.
When Catherine was a child, Leonora was busy spinning this
amazing web of evil.   For generations afterwards there seemed
to be no end to it.

Isabella of France, Joanna of Naples, Doña Leonora : an
unpleasant group. Consider them long and one is almost
ready to applaud John Knox's famous " First Blast of the
Trumpet against the Monstrous Regiment of Women." They
would have understood one another perfectly.   The influence of
their type was enormous. They were securely entrenched.

On all counts, therefore, Catherine's fame was unprecedented
and unique. To make Truth even audible in that confusion
of voices meant to prevail most powerfully. And around her a
silence fell. This pre-eminence made her final defeat all the
more spectacular. Subsequent history of course has reversed
this verdict of failure and vindicated her action. But the
judgment of later centuries must not obscure the truth that in
her own day, in the general view, she failed disastrously. Her
real story is one of overwhelming disgrace and disappointment.

PART ONE

CRUSADING

" It is the rule of God's Providence that we should succeed by failure."
—CARDINAL NEWMAN.

SAINT CATHERINE OF SIENA

CHAPTER I

AN UNUSUAL VOCATION

I

WHERE the three hills of Siena meet, there is an open space which must remain forever isolated from all squares in all other cities of the world. The Piazza del Campo is incredible. Semi-circular and concave, it is shaped like a shell and paved in segments with pale pink bricks through which the vivid grass appears in timorous blades. Under some aspects of the clear Tuscan sky, the illusion is perfect. In the last flush of daylight for instance, the pavement glows with a pearly lustre at the foot of the dim, steep streets converging on it. It waits for the descending pedestrian, as improbable as a fairy scallop. There is a stir of movement in its stones nearly as strong as in the straight Tower of the Mangia springing into the air beside it. It holds all the dead Republic's memories. That far-off liberty still resounds in it, like the freedom of the sea booming forever in a shell. All the history of old Siena is illuminated by that single word, liberty. The free commune was so turbulent as to bewilder us, but its sons had the fullest power of choice that men could aspire to. Their very turbulence is explained by their freedom. They gave authority to rule and as freely took it away when they considered it abused. They fully obeyed only when they trusted. One has ceased even to dream of such liberty to-day. Here, too, women occasionally soared into a freedom which makes modern feminism look foolish. They did not do it by suffrage or by adopting boyish dress, but by cutting the thongs of their own futility.

Of all the Sienese who have made history, Jacopo Benincasa was perhaps the most unconscious. He was a dyer, who prospered here about the middle of the fourteenth century. He should not, however, be confused with an artisan of to-day, with whom indeed he had nothing in common. Words rang truer in his time and the difference between an artist and an artisan had not yet so widened. He was proud to be absorbed in his work, as in an *art*. He lived in a roomy, detached house with a battlemented roof, such as the average professional man to-day would think pretentious to rent. His workshops were beside it and he owned a farm and vineyard outside the city for his own use. (He gave this property later to a daughter as her marriage dowry.) The vineyard supplied his wine cellar, which was a good one. Three of his sons helped him at his work and he also employed a number of apprentices, whom he ruled while he taught them all about colours and what dyes to mix for different textures. His wife, Monna Lapa, had twenty-five children of whom hardly half survived their infancy. But Benincasa had a great heart : he also adopted as his own son Thomas della Fonte, a boy of ten who had been left an orphan during the plague of 1348. He was in a position to give liberal charity all his life, without infringing on his children's rights. He could even be magnanimous : once he was prosecuted for a debt that was already paid. Condemned unjustly, he paid up again and never afterwards expressed the slightest resentment over the affair. He was great enough to forget it. This was sufficient to make people stare at him in the street, in a country and epoch when much smaller injuries were commonly made the pretext for an everlasting feud between families. No doubt all these actions were suggested by the Faith : that luminous and detailed philosophy of life, which can so easily give a man worth and dignity. Benincasa has passed into a wide literature for reasons which will be obvious later on. But he is described as " the poor dyer of Siena," or " the poor, humble dyer of Siena," with an insistence that may be misleading. He was not poor as we understand the word to-day. He was not humble in that spiritless sense in which Uriah Heep was humble : a fellow in an apron, rubbing his hands as he bowed his patrons out the door, would be a most distorted picture of him. His was deliberate Christian humility, *inspired from within*; not an attitude forced upon him by external circumstances. He was not self-conscious of low estate; he had not that craven spirit of the dispossessed and the powerless. For Jacopo Benincasa most emphatically had *status*.

True, he was of the people, but what of that in a society whose framework was so different from ours? Aristocratic birth or great wealth, *as such*, did not matter a straw to the Sienese of his day: what mattered most in every Italian republic was *power to rule*. To command men's actions and guide the commune's destiny, that was thought a splendid thing and that alone was bitterly envied. Lust for power was the really uncontrollable passion and the one constant motive in that period of bewildering changes. The only nobility envied was that which was invested with authority. Now, this coveted power was in the hands of the people at least forty years before Benincasa was born and continued so all through his lifetime. (The Government of the " Lords Nine " lasted for seventy years in Siena, practically excluding the nobles; the subsequent rule, of the " Twelve," was also by the people). He knew no other form of administration and therefore, to him, it was the accepted order of things. Being of the people, he had a definite voice in the government and there was then no stigma attached to the name plebeian. For instance, after the revolution of 1368, the Salimbeni (one of the oldest and wealthiest Sienese families) were rewarded for their services to the people by being declared " of the People " (*popolani*): *that is, eligible to rule*. Curious little ceremony with a hint of humour in it: like cupping the blue blood which produced disorders in the system. There was overwhelming precedent for this at Florence in 1343, when five hundred and thirty noble families were admitted to the burgher class. Their long lineage had become a positive encumbrance and it was wiped out as an act of favour on the part of the government.

Monna Lapa's father had won some fame as a poet. She

did not inherit any poetic imagination and she had the gift of words in an unfortunate way. It must be admitted she was a shrew. She was always so aggressively busy that it weighed uncomfortably on the whole family ; her outlook was so sourly practical that it was colourless and depressing. To " settle " her children—that is, to get her daughters married and make her sons independent as early as possible—was the single enterprise of her life. Any idea that did not bear on this supreme end was ruled out as nonsense. However, if she did not diffuse serenity, she ruled her large household effectively. Probably a gentler woman could not have done it. By her uncompromising precepts and tireless energy, she set her children an excellent Christian example. Compared with the Sienese *type* of her day, mostly women notoriously vain and shallow, the figure of Monna Lapa assumes almost an heroic grandeur.

This was the household to which their youngest child, Catherine, had to adapt herself. The little world to which she opened her eyes was all sunshine (for Monna Lapa, if shrewish, was a great mother). As she grew from infancy to childhood, she was so excessively merry that they thought her almost fey. They gave her the pet name of Euphrosyne because of that irrepressible gaiety. But too much stress need not be laid on this, nor the ideas of our own time read into the fourteenth century. The Benincasa were very remote from the adult generation that goes to " Peter Pan " expressly to weep. There was then no maudlin cult of childhood. To-day, in countries where large families are the rule, children are still taken for granted and left to fit into the existing scheme of things. The truth is that, despite the classical appellation, no-one took very much notice of Euphrosyne. She had no particular claim to beauty, unless indeed the hair which framed her pallid, eager little face. It was golden brown hair : the fashionable colour, because rare. Nearly all the Sienese women are dark and the elaborate recipes they used for bleaching the hair are still extant. We know from preachers who fulminated against them that married women often spent whole days on their balconies, with their hair spread out in the sun, to make it lighter in colour. For the rest, the affairs of Catherine's elder brothers and sisters claimed an attention which quite obscured her.

The big house in which she lived was built against a sharp incline. It had two doors in front : one gave access to the workshops, full of the odour of dyes and crowded with apprentices : the other opened on a staircase leading to the dwelling rooms. There was a fantastic touch about this staircase, because there was a back door at the top of it giving on to the level road ; so that what seemed the ground floor viewed from the back, was the first floor from the front. Through the back door, one entered Monna Lapa's kitchen on one side and a little terrace with a garden on the other side. The staircase indeed was the best coign of vantage to see all that was going on and Euphrosyne took possession of it. On it, she could fly from the wonders of one street to the magic of another ; from the mysteries of the workshop, to the kitchen, which was always interesting. Tremendous meals were prepared at the open hearth ; it was also the room in which the Benincasa dined, and the women sat there weaving, when evening came on. Catherine found other uses for the stairs : checking her childish devotions by saying as many Hail Marys as there were steps. For this, it was better than a rosary of beads. Sometimes she sped up and down so blithely, angels might have borne her. No doubt while Heaven still hung so visibly around her the staircase was a kind of Jacob's Ladder.

The next place Catherine knew, after her home, was the church of St. Dominic. It was a vast red-brick Gothic building on the hill of Camporeggi, five minutes distance from her door, dominating all the valley in which the dyers and tanners congregated. Its bell summoned them to worship God. It had been built in the time of St. Dominic ; the wise and humorous Aquinas had walked its nave. The friars in black and white who lived there were men of peace among a congregation always armed, always thinking of war and discussing war : war with a neighbouring republic, perhaps Florence or Perugia ; war between the different strata of Sienese society : nobles and burghers, or burghers and the very poor ; relentless, unceasing war between the five or six principal families of Siena. The precocious, impressionable child began to distinguish early : life up there in that building glowing warmly in the sunlight was ultimate, sane reality ; life down here in the valley was a fevered, futile delusion. It was the calm-faced priests who dominated the situation ; who really lived to some purpose ; not the heaving mass of the people, who sweated and fretted their little hours away. Catherine had also a powerful Dominican influence in her very home. Thomas della Fonte, the adopted son, had a vocation to the priesthood, and the Benincasa were helping him to be a Dominican. By the time Catherine could frame questions, he was revisiting them, a tall novice. He talked to her willingly, with a patience and knowledge her brothers did not possess. He told her with kindling eyes the great adventures of him whom she always called, " the sweet Spaniard." A little later, Della Fonte was ordained and sent to Camporeggi. In their gladness the family talked of nothing else for weeks. They had now a personal claim on the friars.

About this time, something mysterious happened. Catherine was returning home one day with her brother, Stefano. They had been visiting their married sister, Bonaventura. At a certain turn in the valley, St. Dominic swings suddenly into view, and the children were looking out for this sign that they were nearing home. Suddenly Catherine stood stock still, her eyes distended. The sky over the church was full of shapes and colours : a panoply that was not of any sunset. Stephen, who distinguished nothing, dragged her on impatiently. She took a dazed step or two, like one stricken blind ; then raised her eyes again, but the vision had gone. She burst into tears. Long afterwards, when pressed to explain what she saw, she stammered something about Christ having looked directly at her with a loving smile, blessing her in the manner of a priest. In whatever way the veil had been lifted, the effect on the child was profound and permanent. Though she was then only six years, the old legend says, almost grimly, " after that, she was no longer a child." At any rate, it was the end of Euphrosyne. The precipitous flights on the staircase faltered ; the elfin glee sobered into gravity. She went about with a listening air. And the dogs of the Lord—*Domini canes*—ceased to obsess her imagination, now that the pursuit of the very Hound of Heaven had begun.

2

Monna Lapa was the first to notice something wrong. She thought the child was moping, and took her in hand, as it were. Since the day of the vision, Catherine was tormented with a longing to be left alone to think even for the shortest time. But this was never allowed. She was harried from morning to night with small tasks and innumerable little errands, in which her mother's shrill admonitions followed her everywhere. Although perfectly obedient, a secret anguish swelled in her soul. That burning, unplacated desire made the material life in which her mother held her ruthlessly something choking and intolerable. She made bewildered little efforts to beat her way out : begging permission, for instance, to go to see Bonaventura, because her sister's house was a long way off and, in going and coming, she could appease to some extent her passion for prayer. Once she ran away to be a hermit and spent a whole day in a little cavern on the outskirts of the town. Those hours of peace were exquisite relief but, by divine intimation, she went back home in the evening, a forlorn little figure. Then she built a truly gorgeous castle in the air : she would follow in the footsteps of Thomas della Fonte, cutting off her hair and entering a monastery, disguised as a boy. With this dream, she assuaged the discomfort of several days. But never for a single instant did it cross her mind to end the suffering by being, quite simply, a nun. Meanwhile, Monna Lapa considered her often with a puzzled frown and concluded with a shrug : " She'll be all right

when we get her married." Indeed that word " marriage," the
only word that ever troubled Catherine's earliest years (being
always said when her hair was under discussion), was now
repeated over and over again in her presence. It began to
cause her the most acute apprehension.

In southern Italy to-day, and in Sicily, no daughter of a
respectable family is allowed to go out unaccompanied after the
age of twelve or fourteen. It was so in mediaeval Siena, only
then the convention was applied with the utmost rigidity.
Even the very lowest stratum of the people observed it scrupulously, as the most sacred duty to daughters. No girl of that
age was ever seen on the streets alone, in any circumstances
whatsoever. This meant that when Catherine reached the age
of twelve, her liberty was suddenly and completely curtailed.
Gone were the brief escapes to Bonaventura's house, or to St.
Dominic's. She could not henceforth go three yards from the
door, alone. All the girls of her acquaintance took this as a
matter of course, and indeed enjoyed it. They began to learn
every detail of housewifery, to wear pretty dresses and ornaments, and to wave their hair. Catherine did not want to
do any of these things, and she thought it terrible beyond
words when the walls of her father's house closed in upon her
relentlessly. Monna Lapa's energy became more than ever
exhausting ; her harangues more trying. Indeed, the mother's
discomfort began to explode frequently in harsh outbursts.
She complained about her constantly to the neighbours, and to
her married daughters, including Bonaventura, who was
Catherine's only confidante among her sisters. Instead of
blame, Bonaventura tried coaxing. She persuaded her young
sister into a promise of submission. Catherine shrinkingly
acquiesced in the process of adornment, and for the moment
there was a semblance of peace.

Then Bonaventura died unexpectedly, on the 10th of August,
1362, when Catherine was in her sixteenth year. It was her
first experience of death and her grief was poignant. While this
sorrow was still fresh, a chance remark at home made her heart

leap with panic. She heard the very name of her prospective suitor ; all his advantages were being discussed in detail. Catherine broke in on the family council, shaking with excitement. This time it was complete and absolute defiance : " I will not be married, I tell you all. No, No, NO."

Monna Lapa went to see Father Della Fonte to ask him to bring her daughter to reason. He walked down from Camporeggi, with a grin, half distaste, half amusement. He could not take Euphrosyne seriously as a rebel. But he found her desperately in earnest. From her passionate, disjointed defence, two things emerged : she would not get married, and they should leave her hair alone. The friar gravely agreed that it was unfair to force her into marriage. " Then, you must be a nun," he said, briskly. But No, she was just as emphatic about not doing that. She wanted to remain at home, and serve God in her own way. Here Della Fonte began to knit his brows : she was very sure of herself for one so young ; then this " via di mezzo " was unusual. It was always either marriage or a convent. He groped for a solution : " How can you stay on here and be an old maid ? People will laugh at you ? " Catherine was not dismayed at the prospect. " Well, who'll keep you when your parents are gone ? " " God will take care of me." Della Fonte shrugged, and began to think of his other engagements. Oh, then that hair ! The priest considered the shining tresses quizzically. " Cut it off," he said, jokingly, as he rose to go. " Then perhaps they'll know you mean business ". In his heart he wondered how far her resolution could be tested. He had hardly left the house before she followed his advice. Reckless of what might follow, she cut off all her hair clumsily, in jagged masses. Then, appalled at the ruin of her appearance, she covered her head with a veil, and waited for the storm to burst.

The scene that followed was painful. Monna Lapa shrieked when she saw Catherine (her one title to prettiness gone). She cursed. (In general, the language of the people was violent and Lapa's was exceptionally so.) Her brothers and sisters jeered—needless to say. Even indulgent Jacopo Benincasa was deeply offended. They all felt that Father Della Fonte had failed them completely, and that they must manage the girl themselves. Divining her one little luxury, the refuge of her own room, they decided to take it from her. Henceforth she must share with Stefano. Then Monna Lapa sent away the servant, and gave all the most menial work to Catherine. She was made serve the family at table, and no-one spoke to her, save to give orders. In short, they deliberately persecuted her, hoping that the very misery of her life would break her will. And they continued to assure her : " Your hair will grow again and you *shall* marry, even if it breaks your heart."

Some time passed, and the persecution abated in spite of themselves (they were secretly weary of it). The pariah was sweet-tempered and submissive, but her resolution remained unshaken. Indeed she did not seem to mind. Sometimes they glanced at her furtively, as she stood meekly by the table with the dishes, and they often saw her face transfigured. She looked as if she were enjoying a secret joke. Benincasa of course had a special affection for this poor Maggie Tulliver of the shorn locks. One day, entering Stefano's room unexpectedly, he surprised her praying. He withdrew hastily, as if he too had seen a vision. Acting on some sudden illumination, he decided to bring the domestic unhappiness to an end. On his orders Catherine was, as it were, released from Coventry. Her brothers and sisters were warned to leave her in peace. Supreme concession, she was given back her own room. It was tiny (only twelve feet by nine), with a red brick pavement, and one high window, approached by three steps. It contained no furniture save a coffer for her clothes and a bench. Such as it was, it was *hers*, and she ran back to it with the vehement joy of a prisoner suddenly set free.

Despite Benincasa's injunctions, however, Monna Lapa did not understand letting a young girl like that literally alone. Catherine soon found that the old bondage continued, only under a new guise. Where force had failed, her mother tried persuasion. One can understand, indeed, that under Lapa's spiky exterior was a generous, affectionate nature that was suffering. Now she overwhelmed her daughter with caresses (very distasteful to Catherine's growing consciousness). The girl was tortured by the old close companionship, the jealous supervision almost of her very thoughts. When Lapa suspected she was depriving herself of sleep, she insisted on sleeping with her. But night brought the only delicious moments of freedom. Small wonder that every time the mother woke, she found her daughter had slipped away. This too was prohibited. Then Lapa discovered Catherine had put a board under the sheet where she had to lie, and in the morning she would be there obediently, her eyes wide open, faint shadows under them. In the same way all her first attempts to fast were pursued and frustrated. She was taken for walks, and given little treats to distract her. In the Val d'Orcia, south of Siena, there were thermal springs, called the Baths of Vignone, reputed to cure disorders of the liver and stomach, and all kinds of nervous affections. It was a popular place of resort for the Sienese. Persuaded that Catherine's oddness had a physical origin, Lapa decided to take her there for a course of the baths. The girl had never been away from home before ; perhaps a change would effect an improvement—make her " normal " again. They set off. When Catherine for the first time saw the boiling water foaming into one end of the bath she stopped abruptly to look at it. It frightened her : an unusual sensation. She asked permission to bathe alone and she then went as near as possible to the bubbling source, at the risk of being scalded alive. Queer zest for pain—but she wanted to rise above terror of it, to contempt for it. Then she considered the shock her quivering flesh sustained. It must be something like the pain of Purgatory, and she would offer it up every day to help the souls there. That was making some sense out of the trip. Monna Lapa soon perceived that the treatment was not doing Catherine much good, rather exhausting her. She took her home again, and when they got to Siena, found Catherine had contracted small-pox. Lapa hung over her bed day and night, nursing her through it with the tenderest solicitude. And it was during one of the intimate talks which sickness occasions, that Catherine confided to her mother the desire which was growing stronger every day : she must join the Third Order of Saint Dominic. In other words, by inspiration, she had discovered a way of escape.

Here a momentary digression will be pardoned to explain the new move. When St. Dominic went sweeping through Europe on his mission, he found that one of the worst injuries offered the Church by states, was the frequent confiscation of Church property and tithes. He, therefore, rallied lay men and women to pledge themselves to the defence of ecclesiastical property and liberty. These recruits were called the Militia of Jesus Christ. They did not take religious vows, but aspired to lead exemplary Christian lives. Later, when Church property was less open to attack, and such a military organization therefore unnecessary, it persisted under the name of the Third Order of Penance. Still later, this order divided into the conventual and secular ; those members of it who lived in community taking solemn vows. The secular Third Order still exists to-day, but it is hardly more than a pious association, a shadow of what it was. Though implying real membership in the Dominican Order and enriched with tremendous privileges, it has lost almost all its character of Penance. It is interesting in this respect to compare the original Rule with the last approved version of it. The difference is great. Here are some of the lost articles, which were observed in the fourteenth century :

1. Rigorous fast was observed every day of Advent and Lent, every Friday in the year, and on all other fast-days prescribed by the Church.

2. Meat was permitted every Sunday, Tuesday and Thursday. All other days of the year were days of abstinence (unless for special reasons).

3. They had to rise all the year round at Matins (that is,

3 a.m.), and during Advent and Lent they rose twice during the night.

4. The Dominican habit was worn and the details of it were prescribed, such as sleeves closed at the wrist, and a leather belt worn *under* the tunic.

5. The Divine Office was said daily or, if not, seventy-seven Our Fathers and Hail Marys, divided into the canonical hours, and the Creed twice. A form of Grace before and after meals was also prescribed.

Briefly, that was the rule of life observed by the Dominican tertiaries in Siena, when Catherine Benincasa resolved to join them. It must be observed that, despite Monna Lapa, she had already been leading a far more rigorous life than that prescribed by the Rule. In spiritual athletics, she was in excellent training. Certainly, then, her motive was not to get screwed up to austerity by the community spirit. Still less could the specialized instruction have made any appeal. She learned more from five minutes' solitary meditation than from fifty sermons. Infused knowledge was beating in on her soul with the steady increase of a great tide. But she wanted to *belong* to that family, with its notable privileges and, above all, to secure both protection and liberty by a religious dress. Needless to say, Monna Lapa objected. She did not like the idea, because she understood it would be the end of all hope of marriage. Catherine forced her at last to call on the Prioress about it ; she returned alertly with the news that all the tertiaries were widows or elderly women, and they did not care to admit a young girl to the group. But her daughter persisted, debating the question day and night. She knew there was nothing in the Rule to exclude her, and prejudice could be overcome. Poor Lapa was obliged to make another effort on her behalf. It was hard to refuse her anything while she was tossing in fever, reiterating the same request in a cracked voice, from a swollen throat. This time the application was more successful. Several of the sisters came to interview Catherine to find out if she were the light and giddy type. Completely disfigured by smallpox, she certainly looked harm-

less, and they consented to receive her. From that moment
her recovery was rapid. About a month later (there was
no going back on it now), Monna Lapa took Catherine
up to St. Dominic's for the little ceremony. A number of the
sisters were present, and at least two Dominicans, Father
Adimari and Father Montucci, who invested her in the habit,
cloak and veil which he had blessed. Mother and daughter
returned home silently, Lapa sighing frequently and shaking her
head. Catherine's face was rapt. Symbolism always affected
her profoundly. She looked down at her new dress and pon-
dered Dominic's idea of sheer purity and utter humility. When
they reached home, she went up to her room and closed the door
behind her. The struggle with her family was over. But with
her marvellous intuition of the truth, she had no illusions. To
borrow her own phrase, she knew well it had been " milk and
honey " compared with the conflict upon which she was now
entering alone.

CHAPTER II

THE RE-ORDERING OF A LIFE

THE moment Catherine was enfranchised by a religious dress, she set about ordering her life with impetuous energy. Now she carried the pursuit of freedom into a region that was quite uncharted as far as any human guidance went. No ordinary mind can hope to penetrate fully her actions, still less her thoughts, in this first rush of escape. At most one can only indicate her direction.

Obviously Father Della Fonte, to whom alone she could appeal, was unable to guide her. He was a good priest, inheriting all the strong faith and fervour of the first Dominicans. His rugged simplicity was even impressive in this unfortunate time, when the strife which convulsed Italy was inevitably producing a certain decay in the religious orders. Otherwise, his equipment was mediocre : he was not a skilled theologian ; his experience of souls was neither long nor varied. He did what any conscientious confessor in his position would have done : dissuaded her to the extent of his power. He restricted the number of her Holy Communions ; set bounds to her penances ; urged her to live normally. One can sympathize with him. His usual work was fighting sin. There were times when Catherine's outbursts of grief over the slightest hesitation in responding to grace made it almost impossible to believe her genuine. She had, above all, a disconcerting effect.

This girl of sixteen then, who had undergone a martyrdom of desire for solitude, became suddenly so immersed in it as to be almost overwhelmed. Alone, she had to discover how to win her freedom and she found no other road save the stony one

17

trodden by all the saints : absolute dominion over the heart and senses. It is important to dismiss here the popular notion that this sort of captaincy is gained by a mere series of cold negations. It is mainly a constructive process : a fundamental re-creation of self, with God directing and assisting. Catherine followed this up in her narrow, brick-paved room, in which the light was always dim because she kept the outside shutters of her window closed against the street. At night, the shadows were stirred by the flickering of a lamp constantly burning before sacred images painted crudely on the wall. She never left this place, except to go to Church. She never spoke, except in Confession. Such a silence might dismay even a Trappist, yet one would hesitate to include this in the rigours of the new struggle. Clearly the conversation of her family and companions had become impossible : she had far outgrown it. What remained, unless the conversation of the women drawing water from the fountain of Fontebranda, a few yards away : gossip of prices, and dishes, and dresses ? It was out of the question that she could take part in it. Silence then was her sole refreshment : the relief from " words, words, words." Fasting certainly cost something : she retrenched steadily until bread and water and herbs seemed a luxurious repast. Herbs alone had to suffice in sterner moods. Vigil was the hardest of all. But consider what she called " paying the debt of sleep to the body " : one half-hour in the space of two days and nights, lying fully-dressed, on a plank. In this way she succeeded in cutting out all pre-occupations about dress, food and health—this vast concern which gluts with its details all ordinary daily life, and keeps men scurrying around like ants. When Catherine got away from all that, she had already travelled a great distance into a wide, clear world where she was free to think about something more interesting. And because life is so short as to seem God's greatest joke on man, she experimented with sleep until she reduced its exigency to the veriest minimum.

It is hardly necessary to remark that the other tertiaries in

Siena, the elderly women and widows into whose society she had almost forced herself, misliked and distrusted profoundly what they knew of Catherine's ideas. Though she never mingled with them, it was inevitable they should insist that she wanted to teach them all what to do. There was the Rule, why should she persist in outdoing it ? Was not what the Master-General of the Order prescribed for them good enough for her, the youngest and the newcomer ? And their resentment increased when they knew Catherine was aware of their murmurs, but continued her way undisturbed. Already everyone sensed in her a quality which was not at all the irritating obstinacy of the meek : rather a strength of will which was almost frightening. The pressure of these women's displeasure was brought to bear on harassed Father Della Fonte, who in turn vented it on Catherine. Thus, every stroke she drove home in her spiritual combat produced this unhappy kind of reverberation in the exterior religious life of her little circle.

The opposition to her widened as time went on, and presently the friars in St. Dominic's began to be sharply divided among themselves in their opinion of her. This was when her ecstasies became publicly noticeable, growing frequent and prolonged. She would collapse suddenly forward on her face after Holy Communion and remain so, perhaps for hours. Every effort to rouse her was useless. She appeared neither to see nor hear, and her limbs were rigid. Pressed to explain this experience, Catherine answered that God had explained it to her in words somewhat like these :

" . . . the bodily powers alone departed, becoming united to Me through affection of Love. Then is the memory full of nought but Me ; the understanding uplifted to contemplate My truth as object ; the will, that follows the understanding, loves and unites itself to what the eye of the understanding sees. These powers, being united and gathered together and immersed and inflamed in Me, the body loses its feeling, so that the seeing eye sees not, and the hearing ear hears not, and the tongue does not speak, except as the abundance of the heart will sometimes permit it for the alleviation of the heart and the praise and glory of My name."

But the recurrence of the phenomenon was creating a mild sensation in the district. The Dominicans were uneasy and embarrassed (Della Fonte always moodily inclined to defend her). One way to end it was to deprive her of Holy Communion. This was done. However, they *had* to permit her to receive sometimes. They ordered her to leave the Church immediately afterwards and she promised. But the moment the Sacred Host touched her tongue, she dropped insensible. Other tertiaries were told to carry her out. They laid her on the pavement, where the Sienese urchins kicked her, thinking the whole pother was a fine joke. One or two women waited by out of compassion, but they could not make her hear until the sun was high in the heavens, scorching down on them. Catherine prayed and prayed that these things should be hidden, at least in her own home, but of all her prayers, this one never prevailed. Apparently a sign had to be given, and this was how she was branded. One very young Dominican was absolutely convinced she was an impostor, and just as determined to prove it. He waited one day until his brethren were all in choir, then went to the motionless form and pierced her foot several times with a sharp instrument. She did not give the least sign of life but long afterwards, when she rose to go, she became aware of the wounds. Another older friar came all the way from Pisa to see the prodigy. *He* looked at her with the most profound reverence, then bent down and timidly touched her clasped hands with the tip of one finger. Afterwards he said that that finger exhaled an ineffably sweet perfume for forty-eight hours, refreshing him in body and in soul.

Light and shade, victory and defeat alternated in the same way in the girl's interior conflict. She had visions so vivid and tangible, of such inexpressible delight, that the glory remained in her eyes and, for days afterwards, everything she looked on was touched with gold. Little attempt shall be made here to describe what she saw, so not, as Huysmans has it, " to inflict on the Lord the shame of our words." It is well to remember that she herself never discussed such things readily, and apparently disliked any reference to them. In later life she was always being pestered by bores, asking her with a kind of greedy curiosity : "What did you see ? " She was never very descriptive. Sometimes, when ordered to do so in the name of religious obedience, she made attempts to describe and it is curious how her speech, naturally eloquent and forceful, then became stammering and weak. She said : "It is too like blasphemy. I cannot speak of these things which transcend words ; they are ineffable. It would not be lawful for me to explain them, because the memory is not strong enough, nor human words sufficient to express them. It would be like proffering mud in the place of gold." The light of these divine colloquies never quite died out of her countenance. Such grace began to provoke a vague, almost sorrowful response from suffering humanity. People craned to see the pallid, oval face under the dark hood. They followed her about with their eyes, and found themselves longing to see her again.

These hours of exaltation established a sort of counterpoise for the hours spent in an abyss of misery. She, too, had to descend into that gulf where demons snigger at the Faith, where only the material realities of life remain, and belief recedes like a pallid dream. Then she saw nothing but her coarse dress ; her narrow, mean little room ; the dust on the staircase. She heard nothing but the loud voices of her family, as jarring in laughter as in dispute. She went to Church for relief, but shrank from the white glare of sunlight on the incomprehensible streets, from the hostile faces of her companions, from the annoyed glances of the priests. Running back like a stricken animal, she found no refuge in heaven or on earth. "Then it seemed she never remembered God, nor will she remember Him ; and when she heard His name, He seemed to be one whom she had heard spoken of a long time ago." In that abandonment, a voice that was not a voice, would yet be audible : " Why go on with it ? After a lifetime of this travail, you will still not win through in the end. Poor child, do not destroy yourself. You are young and can still enjoy the world Give it up before you go too far. You would be stronger if you were married. Think of Sara and Rebecca and Leah and Rachel, how they pleased God." Then her room would be invaded with troops of impure spirits, from whose obscene suggestions and gestures she found no means of defence, until she seemed to lose her own chaste soul and become inhabited by the very demon of uncleanness. And when she prayed, her broken words sounded like a foreign language in her ear, and she did not know for what she prayed.

Once only, in the space of three years, does she seem to have broken the silence in which she sweated and laboured alone. It was to ask a companion, less scandalized than the others, to teach her the alphabet. She wanted to learn to read, which meant she had to learn Latin, in which language most works were preserved. The enterprise was deprecated, like all her movements. The popular opinion then was that learning spoiled a woman. A Tuscan proverb says : " Dio ti guarda da nobil proverino O di donna che sa latino "—God preserve thee from an impoverished grandee, or from a woman who knows Latin. Things like that were said, with many headshakings, with reference to Catherine. For a long time, she seemed to make no progress whatever, but one day picked up a manuscript and found she could easily read it. It was like an answer to prayer. From that moment she could read but, almost to confirm the miraculous nature of the gift, she could neither spell nor distinguish separate words or letters. Henceforward, she could meet a priest with his finger in the breviary, or watch the leaves of the Missal being turned over at Mass, without that painful sense of exclusion. She read most of the Bible, and learned how to say Divine Office. In the Psalms, she found praises more rapturous and true than any she had yet framed, petitions more divinely inspired, sorrow more poignantly uttered. She substituted the canonical hours for the seventy-seven Paters and

Aves of the Rule, and every day at Lauds, in the Canticle of the
Three Children, her spirit floated wide over the universe and
whispered throughout all creation. In St. Paul's Epistles
she found a garden of delight. She penetrated the great
apostle's mind, understanding perfectly his burning phrases,
his tremendous ellipses, his cries to his friends to bear with his
folly. To her he became, " that lover, Paul," " that glorious
trumpeter," or even—supreme expression of kinship—" quel
Paoluccio " (that little Paul).

In this wise passed her sixteenth year, her seventeenth, her
eighteenth. During this time, she knew nothing of the city
life outside her home, except what intimations were borne in
upon her by bells. They were the voices of the Church and of
the State, speaking continually, ordering a just and sane division
of the Sienese day. St. Dominic's bell began, cutting the air
crisply at three a.m., when the friars rose for Matins. Then
the great bell of the Cathedral clanged out at dawn, giving
permission to open the gates of the city and admit the country
folk with their carts of produce. Until that peal was heard, no
citizen was allowed to leave his home. At seven a.m., a bell
announced that the Town Hall was open for business and any
official was fined who did not arrive there before the strokes
ceased quivering. Then the churches took up the sound,
advising the hours of Mass. The *Misericordia* was tolled when a
prisoner was being led to execution. A bell gave the alarm for
fire. Furious, disquieting clamour of all the bells, *a stormo*,
meant that the citizens were to take arms to fight. Curfew
rang out at nine in winter and ten in summer, ordering the
city gates to be closed for the night and all citizens to retire to
their houses. Anyone who went out after that bell had ceased
was compelled by law to carry a light, because the narrow
winding streets were not illuminated, save for a rare lamp burning before some shrine. Except for the Mass bell, which she
always obeyed, and the *Misericordia*, which induced her to
intercede, these sounds reverberated unheeded in Catherine's
little room.

There was one season of the year, however, when even a deaf man could not ignore what was going on in Siena. That was during Carnival, when Italy was in her lightest and most dangerous mood. Unless in the seclusion of a cloister, or a high-walled convent garden, it was next to impossible to resist the strong current of city life, which swept everyone along before it. Catherine had at least to be aware of it in her room—so close to the street. The revelry began each year at Epiphany and continued with increasing momentum until Shrove Tuesday. During those last three days before Lent, the whole city was given over to it. Fontebranda then was like Hampstead Heath on August Bank Holiday, in its noisy abandonment to special sorts of buffoonery. Here, however, the resemblance ends (the sanction for Bank Holiday gaiety being too obscure). There was always some small section of the Italian communes which remembered that the festival had a religious origin, and treated it as such. It was the " carne levarium," the last outburst of merriment before the " putting away of the flesh," or the serious days of Lent. Also, not only the populace, but nobles, governors, everyone joined in. The streets were crowded from morning to night with masked revellers : the air was filled with the thrumming of mandolines, outbursts of laughter, cries of admiration and applause at the gorgeous pageants that succeeded one another. Country folk packed the city, to gape, or take part in the fun. At night there were torchlight processions, and great feasts, at which the ladies and young fops vied with one another in the sumptuousness of their apparel. Quarrels were invariably bred. During the last three days before Lent, foodstuffs got more scarce and dearer, and the traders in the booths set up in the streets would inevitably fight with buyers, or with each other, until they came to blows. Eggs, cheese, bread, would be seized in the scramble. It was a common sight (not even exciting) to see a whole street abandoned to fisticuffs, a heaving mass of struggling combatants. It is said that this is how the Sienese version of boxing originated. Of course nobles and rulers could hardly be trusted to meet without one offering another some mortal offence. What happened in Venice the Shrove Tuesday of 1355 is typical. The doge of that time, Marin Falieri, was a man of seventy-seven, who had a very beautiful young wife of whom he was morbidly jealous. Naturally it was *the* joke in government circles. At the final carnival festival in his palace, Falieri thought a certain Steno (member of the criminal tribunal) too free in his manner towards his wife, and ordered him to leave the assembly. Steno obeyed, but in a furious temper. On his way out, he scrawled two scurrilous lines on the ducal throne in the hall :

> " Marin Falieri della bella moglie,
> Altri la gode ed egli la mantiene."

(Marin Falieri with the lovely wife : he maintains her, but others enjoy her.) Falieri took this as a deadly insult. He prosecuted Steno, who received only a month's detention. This irritated the old doge more than ever. He brooded over the affair, and finally entered into a plot with several citizens to over-throw all the nobility. Someone betrayed him (there was always a traitor in those plots) and the ruler of the maritime republic was thereupon beheaded on the staircase of his home.

Catherine was familiar with such stories, which was why the wild licence of Carnival always dismayed her. On this Shrove Tuesday of 1366, when she was almost nineteen, she prayed particularly for unassailable faith, such as would resist the most formidable assault. Impelled by her sense of isolation in the empty house (all her family having gone off to the festival outside) she asked with intense fervour to be delivered from the recurrent nausea of doubt, from even the occasional dominion of the abominable spirit of confusion. Her prayer was heard. Into that cold, dark chamber advanced with solemn majesty a pageant incomparably more gorgeous than any thing seen on the Sienese streets. Preceded by dazzling light, celestial music, with warmth, perfume, colour, and sheer joy (all that she was so

heroically denying her senses) there came towards her the
Redeemer, His Blessed Mother, St. John, St. Paul, St. Dominic,
David and legions of angels. While the grave and kindly looks
of this heavenly cohort were bent upon her, with the formality
of a betrothal ceremony, she received the eternal assurance of
Christ that, as she was espoused to Him in Faith, His strong support would never fail her. When the vision faded, Catherine had
succeeded in escaping from Carnival. Her forehead remained
pressed to the wooden coffer which served her as couch : she
was ravished in ecstasy.

A few days later, she realized the full meaning of those mystical
espousals. It was the climacteric ending to her long retreat ;
the seal of approval on her solitary and painful novitiate. She
understood it when she received the clear intimation from God
that her life of seclusion was to end. She was told to mingle
with her family again and with the world outside. By this time,
she had established a kind of equilibrium amid the trials which
beset her. She believed her soul had found its final poise, and
her first movement was one of dread. She prayed with tears
to be left in her retirement. In this involuntary shrinking, she
learned her final lesson : that the will is the last possible residence
of sin ; that there was here the subtlest of all temptations against
charity : " I cannot help my neighbour without losing my
peace of mind." She saw in a flash how cunning the snare is :
when the spiritual will divides, as it were, and the soul protests :
" I want only to do good ; but let it be in *my* way." Willing with
all her strength to do the good that was God's choice, she walked
out of her room to the terrace and looked out over the towers
and spires of Siena. It would be the opposite of the truth to
suppose that her horizon widened now. Rather did it close in
around her disquietingly. Catherine felt that she had outgrown
not merely her family, but Siena. Her very language was different. She shrank from resuming home life with every possible mental and physical revulsion : the smell of food alone, the intense
pre-occupation about trifles, that curious coarse insensibility to
facts beyond experience. Clenching her hands, she felt she

could not turn back and bridge again the gulf over which she had passed.   Then she swung round resolutely from her contemplation of the city, and walked into the kitchen, where her family were eating their dinner.

Chapter III

IN THE PUBLIC EYE

THE Benincasa were connected by marriage with a notable Sienese family, the Colombini, in this way : Jacopo Benincasa was Monna Lapa's second husband. Bartolomeo, her son by the former marriage (that is, Catherine's half-brother), had married Lisa Colombini, first cousin of that Giovanni who had made the name famous some ten years ago. Giovanni Colombini was a rich merchant and city ruler (one of the " Lords Nine "), who had given up his wealth and power to become " a poor man of Christ." Reforming his whole life with startling suddenness, he had then founded the order of the Gesuati, which provoked a tremendous religious revival in Siena and throughout Tuscany. The great and ephemeral success of this man's movement is explained by the temporary enervation of the Franciscan and Dominican orders. A simple remark sometimes illustrates a period marvellously and nothing need be added to this remark of a friar minor to Colombini : " If religious will once more begin to speak only of God, the spirit of holy fervour will return among us, and we shall set the world on fire."

Now Lisa Colombini and her children were living with the Benincasa when Catherine resumed family life, diffidently at first and a little awkwardly. It was an altered household from what she had known three years ago. All her sisters were married by this time and living elsewhere. But her brothers had brought their wives to the home, as was the custom, and there were several strange faces around Monna Lapa. Lisa immediately stood out from all the others in her sympathy for the young recluse.

Perhaps there was in her blood some of her cousin's mystical fervour. She had no great gifts indeed, but she had a woman's supreme quality : she was a peace-maker. The family's attitude was still a little sore towards the daughter who had been such a disappointment. They were uneasy too at that explosiveness which they still discerned in her nature ; she was always the potential rebel who took nothing for granted. This was suggested by even the deliberate speed of her least actions. Their one idea was : what will she do next ? Often when some domestic task would fall from Catherine's nerveless hands, ecstasy having seized her, Lisa would take it up with a compassionate shrug and finish it. In this way, she won over her young sister-in-law to talk to her readily. She was the first to discover that the girl was golden-mouthed, like another Chrysostom. She did not understand one-tenth of Catherine's outpourings, but within a short time she worshipped her.

If ecstatic seizures were an embarrassment in housework, Catherine's power of vigil enabled her to give tremendous assistance. She loved absolute cleanliness and it was an ideal not easily attained in that crowded house. Therefore she formed the habit of going through all the rooms at night, collecting the soiled linen, which she washed while the others slept. She helped in the preparation of the big meals (which she never tasted) ; made bread ; set the house in order daily, and in all those tasks she was thorough and so rapid that even the servant was amazed.

Her father gave her permission to distribute alms according to her judgment. Soon she needed Lisa's championship too, to defend her in this, because her liberality was startling enough to set the whole family by the ears. It must be remembered that Monna Lapa herself was a generous alms-giver and when she was forced to protest against her daughter's actions, she was touched on a sensitive spot. It is essential to seize this point. Avarice, in mediaeval Siena, was not only unchristian, but utter bad form. The idea was that a *gentleman* could not be mean. Such was the atmosphere of that famous Sienese club of young bloods, the "Spendthrift Brigade." They never feasted without flinging one table of viands through the window to the poor. In the sonnets addressed to this club by a contemporary poet, he reminds them repeatedly that liberality is *the* lordly quality. He augurs them not so much " a full purse wherein to dip," as a full purse from which to distribute :

> "And from your purses, plenteous money-fall,
>   In very spleen of misers' starveling gall,
>   Who at your generous customs snarl and snort."

They who, he said, inherited the cream of Christian life, were to consider avarice the only outcast thing amongst them. The miser, in fact, was the joke of society :

> "And make your game of abject vagabond,
>   Abandon'd miserable reprobate,
>   Misers : don't let them have a chance with you ! "

And when this same poet would praise a man, he makes this the culmination of all virtue :

> " He holds not money-bags, as children, holy."

Clearly then, largess was the order of the day. The Sienese would have been blankly bewildered at our phrase : " the deserving poor " ; they abominated any meanly measured doles. But far beyond what social etiquette demanded, the Benincasa were inspired to the *interested* (and not contemptuous) charity of the Faith. Catherine's almsgiving had to be really drastic before it provoked opposition. Such indeed it was. Joints of meat, bread, flour, oil, eggs, whole hogsheads of wine disappeared. Poor Monna Lapa could hardly hope to keep the larder replenished under such conditions. The linen cupboard was rifled. Catherine even cut sleeves out of the servant's new dress hanging on the wall to furbish up a tunic, which a beggar complained had no sleeves. The whole family put what they had under lock and key. Then she gave everything she possessed herself : the little silver cross on her rosary beads, every garment she wore that she thought she could dispense with, even her cloak. This latter was retrieved with difficulty and indignantly restored to her. First of all, it was part of her habit. Then did she not know that only women of bad repute went about the city without a cloak ? It was the sign by which they were recognized for what they were. Why, the very law forbade respectable women to go out without one. Catherine's reply, though hardly soothing at the moment, will never be forgotten : " I would rather go without a cloak than without charity."

All the Dominican tertiaries who could, helped voluntarily in the Sienese hospitals, in fulfilment of that article of their Rule which bade them visit the sick. In her return to a " normal " mode of life, Catherine now did likewise. Accompanied by the accommodating Lisa, she became familiar with all the charitable institutions in the city. Of these, the most soaring triumph of goodwill to men was the building known as the Scala, whose great Gothic facade ran along one side of the Cathedral square in the centre of Siena. It surpassed anything one could find in Europe to-day. Besides an ordinary hospital, equipped as completely as contemporary scientific knowledge allowed, it included a free hospice for pilgrims and a home for foundling children. It provided for the marriages of the orphans, even down to the girls' trousseaux. The poor of the city could always obtain food there. But neither the city nor the commune financed it ; the staff were not paid ; they did not beg for alms. It was conducted by a pious confraternity, who devoted themselves *and their possessions* to the relief of the poor and the sick. The confraternity admitted men and women and lived according to a Rule, which was almost monastic, regulating their lives even in the least minutiae. The brothers and sisters assisted at daily Mass, recited the Office, observed silence at meals, and of course occupied separate quarters. They were not allowed to eat or drink outside the hospital, or even to sit down in the houses of lay people. There were periods when Catherine almost lived in this building. Here again her victory over sleep stood her in good stead. She took the night cases by preference, and they allotted her a little cell in the hospital to which she could retire for a brief repose. In certain respects, the Scala was the most interesting place in Siena. Catherine saw life there as she had previously only imagined it. She made a wide circle of acquaintances, from whom she received a clear knowledge of contemporary affairs. All the news of the day filtered through this institution. Pilgrims always had much to tell. All the suffering and broken humanity of the countryside around found its way there. Most of the priests and doctors in the city had occasion to visit the place every day.

Catherine also favoured greatly the Mercy Hospital, a smaller institution, of which the rector was then one Matteo Cenni, or Misser Matteo. There was a quality about this man's charity which immediately appealed to her. He directed his little world with an impassive kind of efficiency which spoke of the burning flame in his breast. Cenni, on his part, admired the notable physical endurance of the young tertiary, whose service was so good, and whose conversation was so remarkably intelligent. A friendship sprang up between them. One day, Cenni confided to Catherine that his youth had been dissolute and that his present life was an act of reparation. He also told her all about William Flete, the extraordinary Englishman, hermit of Lecceto (a wood outside the city), who had brought about his conversion. And, through her bond of sympathy with the rector, the Mercy Hospital, of all the hospitals in Siena, assumed for Catherine the air of a friend's house.

One other institution must be named, which she penetrated though it was taboo to even the most intrepid : a hospital where disease could be only assuaged, not cured, the fetid lazar house outside the southern gate of the city. Catherine took charge of a leprous old woman there named Tecca, whom everyone had abandoned because her wicked tongue was almost more insupportable than the hideous ravages of her disease. The place was a good half-hour's walk from her home, but Catherine went there twice daily while attending Tecca, walking quickly with

her light, free gait. By way of recognition, Tecca slandered
Catherine's honour in the most vile fashion. Some murmur of
this reached Monna Lapa, who furiously forbade her daughter
to go there again, telling her that anyhow she would not only catch
the disease herself, but infect the whole household if she did not
cease from such folly. Yet Catherine insisted on going on
with the case. The old woman's incredible malice afflicted her
profoundly, but she said nothing and continued to nurse her
lovingly. A suspicious eruption then appeared on her hands,
which she strove in vain to hide from her mother. She was
consoled when Tecca died repentant, a little later. Catherine
performed the last offices and even buried the horrible corpse
herself. On her way home, she glanced resignedly at her hands,
to find the eruption had suddenly cleared away, leaving them
so white as to be almost luminous.

About this time, ecclesiastical affairs were the burning topic
of conversation in Siena, and Catherine, in her round of the
hospitals, became fully informed of what was taking place. She
knew, of course, that ever since the French soldiers laid hands on
Boniface VIII (in her grandfather's time—almost a generation
ago now) Rome had been abandoned by the vicar of Christ.
All this time the soil sanctified by the blood of hosts of martyrs
and the true papal seat were deserted for the security and peace
of pleasant Avignon on the banks of the Rhône in Provence.
But so powerful an effect has the mere passage of time that the
residence of the Popes in Avignon was now almost generally
accepted with indifference. None but the best minds in Catherine's day deplored it. But *she* grasped perfectly the point of
Dante's bitter scorn and Petrarch's invective.

Ever since the transfer of the Papal See, anarchy had been
increasing in Italy. The Popes governed there through French
Papal Legates, who misunderstood and misruled the people,
and were cordially detested by them. Catherine knew, and
grieved to know, that the Papacy was every day losing prestige
thoughout the peninsula. Just now, Siena was at war with
Perugia ; Florence with Pisa, Milan with Bologna. Rome was

the scene of a bitter struggle between the papal Legate and the
people, and among the Roman barons themselves.   France was
at war with England, and all Christendom was exasperated by
suspected French influence on the Papacy.   There seemed no
hope of peace in Christendom until the Pope returned to the
independent see of Peter.   Both Dante and Petrarch had
implored it.   St. Bridget of Sweden, in her dark mystical effusions,
prophesied the doom of the Church unless the Papacy broke
the fetters with which Philip the Fair had bound it.

Siena was familiar with Petrarch's sonnets, in which he fiercely
condemned the corruption of the Avignon court, and sorrowed
for the desolation of Rome, ancient and true centre of government, where cattle were now grazing round the altars in St.
John Lateran.   Rome, indeed, was a cemetery " wherein nothing moved save the shades of ancient heroes, and the wind of
glorious memories."   Italy, which had given such great leaders
to the Church, could not admire the French Popes.   Here again
a single remark conveys much.   Said a French Prelate of the
Curia to Petrarch :   " Our two Clements have destroyed more
of the Church in a few years than seven of your Gregories could
restore in many centuries."

But the very name of the present Pontiff reigning in Avignon,
Urban V, was held to be propitious.   From the time of his
accession in 1362, great things were expected from him, for he
was a man of blameless life.   A thrill of hope ran through
Europe five years later at the news that he was restoring the
Papal See to Rome.   In fact, Urban made a brave effort to do so.
Ignoring the French king's opposition, he left Avignon April
30th, 1367, and landed at Corneto the following June 4th.   A
great host of nobles and envoys were waiting to receive him
(among them Giovanni Colombini and his little band).   The
Romans sent an embassy to confer on him the lordship of their
city and present him with the keys of the Roman fortress,
Sant' Angelo.   A few months later, amid scenes of the wildest
rejoicing, the Pope entered Rome in a great procession of
triumph.   But when he looked around him at the ruin into

which the Sacred City had fallen, it is said that he wept and flung himself in prayer by the tomb of Peter.

In distant Siena, Catherine shared in the universal gladness. It was believed that a new era of peace and reform had now opened for the Church. Just at this time too, an event of some importance befell the Benincasa, touching them more nearly than Urban's return to Rome. The second son, Bartolomeo, was elected one of the Twelve rulers of the city for the months of September and October, 1367. His correct title was : " Magnificent Lord, One of the Twelve Governors of the City of Siena." These governors were chosen by an elaborate system of rotation, and held office for only two successive months. During this brief period, the family belonged to the ruling class in Siena, and rejoiced in their political triumph.

Catherine now made her first friend among her religious companions, the tertiaries, in Francesca Gori, or Cecca—for short. This Cecca was a widow of high rank, about twice Catherine's age. She had tremendous enthusiasm for the Dominican order, having three sons novices in it. Lisa told her the intimate details of her sister-in-law's life and Cecca soon began to express a devotion for Catherine as intense as Lisa's. There is something pathetic in the admiration of these two elderly married women, mothers of families, for this inexperienced girl of twenty. They interposed their matronly persons between her and the harsh wind of censure, defended her vehemently, accompanied her everywhere, ordered their lives at her suggestions, treasured up all her words. Henceforth Catherine was rarely seen outdoors except in their charge. It was a new experience for the Sienese who had known only the solitary. Catherine was a changed being when animated by conversation, her face becoming sweet and gay, her regard frank and penetrating.

Jacopo Benincasa never saw the results of his son's elevation to power. In the hot July and August of the following year, he seemed to be ailing and took to his bed. Suspecting the truth, Catherine never left her father's side. He died and, at the instant of his death, she laughed for joy, comforting the others as though she were in nowise concerned, " for she had seen that soul pass out of the darkness of the body and enter immediately into the eternal life." The Dominicans chanted the Dead Mass for him on the day of his burial, August 22nd, 1368. This bereavement was to affect the family fortunes profoundly, but no change was evident for the moment. The three eldest brothers took over the dead dyer's business and things went on as before.

Della Fonte decided at this time to keep some record of Catherine's extraordinary conversations. But he had had only the education necessary for his ordination and not a ready pen. Therefore he enlisted for the task a friend of his, a younger Dominican named Bartolomeo Dominici, to whom he dictated an account of the most miraculous manifestations told him by his penitent. Several notebooks were soon filled in this way, Della Fonte dictating and Bartolomeo writing. This latter became so enthusiastic for the subject of the record that, at his instance, Della Fonte introduced him to Catherine, who thereupon acquired a new friend.

Not that Bartolomeo was immediately captivated. It took time for their friendship to ripen. He had gone to her in a spirit of enquiry and he was very much on his guard. He suspended his judgment for some time. Many of her ways irked him, for instance her perpetual self-revilement. He wondered if there was a shade of hypocrisy in this, and even challenged her about it. Did she not know she was blameless ? Catherine explained with such sincerity that she measured her service to God by the graces received from Him—in which illumination her efforts were feeble and spasmodic—that he was silenced. Then one day he was startled and incredulous to hear her almost lay claim to the gift of double sight. She referred casually to what he and three of his brethren had been discussing the previous night. In amazement he asked her to name the others and she did so. But he still suspected that one of them might have told her, and therefore prepared a little test. One day he asked her what he had been doing at a given hour the previous evening. He had been absolutely alone then and knew no-one but God observed his actions. She answered him : " Writing." "About what ? " persisted the priest, with something like a pang of dismay. She told him the exact subject and he threw up his hands in a little gesture of resignation. Henceforth she had in him a fervent supporter.

This friendship with Bartolomeo Dominici had a profound and lasting influence on Catherine's intellectual development. He was the first learned priest she knew. He had taken his doctorate at Bologna and was a lecturer at the University of Siena. A true Dominican in his life-long passion for discovering fresh expositions of the truth, he was at this time rapidly acquiring renown in his Order.

But on the opposite side of Siena, in the Franciscan Church, a voice was now raised in public, denouncing Catherine Benincasa. Her growing circle of friends grew hot with indignation when reports of this were brought to them. Especially as the condemnation was made by a man of undoubted authority, one Father Lazzarino from Pisa, then lecturing on philosophy in Siena. Moved perhaps in some measure by the rivalry between the two great religious orders, he poured out a torrent of scornful invective on the Dominicans for tolerating the deceptions of the young tertiary.

Father Bartolomeo, in particular, found this intensely disagreeable. He, too, had to go to the University occasionally to lecture on the " Sentences " of Peter the Lombard, and he found that, because of his friendship with Catherine, Lazzarino was making him unpopular with the students, who took up the debate. (Naturally, it was far more interesting than either philosophy, or the " Sentences.") Even those who disliked Catherine in Camporeggi were annoyed at Lazzarino. He thundered unceasingly against her from pulpit and rostrum ; going about the city like one whose sole mission in life was to set Siena right about Catherine. Bartolomeo protested that he claimed nothing for her but that she was an extraordinarily good Christian, with an infused knowledge of divine things and certain remarkable gifts.   One evening, while the controversy was raging, he was surprised by Lazzarino entering his room and asking to be directed to Catherine's house.   Thinking his opponent's heart was touched, the Dominican willingly offered to accompany him the short distance to Fontebranda, and they set out together. But, as a matter of fact, the Franciscan merely wanted to strengthen his case by personal observation.   The proud teacher of men was thinking, as he paced along in his habit : " These women ! As if the devil doesn't *always* use a woman when he wants to ensnare souls ! "   And he shot a look of mingled disgust and pity at his companion.

When they entered, Catherine was alone.   She greeted them courteously, and then fixed the visitor with her dark questioning eyes.   There was an awkward silence.   The friar had expected a voluble talker, and he was annoyed at the queer nervousness taking hold of him.   Making an effort, he said :

" I have heard of your holiness and how God has given you understanding of the Scriptures, so I have come to you to be edified and comforted."

" I am glad," said Catherine, " that God sent you to me. With your knowledge of the Scriptures you daily feed souls, and now perhaps you will console me a little."

This stilted conversation of thrust and parry continued for some time.   Catherine seemed determined not to uncover her guard. Her expression was brighter than usual ; there was even a hint of laughter in her face.   At last Lazzarino rose to go, muttering something about the lateness of the hour, and that he would return another day.   She knelt for his blessing and begged his prayers.   Negligently tracing the Sign of the Cross in the air, he said over his shoulder, " You pray for me too."   She promised fervently.   Bartolomeo parted company with him at the foot of Fontebranda.   Lazzarino pursued his way across the city, puffing disdainfully to himself : " Oh, she's good, I suppose, but not at all the great one they make her out to be."

He rose during the night, as was his custom, to prepare his

lecture for the following day. But he found himself pervaded with an indescribable languor and melancholy, so that tears coursed helplessly down his cheeks. The learned professor abhorred softness and he tried in vain to ascribe a physical cause to this tremendous woe. But he was shaken by sobs which he could neither check nor explain. Angry and wretched, he could not deliver his cherished discourse and the whole day passed in the same humiliation. Furious with himself, he was obliged to keep to his room. Quite broken, as evening drew on, he began to search his conscience to find some explanation of such obsessing grief. It was not until night came that a scene rose accusingly before him : the poor, bare room ; the slight figure of the girl he had spent such energy in deriding ; her grave regard. He threw a desperate glance round his own comfortable quarters : his magnificent library, his silk-curtained bed, his padded chairs. Discovering himself in a blinding flash, he paced up and down waiting for the dawn. Then he flung out of the monastery and was hastening across the city to Fonte-branda before the sun was risen. Catherine was up (no-one seems to have ever found her asleep). Hearing the footsteps ringing on the silent street, she ran lightly down the stairs and opened the door. Lazzarino threw out his hands to her with a haggard look. He implored her to take him as her son, to tell him what to do. They had " a long and holy colloquy." That day, Lazzarino gave away everything he possessed, including his books. He retained only a commentary on the Gospels for his sermons. Then he retired to a hermitage, from which he emerged at intervals to preach.

The thoughts of the Sienese were soon diverted from these little domestic incidents to external affairs. Urban's transfer to Rome was going to affect them personally, because the Emperor was now on his way to join the Pope at Viterbo, and would pass through Siena. The monarch who at this moment exercised vague sway over that realm of shadowy boundaries called the Holy Roman Empire was Charles IV, King of Bohemia. He was Clement VI's nominee to the title and was therefore called " the priest's Emperor." He was son of that blind King John who had fallen at Crecy. He was not in the least worthy of his father. The Italians' disillusionment in his regard is almost comical in its bitterness. They who, we may suppose, inherited the truest idea of what a Roman Emperor should be, called him : " That ignominious Charles of Luxembourg." The last time he had crossed the Alps into Italy (thirteen years ago) he had brought an empty purse, which he contrived to fill before he went home. That was all he had to his credit. To relieve the tedium of audiences, he had a habit of stripping the bark off a willow twig with a little knife, while his eyes wandered vaguely over the kneeling ambassadors. They were always positive that he had not listened to a word they said and they were astonished if he made a pertinent remark.

It will be remembered that the people of Siena had now been in power for over seventy years and the nobles were practically excluded from the government. But the aristocratic families were never reconciled to this exclusion and they welcomed any pretext for provoking a revolution, in which they might have a chance of coming uppermost again. On the occasion of Charles' last visit to Siena, the nobles had helped eagerly in the overthrow of the " Lords Nine," but the next form of rule, that of the " Lords Twelve," was equally restricted to the people, and the aristocratic families had now been chafing under this for thirteen years. As Charles' coming drew near, it was obvious that revolution again menaced Siena. Since Catherine's family was involved in this, the reader cannot be spared the details.

The Benincasa were perturbed because, through Bartolomeo's term of office among the Twelve, they were committed to the support of the Government party and anything might happen. The partisans of the Twelve had split into two, sundered by the divisions between the warring nobles. These latter secretly brought troops into the city and on September 2nd, forced the Twelve to surrender the Palace and resign control of the State. A new government of thirteen consuls was set up, ten of whom were nobles. These sent an embassy to Charles IV, but a rival embassy was sent by the dispossessed, supported by one powerful family, the Salimbeni. Charles accepted the offers of the latter and sent one Malatesta to Siena with eight hundred horsemen. When the cavalry arrived in the city, there was hand to hand fighting in the streets, culminating in a fierce struggle round the government Palace, which was finally sacked by the infuriated populace and the imperial troops. The nobles and their families fled. A new lordship of Twelve Defenders was now created, representative of all classes. When the Emperor arrived at last, he knighted two of the Salimbeni family, who received a more signal honour from the government by being declared " plebeians," that is, eligible to rule.

But the moment Charles had proceeded on his way to Rome to be crowned by the Pope there, things got worse in Siena. The exiled nobles, in their secure fortresses outside the city, plundered all around them and refused to come to terms. On December 11th, there was another rising ; the mob broke into the Palace and drove out the rulers. A new council of Fifteen Defenders, or Reformers, was set up, still tenaciously *of the People*. But the Salimbeni and their partisans were disgusted at this issue of the struggle, and they sent another embassy to the Emperor, imploring his help.

Charles was now on his return journey from Rome. He re-entered Siena on December 22nd with his troops, and alighted at the Salimbeni Palace as before. A few days later, reinforcements joined him. He demanded the surrender of five important fortresses and this audacity practically united the whole city against him. One morning in January 1369, there was a sudden clamour in the streets. The Salimbeni and their allies rushed through the city, killing and destroying. They were in concert with the imperial troops to force the new plebeian government to yield office. Charles himself set out for the palace with three thousand horsemen. All Siena was thrown into the wildest confusion. The bells clanged their furious summons to arms, and the citizens responded in a great rally for their liberty. They

attacked the Imperial troops and there was a fierce struggle in
the streets. The Emperor was driven back to the Salimbeni
Palace. A proclamation was issued forbidding food to be sold
or given to him or to his troops. Then Charles lost his head.
"Alone in the Salimbeni palace, the Emperor was a prey to the
most abject terror. He wept, prayed, embraced everyone, and
begged pardon for the mistake he had made." Such horses and
baggage as could be recovered were restored to him. He was
given a large sum of money on condition that he left the city
immediately. He accepted with alacrity and went off on
January 25th. However fiercely the rival parties in Siena
disputed, they seemed to be agreed on this : Charles was of no use.

After all this turmoil, the government of the Fifteen Defenders
remained in power, but there was little satisfaction, and risings
and tumults continued in the city. The nobles outside the gates
were still unreconciled and they plundered and ravaged the
countryside. These disorders convulsed Siena for over a year.
The hospitals were always crowded with wounded and dying.
Armed guards patrolled the city day and night, giving the alarm
by lighting fires, and by a great clanging of bells. Catherine
was now twenty-one years old, an intelligent and disgusted on-
looker. She spent her days binding up wounds in the hospitals
and, as her sensitive fingers moved, her mind was working on
the problem. She bitterly resented the insane fratricidal strife,
and a strong political programme was slowly taking shape
in her ideas. This year's events gave great impetus to its
formation.

The two eldest Benincasa were active members of the former
government party, that of the Twelve ; their lives were, therefore, constantly in danger in the continual rioting. One day a
friend rushed into their house, gasping that an armed mob was
on its way to take the brothers' lives and that they were to fly
to the church of Sant' Antonio, whither others of their faction
had rushed for security. Catherine interposed authoritatively
" No, they must not go there, and I am sorry indeed for those
who have gone. I will take them to a place of safety." She

hurried out her brothers and, walking between them, passed quickly through the tumultuous streets, the crowds drawing aside respectfully to make way for her. She led the boys to the Misericordia and left them in Cenni's charge, telling them to remain there three days. At the end of that time, the commotion had subsided. The brothers got off with a fine and were left in peace. But all those of their party who had rushed to Sant' Antonio were found there by the furious mob that fatal evening and slain.

At length, when all order had come to an end in Siena, both nobles and people sent ambassadors to Florence for an arbitration of their differences. The neighbouring republic made a settlement and peace was proclaimed in the city, with great rejoicing, early in 1369.

A new friend had entered into Catherine's life during these months of disturbance ; this time from among the great Sienese families, Alessa Saracini. From the remote beginnings of this republic's history, there had always been five great families, dividing (and disputing) wealth and power. They were the Saracini, Salimbeni, Piccolomini, Malavolti and Tolomei. Alessa was a widow, but she had no children and was not much older than Catherine. This explains why her attachment was so much more passionate than even that of Lisa or Cecca. She was different in other respects : cultured, intelligent, a forceful character, with all the poise and assurance her family name conferred. She not only read Latin, but wrote it excellently and therefore she could laugh at prejudices about the education of women.

When she met Catherine Benincasa, she felt as though she had never lived until that moment. She regretted all her past life as a stupid waste. She, too, became a Dominican tertiary. Catherine's conversation so entranced her that she found the days unendurable on which she did not see her. Having no ties in the world save an aged mother whom she looked after, Alessa sold up her house and bought one near that of the Benincasa that she might be closer to her in whom all her thoughts and affections were now centred. Catherine then began to go frequently to the Saracini's, a quiet and restful home compared with her own. Alessa (wise friend) knew how to leave her in peace. Catherine soon came to spend weeks there, sometimes months on end. She had now two homes in Siena : one with Monna Lapa and one with the Saracini. It is certain that of all the women she loved and pitied, none ever came nearer to her than Alessa. In their long talks, the latter was in a position to explain exhaustively to Catherine the Guelph and Ghibelline passions of the Sienese aristocracy ; the detailed history of all their ancient and everlasting feuds. Thus all the events and the friendships of these years contributed to Catherine's clear knowledge of the politics of State, Empire and Church.

At the close of this phase of her life, something very mysterious happened, which showed how famous she had become in her native city. Father Bartolomeo was preaching one August Sunday morning of 1370, in St. Dominic's, when there was a sudden commotion among the congregation. A wave of some shock has passed through the church ; the tertiaries were all whispering together ; no-one was listening to him. He thought he caught the words : " Catherine Benincasa is dead." Concluding his sermon hurriedly, he hastened to the sacristy where he found a lay-brother named John, wringing his hands in despair at the news. They both set off at top speed for Fontebranda. The street where she lived was crowded with groups of people, talking excitedly. The staircase of her house was jammed with enquirers. The two Dominicans forced a passage through and entered the room where Catherine was lying motionless on the wooden coffer. Monna Lapa and Father Della Fonte were bending over her ; Alessa and Lisa were whispering by the window.

Bartolomeo had seen Catherine in a trance over and over again, but he saw at once that this was different. " When did she die ? " he asked with a tremor in his voice. Lapa explained she had found her like that at six in the morning. At sight of the marble face, Brother John burst into sobs so rending that he ruptured a vein in his breast, causing a hemorrhage, so that blood poured from his mouth. Alessa tried to assist him, but he was evidently in grave danger and the woe in the little room was indescribable. Della Fonte thought of lifting him towards the couch. He took Catherine's lifeless hand and touched with it the breast of the fainting lay-brother. The hemorrhage ceased immediately. A few seconds later, they were overjoyed to see a faint tinge of colour appear on the girl's face, her eyelids fluttered. They pressed around her eagerly to meet the familiar bright glance, but her look of returning consciousness expressed some horrible desolation. She turned her face to the wall and cried as though broken with grief.

One by one, they retired comforted, leaving only Alessa with her. The good news was taken outside and the street cleared. It was then only a prolonged trance (she had been reputed dead for four hours). But Catherine's tears never ceased for two days and two nights. The little procession of her friends of these years tried to console her : Lisa, Matteo Cenni, Cecca, Father Bartolomeo and Alessa. She could say nothing but this : " *Vidi arcana Dei* (I saw the hidden things of God) and now I am thrust back again into the prison of the body." This mystical death had been an experience different from the ordinary ecstasy. To the end of her life she never spoke of it without strong emotion. No attempt shall be made here to describe the reverse position from which she had looked back on the world. Whatever glory she had glimpsed, it made her life on earth seem a dark and solitary drama in comparison, and her tears were like a supplication for courage to play her part.

In the Autumn of this year, the hopes of all those who had hailed Urban's return as the beginning of a new era were bitterly disappointed. Rumours had been circulating for months that he had made up his mind to go back to Avignon, but men would not credit it, as news too horrible to be true. He was a Frenchman and longed for his own country again. During his three years in Rome his health had been failing steadily. The French Cardinals (far in the majority in the Sacred College) never ceased urging him to return. The French war with England was put forward as an excuse : he could interpose more successfully in Avignon. When his preparations were unmistakable, anguished efforts were made in Italy to hold him back. A Roman embassy pleaded with him in passionate terms. Petrarch sent a courier speeding with a letter, described as his noblest composition, in which he makes Italy implore the fugitive Pontiff. The Swedish princess in Rome, afterwards known as Saint Bridget of Sweden, rode on her white mule up the hill of Montefiascone, where the Pope was in residence, to add her entreaties. The interview was a failure. Then she gave a document, purporting to be a divine revelation of the will of God, to a young French Cardinal, named Peter Roger de Beaufort, to present it to the Pope. De Beaufort read it and was profoundly moved, but would not dare give it to Urban. In the end, Bridget insisted on presenting it herself, but when the Pope had read it he did not seem impressed.

Early in September, they learned in Siena that it was all over. He sailed on the 5th from Corneto. Rome was again abandoned, but the sting to Christendom lay in this : it was now by the deliberate choice of Peter's successor. He never saw the close of that year, as he died three months later in his brother's house in Avignon, and was buried as he desired, clothed in the habit of a simple Benedictine monk. On December 30th, 1370, the new pope was elected. He was that Peter Roger de Beaufort whom Bridget of Sweden had so much impressed in Rome. He chose a name great in papal history, Gregory, being the eleventh of that title. He had one thing which distinguished him from all his predecessors in Avignon, an enthusiasm.

CHAPTER IV

THE SCHOOL OF MYSTICS

THOSE hastening feet of Father Lazzarino in the early dawn were like the first sounds presaging the approach of a great multitude. The moment Catherine's discernment of souls was bruited abroad, people flocked to her from all sides. Those burdened with mental trouble claimed her attention in far greater numbers and more importunately than the poor and the sick : because charity to the mind is so much rarer and more delicate than that extended to the body. She was never known to disappoint anyone. Indeed she was profoundly interested, even absorbed, in every human being she ever set eyes on. She understood every emotion that ever vibrated in the human heart. Her intuition was immediate, infallible, expressed in incisive phrases that went straight to the core of every matter. Her method varied with the individual, but always it was unique. To the weak she said : " Sensuality is a lie, you know, based on the vilest illusions." But to the strong she explained : " By sensuality, I do not mean the weakness of the senses. I mean condescending to our sensitive natures even in what is lawful, even in spiritual things, even in pious little fads." To some forms of grief, she would retort : " Oh grieve—over your weak grief." To the discontented : " Be impatient—with your miserable impatience," or with powerful emphasis : " Do you know that you *pester* God with your great impatience." Her lightest remark was electrifying, like this, to a man puffed up with his learning : " Don't be proud—it will coarsen your understanding." Or she would charm the shrinking with a paradox : " Hate yourself and think always in what way you can endure pain for love of that hatred." To a monk who complained of not having time enough for prayer, she said : " Pray the prayer of action, which is the fragrant flowering of the soul." Then swiftly she added : "A good man *is* a prayer."

Two factors now induced her to commit her ideas to writing. Her family began to feel at this time the full effects of their bereavement. After the death of Jacopo Benincasa, which took place in 1369, the firm did not prosper and her brothers began to fear poverty. Also they were not happy in Siena and possibly not safe, since their political downfall. Therefore, in 1370, they applied for naturalization as citizens of Florence and left for that Republic with their families. In their father's lifetime, they had always had a branch of the business there and this they now tried to develop and extend. It meant a great change of life to the small remnant of the family left in Siena. The moment her brothers had gone, Catherine naturally thought of letters as a means of maintaining her influence over them and holding the exiles together. In addition to this, she was constantly receiving letters which demanded answers. Father Lazzarino, for instance, wrote the moment he was settled in his hermitage, complaining of the persecution he had to endure from his brethren and of how he missed his books. Now as Catherine could not write, Alessa offered to write her letters for her. Lazzarino was, therefore, consoled by a reply, written by Alessa on a sheet of parchment at Catherine's dictation, in which all his difficulties were examined in order and concluding as follows :

" Let us endure, let us endure, dearest brother ; for the more pain we suffer down here with Christ crucified, the more glory shall we receive ; and no pain will be so much rewarded, as mental pain and labour of the heart ; for these are the greatest pains of all and therefore worthy of the greatest fruit."

Probably through his acquaintance with the University students, Father Bartolomeo had formed a friendship with a young Sienese poet, then enjoying considerable fame in the city, named Ranieri di Landoccio dei Pagliaresi, or Neri to his intimates. He belonged to one of the lesser noble families of Siena and often consulted the Dominican about his spiritual difficulties, which were certainly complex. He was melancholy and hyper-sensitive. The mere facts of life seemed to dismay him. The world disgusted him, but religion did not draw him with sufficient impetus to sever him from what he detested. Perhaps it was his poetic faculty which made legion his perplexities. He seemed to see everything with blurred edges. This dreamer used to make the energetic preacher sigh. In the end, Bartolomeo persuaded Neri to approach Catherine, assuring him : " She will explain everything to you." Being an aristocrat, Neri was careful to do the right thing. He wrote a very correct, but naïve letter to Catherine, asking to be received in the circle of her acquaintances. He received the following reply :

" You wrote asking me to receive you as a son : wherefore I, though miserably unworthy, have already received you and do now receive you with affectionate love and I hold myself responsible, and will ever do so before God, to pay your debts for every sin committed, or which you may commit. But I beseech you to fulfil my desires : conform yourself with Christ Crucified and cut yourself off completely from the conversation of the world."

Neri was moved by the tone of this letter. He ventured to present himself at the Benincasa's and, after five minutes conversation, he was enamoured of Catherine's genius and of her natural eloquence. He asked her if he could serve her in any way and she answered readily : " Yes, write my letters for me." It will be remembered that she led a strenuous life. She never neglected the myriad duties in her own home, nor the hospitals, nor other sick persons who were constantly sending for her. But it grieved her to leave unanswered the plaintive letters which couriers were constantly presenting at her door, sometimes kicking their heels outside, waiting for a reply. She found that

Neri could follow her rapid dictation much better than Alessa and, in this way, he took over the main burden of her correspondence : providing the parchment, seeing to addresses, finding couriers. He thought it a supreme privilege. Her dictation was more interesting than anything he had ever read : than even Dante, whom he knew by heart. All the poet in him rejoiced in her colourful language : " From the thorns of tribulation, let us pluck the rose of peace and quiet." " If you make a holy resistance to temptations you will find in those thorns the fragrant rose of perfect purity." Or this : " We must perceive among the thorns the perfume of the blossom about to open." He delighted in her swift transitions : " Then let us do like the Cananean woman when we see Christ passing—through our souls." There were certain things Catherine could not name without soaring into poetry. If she spoke of the Precious Blood, her prose ascended to a hymn. Whenever she mentioned patience, she took a lyrical flight :

" Oh true and sweet Patience, thou art the virtue which is never conquered, but dost always conquer ! Thou alone dost show whether the soul loves its Creator or no. Thou dost give us hope of Grace : thou art the solvent of hatred and rancour in the heart ; thou dost free us from dislike of man ; thou dost take all pain out of the soul ; through thee the great burdens of many trials become light and through thee bitterness becomes sweet : in thee, Patience, queenly virtue, acquired with the memory of the Blood of Christ crucified, we find life."

Or, in her musical Tuscan, she would apostrophize the virtue as though she beheld it in corporeal form :

" Oh Patience, how pleasing thou art ! Oh Patience, what hope thou dost give to those who possess thee !

" Oh Patience, thou art a queen, who possessest and art not possessed by wrath. . . .

"And thy garment is of the sun, shining with the light of true knowledge of God and with the warmth of divine charity. Thy vesture casts rays, striking those who injure thee, kindling on their heads burning coals of charity, which consume the hatred in their hearts. Thy vestment is embroidered with the different stars of all the virtues ; because patience cannot be in the soul without the stars of all the virtues, shining in the night of self-knowledge. . . . "

And Neri's dark, serious face would light up with enthusiasm, as he wrote appreciatively the concluding words of the picture.

The point about Catherine's proclamation of patience was this : it was supported by a sense of the value of time which almost amounted to an obsession. She never forgot for a second that " time passes like the wind." She hated to sleep. She was always conscious, in the innermost fibre of her being, that her days were jealously numbered and were racing by. To her every moment was an " *atomo fuggente* " which, like Faust, she would arrest. She saw time symbolized in every swift movement of Nature : the river in flood, the wind passing through the ilexes. The flight of time was the solvent of every grief :

" We must therefore bear this little trial willingly. Little, we may call it, like all our sorrows, because of the brevity of time ; since no trial can last longer than our time in this life. How much time have we ? It is like the point of a needle. Therefore it is very true that sorrow is brief, because trouble that is past, I suffer no longer, since the time is past ; what may come, I do not suffer yet, as I am not sure of having the time, since I must die and I do not know when. I have only this little point of present time and no more. Therefore every great grief is small, because of the brevity of time."

Now Neri had heard patience preached before, by bland ineffectual people who made it the exasperating excuse for their own incapacity. On the other hand, he had heard busy capable people excuse their snarling impatience by their very efficiency : they had too much to think about. But Catherine was a strenuous and most effective woman and, with all her vibrant energy, she had oceanic reserves of patience. He had never before met anyone who was so powerful, yet so patient. He

had always thought the two extremes opposed. It was profoundly interesting to find them meeting in her.

But the condition of Neri's new life was this : " Sever yourself
completely from the conversation of the world." He had many
friends among the gay Sienese society, who pursued him and
flattered him because they admired his beautiful verses, particularly one Francesco Malavolti, a representative of one of the
five great families of Siena. Malavolti's conversation was very
much " of the world." He was a man of about twenty-five,
married to a beautiful young girl of fifteen, to whom of course he
was not faithful. To put it crudely, he was always hunting
women. Needless to remark, he disguised this as the quest of
the great and noble fervour. Every episode was " love at last "
—this time surely the real splendour ! He talked of nothing
else, except perhaps his horse and his falcon. He was a very
fine gentleman, with graceful manners and a genuine affection
for Neri. But once the latter knew Catherine Benincasa, he
could no longer shrug at Malavolti's episodes. They afflicted
him. Once he attempted to describe Catherine to Malavolti,
who showed no interest. Later he tried to persuade him to go
to see her, only once, but Francesco derided the notion. Perceiving Neri's distress however, he eyed him compassionately,
thinking : " How like a poet ! " To please him he agreed to go.

On their way, Malavolti felt dreadfully bored and contemptuous. He said to himself : " If she preaches to me about the
soul . . . and as for confession ! She'll get her answer from
me." When they entered Fontebranda, the district of the tanners
and dyers, he stiffened at the contrast between his own gorgeous
person and his prosaic surroundings. He glanced right and
left disdainfully and sniffed with fastidious repugnance the acrid,
pungent odour of tanned hides spread out in the sun to dry.
But when they entered Catherine's presence, all the smart things
he had ready to say died away on his lips. " No sooner had I
seen her face than a terrible fear entered me, with so great a
trembling that I almost fainted : and though, as I said, I had
not the least intention of confessing, God so wondrously changed

my heart at her first word that I went immediately to confess myself sacramentally." Shortly after this, Malavolti reordered his whole life ; lived honourably with his wife ; frequented the churches, and was perfectly happy with the company he found in Catherine's circle. He had a saving sense of humour, this Malavolti, and for such as he, who claimed some laughter out of life, there was plenty of material for comedy in the group now rapidly forming in the Benincasa's house. In particular, nothing amused him more than to see other people go through his own experience.

His former friends did not let him escape from them easily. There were two especially ribald at his expense, quondam companions in his episodes of gallantry (one of them a connection by marriage). Whenever this pair sighted Malavolti after his conversion, they bore down on him to abuse Catherine, and they had tongues ! Things got to such a pitch that he had to suppress an inclination to run whenever he saw them turning the corner of a street. To his credit, he never breathed a word of this to Catherine. One day they stung him to such effect that he said sullenly : " Let me introduce you to her. If it has no effect, I promise you to go back to my old ways. But I warn you, if you as much as set eyes on her, she will convert you and make you go to confession." Confession ! The derisive howls of his critics startled the street. Christ Himself could not do it ! But they took up the challenge with alacrity. They would go of course and win Francesco back. They would tell her. . . . They talked indecently all the way. Malavolti led them in and meekly presented them. He waited for the crash of their assault but no word came. They stood there like stockfish, staring at Catherine with their mouths open. She took the initiative and gently reproached them for what they had been saying on their way to her. (Who in God's name had told her ?) The two gallants reddened ; then, to their own utter confusion, they began to weep bitterly, protesting between their sobs : " Tell us what to do, lady. Only command us and we will obey." " Go to confession at once," said Catherine. " Francesco, take them to

Father Della Fonte." Malavolti grinned as he marched them up to Camporeggi. The two black sheep became like little white lambs. Siena was amazed to see them devoutly attending all the Church services the ensuing Lent.

Rossetti said that most literary circles have their Scamp and their Bore. This might also be said of Catherine's Fellowship. Francesco Malavolti deserves the distinction of Scamp in that little group : he had one or two lapses (of which more presently) after the first fervour of his conversion. He was a voluble talker, restless, always independable. And Father Simone da Cortona came nearest to being a Bore. He was a very young Dominican, a novice when he first knew Catherine. He was so morbidly self-conscious and shy that it amounted to neurasthenia. When he went to the Benincasa's with a group of priests, he would hang back in the doorway in an agony of timidity. If they did not remember to drag him in (and he was often forgotten) he would go away again, chafing and wretched that he had had no word with Catherine. Once, when they were all at table, she perceived him outside, scowling as usual, and asked his companion, who had entered : " Why doesn't Father Simone come in ? " " He's feverish to-day." She called out to him, indicating a seat beside her, which Simone accepted glumly, and then she proceeded to put food into his mouth as though he were a sick child ! His letters were the most exasperating documents. He could not send the tritest message without wrapping it in layers of Scriptural quotations, so that it was as hard to get at the good man's meaning as it is to get a silkworm out of a cocoon. But Catherine always showed him particular attention. She tried her best to cure him of his painful timidity—a real barrier in his work. She knew well his innate generosity of heart. Probably she knew also that when it was a case of defending *her* against detractors, this nervous friar became as fierce as a tiger.

One day Catherine was talking to a number of those friends, when she suddenly broke off ; her colour rose and she began to utter fervent words of thanksgiving. " What is it ? " they exclaimed. " Now," she said, " you are going to see two big fish fall into the net." As she was speaking, Lisa came to the door to say two priests wanted to see her. Catherine prepared to go down, but her visitors bustled in. They said it was not necessary to speak to her alone. At their unmistakably hostile attitude, the group around Catherine stiffened. The new-comers were Father Gabriele Volterra, the Franciscan Provincial, and Father Giovanni Tantucci, an Augustinian. They were both well-known in Siena and had a great reputation as learned preachers. They both held the degree of " Master in Sacred Theology " (the Augustinian had been to Cambridge for his). Both of them detested the very name of Catherine Benincasa, as a kind of quack theologian (a woman, forsooth !) who led people astray. They made up their minds to confound her once and for all with a few well-chosen questions.

They seated themselves now, one at each side of her and began to interrogate her " like furious lions." For a few moments Catherine answered them patiently (and they could not honestly cavil at her replies). Then she suddenly cut through the stupid theological trap they were trying to set for her and reproached them vigorously for the tenor of their lives. " Master Gabriel was living in his monastery with more pomp than a cardinal : he had made himself one great room out of three cells, by having the walls removed. It was sumptuously furnished with a most noble bed with silk eiderdowns and silk curtains. He possessed a library and many precious objects, worth hundreds of ducats." Almost at Catherine's first vigorous words : " Oh, you have the shell of Christianity, with your vain science, but not the kernel . . . " he was so overcome that he pulled his keys from his girdle with a dramatic gesture and cried : " For the love of God is there no-one here who will take away all that is in my room ? " Two young men who were present rose up and said : " What do you want us to do for you ? " " Go to my room," said Gabriele, " and distribute all that is in it, leaving me nothing but my breviary."

They took him at his word ; went straight to the monastery

and dismantled his apartment, giving the books to needy students and the rest to the poor, " leaving him only what was necessary to a friar of strict observance." Although still Provincial, Master Gabriele then went to the Florence house and served in the refectory there. Giovanni Tantucci also gave away all he had and became one of Catherine's " sons." Henceforth he figures largely in the circle of her friends. In virtue of his academic degree, they always called him " the Master."

A member of the circle who must be described, because he stood alone in his practical level-headedness, was Ser Cristofano di Gano Guidini. He was older than most of the others : a Sienese notary from a little village outside Siena ; a rustic, therefore, with a thin veneer of city manners. He was an Italian Pepys in his ponderous solemnity, but with none of Pepys' coarseness. He was always telling Catherine he would be a monk if it were not for his mother. Then he decided to get married and he wrote her a careful description of the three ladies whom he had in mind—with their respective advantages set out at length. He asked her to help him to choose. (Alas, it never entered his head that one of them might refuse him !) Catherine, in her reply, protested that it was a matter more for someone in the world than for her ; however, not to disregard his request, she distantly indicated whom she thought best for him. Her letter is a marvel of delicacy. The queer thing is that Cristofano did not take her advice. He married someone else, although he cherished her letter to the end of his life.

At the age of twenty-five, Catherine had so modified her organism by continuous fasting that her stomach was now unable to endure food. Fasting became completely effortless : it was the desirable thing and eating was a torture. It is an absolute fact, testified by hosts of intimate friends, that she lived corporeally as well as spiritually on the Blessed Sacrament.

This mode of life provoked a veritable fury of criticism, so intense, so annoying to all concerned, so unabated, that she was forced to make a pretence of eating in order to appease her scandalized opponents. They said everything possible ; from the gross supposition that she fed well in private and fasted in public to make herself look interesting ; to the idea that obedience would be better, since she disobeyed her superiors by not eating ; that she was deceived by the devil ; that Christ, His Holy Mother and the Apostles ate normally and why not she ? The answer to all these objections was : *she could not eat.*

Her friends often sat down to a simple repast in her house, at which she would preside. She read to them, or talked, while they were eating. To avoid singularity, she too would partake of a morsel, and in this morsel she humorously indulged a capricious taste. Alessa prepared for her a tiny salad, or some raw herbs, or perhaps a nut. She liked also the head or the tail of an eel, or a mouthful of strong cheese. She masticated one such morsel and then drank water copiously to assist it down. But the moment any food entered her stomach, her face swelled and grew disfigured and she suffered intolerable pain until she rejected it again. She would, therefore, be forced to retire from the room with a companion and get rid of the food by inserting a straw or a feather into her throat. Alessa, who often saw blood coming from her mouth in this effort, besought her not to eat since it cost her so much, but Catherine's invariable reply was that she wished she could eat so as not to look so odd.

One little episode must be told here to show how far this singular woman condescended in these little festive gatherings, which she graced so willingly, and to what a mystical height she exalted them. Once, when a number of her friends were seated round her at table, she took a slice of bread, raised it to her mouth, then made a gesture of offering it to someone, and slipped forward in ecstasy. This was nothing new. The company finished the meal, talking animatedly among themselves. The table was cleared and someone gently detached the bread from Catherine's fingers. When she came to herself, she asked for it in a tone almost of anguish. " Why ? " they queried in amazement. She said she had touched with it the side of Christ and had been savouring it with St. Paul and St. Thomas. Complete silence descended in the room. They looked at one another and stared at her as though she already spoke to them from another world. When Neri rose to take leave, swinging his cloak on his shoulder and sweeping his hat low in the doorway, the world which he despised had receded immeasurably. He was no longer drawn against his will by the throbbing of a mandoline up a distant street, by the pale evening sky over the city of towers, by the distracting song of youth within his own heart. It seemed quite easy to dismiss all that after an hour with the circle.

But to the plain people of Siena the school of mystics merely provided more material for slanderous gossip. They were thoroughly out of sympathy with the novelty, and the " Queen of Fontebranda " was the favourite topic of jest. They gave the members of her circle the nickname of " caterinati," which the Sienese urchins jeered after them as they passed. In many respects, it was perhaps the worst moment of Catherine's life when she discovered that a real handle was provided for slander in the serious defection of one of her group. He was in some religious order, but whether professed, or a novice, or a lay-brother is not known. Neither will his name be ever revealed, because they never referred to him by name. After his disgrace, he was known to the Fellowship as " that other." He fell in love with Catherine in the worst sense and, perceiving his wretched state, she ignored him. Consumed by jealousy when he was excluded, his perverse love turned to hatred and he vowed he would kill her. One day, Alessa and Lisa had left her alone for a few moments in St. Dominic's when he chanced to enter. Seizing his opportunity, he drew out a knife and was in the act of striking when his hand was angrily arrested by a man who had just entered the church. This religious was consequently dismissed from his order and returned to his parents' home in the country in a state bordering on insanity.

Catherine had seen nothing of what had happened, being absorbed in prayer, but the scene was related to her afterwards. It caused tongues to wag furiously. " That," said one-half of Siena, " is what comes of those fellowships ! " But, for good or ill, the unique circle was formed and widening rapidly every day.

While Catherine lived and was within reach of her friends, it would be impossible to disband it.

One friend always brought another. Only those who came very close to Catherine and figured prominently in her life have been described here. Her " family," as she called it, was really very numerous. Ser Cristofano brought the artist and politician, Andrea Vanni. There was a representative from most of the great Sienese families : Alessa Saracini, Francesco Malavolti, Gabriele Piccolomini (a married man), young Matteo Tolomei, whose brother she converted in a striking way, and whom she inspired to enter the Dominican order ; Tommaso Guelfaccio, who had been a disciple of Giovanni Colombini ; a youth named Nigi Arzocchi. Neither Matteo Cenni nor the Master rested until they had made Catherine acquainted with all the Augustinian hermits of Lecceto.

The great English recluse who lived there, William Flete (who had converted Cenni), became a humble follower of Catherine's counsel, asking for it repeatedly. He was a man of great religious fame : a writer, too, whose controversial works were carefully copied and treasured. He spent his days in the wood, meditating and writing ; returning to the monastery in the evening. One of his personal penances was to drink nothing but water mixed with vinegar. He and Catherine became great friends, although they never quite agreed. She thought that he was somewhat harsh in his judgment of others and should be more compassionate. Once he complained to her that the Prior wanted him to say Mass for the community occasionally during the week ; he apparently considered this a great hardship. But she answered he ought to say it every day in the monastery, if it were the Prior's wish. She thought him far too self-centred and constantly reproached the learned recluse for his " ignorance." He, on his part, revered her, and he induced two others to the same frame of mind : his chosen companion, Father Antonio, and one Felice Tancredi.

Business connections of the Benincasa joined the circle, like Sano di Maco, an influential merchant. Perhaps the most pathetic of them all was Father Santi, an aged hermit from the Abruzzi, whom they called " the Saint." He had been an intimate friend of Giovanni Colombini. " In his old age, finding this precious pearl, Catherine, he left the quiet of his cell and his former mode of life, in order that he might help others as well as himself and followed her, especially because of the signs and wonders that he daily saw both in himself and in others ; declaring that he found greater quiet and consolation of mind, as also greater advance in virtue, by following her and listening to her teaching, than he had ever found in the solitude of his cell."

All these people, from the young novice Simone da Cortona, to the aged priest, Father Santi, called Catherine " Mother " ; that is the name her sister-in-law, Lisa, gave her, and Cecca : both of whom were twice her age. Neri, Francesco, all the laymen fell into the way of it. It was the only term that could remotely express her position among them ; or the reverent love with which she inspired them. Yet the name irked them vaguely ; she was so unlike the traditional lady abbess. Once admitted to intimacy in the circle, they changed it to " Mamma." (Then it was strange indeed to hear Ser Cristofano, for instance, calling this girl, Mamma.) But it was necessary to establish a difference : such throngs sought her out daily for counsel, calling her " Madre." They decided she was the Mother of thousands, but " Mamma " to them.

The *cenacolo* of Catherine Benincasa preceded all the famous salons of Europe : that of the divine poetess, Vittoria Colonna, came a century later ; there was none in France until the seventeenth century ; nothing remotely resembling it in England until the nineteenth. In the *cenacolo*, as in the salon, conversation was the chief amusement. But in everything else the Sienese movement must be isolated. The French and English groups, say the salon of Madame Récamier and the " intellectual " Sunday afternoons of George Eliot, are utterly unlike the Fellowship. Catherine did not choose the members of her circle according as they could conform with the artificial rules

of the Hotel de Rambouillet. She could not have endured to
foster the monstrous egotism of a Chateaubriand, like Madame
Récamier. Her friends came to her unsought, spontaneously,
and their intercourse has all the freshness of a dewy morning.
In passing from the French to the English model, the transition
becomes still more cheerless. The Sienese girl is poles apart
from the stern, square-faced Englishwoman, with the heavy
jaws and large, drooping mouth.   George Eliot was a great
woman, but it is difficult to imagine her enlivening anyone. Her
conversation must have breathed the chill of her icy philosophy.
In her dark novels she proposes to burdened humanity the
depressing doctrine of self-renunciation *as an end in itself.*
Catherine taught a more triumphant philosophy of life. Being
the truth, it was harmonious, lucid and encouraging. She
summed everything up in the love of God : from the creation
of the world to her own vicarious suffering. And what she
taught—and lived—most eagerly was this : we can express love
of God only in love of our neighbour.

Here is the supreme difference between the Fellowship and
every subsequent group resembling it. Although formed in
the first bright dawn of the Renaissance, the " caterinati " did
not pursue letters, or culture or foster their own genius, or even
seek holiness for their own satisfaction. Catherine would have
dismissed all that as waste of time. She often explained : you
must not love God *for yourself.* When the " Saint " said that in
his old age he began to learn how to " help others as well as
himself," he hinted at the purpose of the Fellowship. *They were
training for action.* Very soon Catherine was to draw out the
steel she had forged and test it. The time was rapidly approaching when she was to rally them imperiously and say, in the tense
accents of command : " Now ! "

Chapter V

DIEU LE VEULT

It has been finely said that " the heart died out of the Middle Ages " when the Christian world lost Jerusalem. Three times already in her history, Europe had spent herself in protracted, sweating efforts to plant the Cross securely in the land where men had first seen that Sign. The shame of that fourth ignoble expedition, ending up in the wrongful taking of Constantinople, had been in some measure atoned for by the long heroism of King Louis of France. But it was now one hundred years since the saint-king had died in his Crusader's cloak on the scorching plain of Tunis. Asia Minor was the grave of over one million crusaders. And the Crescent not only hung over Jerusalem in triumph, but was approaching every day with more ominous menace to the Christian frontiers. Now, there was cruelty enough in the internal wars of Christendom, but nevertheless there was a quality in Mohammedan warfare which filled the Christian mind with detestation and dismay. Christians always had at least one basis of agreement : a common standard of morality. They knew themselves when they fell short of it. But the infidel enemy was wholly incomprehensible and baneful, beyond appeal. This difference is illustrated by an incident of the Fifth Crusade.

It happened in Egypt, not so far from Damietta on the march up the Nile. Harried on all sides by the Saracens, progress was terribly difficult and the Crusaders suffered greatly from famine and disease. They decided to retreat again to their stronghold in Damietta but found they were cut off and King Louis, Joinville (our chronicler) and others were made prisoners. After a period of horrible suffering, a treaty was concluded with the Soldan by which Damietta was to be surrendered again for the king's release and the other notable prisoners ransomed for large sums. Then from galleys moored on the river, the imprisoned Crusaders were horrified spectators of a revolt in the enemy camp, during which the Soldan was killed by his emirs.

"Almoadam had been attacked while he sat at dinner in his tent. Slightly wounded, he escaped and took refuge in the innermost tower of his encampment. Then they threw at him Greek fire, and it caught the tower, which was made of pine planks and cotton cloth. The tower flared up quickly, nor have I ever seen finer nor straighter flame. When the Soldan saw this, he gat down swiftly, and came flying towards the river, all along the way of which I have already spoken to you. The guard had broken down all that enclosed way with their swords ; and as the Soldan fled along to go to the river, one of them gave him a spear-thrust in the ribs, and then he fled to the river, trailing the spear. And they followed after, till they were all swimming and came and killed him in the river, not far from the galley in which we were. One of the knights cut him open with his sword, and took the heart out of his body ; and then he came to the king, his hand all reeking with his blood, and said : ' What wilt thou give me ? for I have slain thine enemy, who, had he lived, would have slain thee ! ' And the king answered him never a word. . . . "

Fifty years before Catherine Benincasa was born, the whole of Asia Minor and all the Greek possessions beyond the Bosphorus and the Hellespont were lost to the Turks. Now these were steadily acquiring all the provinces of the Greek Empire in Europe. The Christian Emperor of the East was only a vassal of the Sultan. Hungary, and through it all Christendom, was seriously threatened. But the Christian world, consuming its strength in fratricidal wars, had no thought for the peril at its frontiers. Europe seemed totally sunk in indifference until Gregory XI succeeded to the Papal throne. True, some of his predecessors at Avignon, notably Clement V, John XXII and

Urban V, had preached a Crusade, but with neither consistency nor great effect. The difference lay in this : that it was the enthusiasm of Gregory XI's pontificate. Among his first acts of administration, he made over to Raymond de Berenger, Grand Master of the Knights of Rhodes, the rich principality of Smyrna, which could be used as a French crusading basis in the East. He also wrote to the King of England, to the Count of Flanders and to the Doge of Venice, inciting them to take arms against the Turk. Then he had the Crusade preached throughout Europe and in due time the ripple of the commotion reached Siena.

In Fontebranda, Catherine welcomed the news of Gregory's efforts with joy. To her it was like the voice of Moses, leading them out of their long night of ignominy. She sprang ardently to the response. Here was the purifying flame for which the Church had been languishing. She had no doubt whatever that the slack, the venal, even the rotten members of Christ's mystical body would recover their baptismal glory in the cleansing power of this ideal. She heard already that martial music of armies tramping eastwards with the Cross for standard. The Crusade was the simple and clear solution of every problem of the day. The fierce commercial rivalry between the Communes, their internal faction fights, family vendettas, class warfare, the catch-cries of Guelph and Ghibelline would all be forgotten in the united effort for this great achievement. Above all, supreme relief for torn Italy, it would rid the republics of that hydra-headed monster which preyed on them incessantly : the wandering companies of free-lances. Here was fighting which promised to be fierce enough to whet the keenest appetite. God knew whether there were not soldiers enough in Italy who battened on warfare ! Let them enroll now in a just war which, were the Christians victorious, could result in nothing but good for the conquered, because these too would then become sharers in the precious Blood of Christ.

Thus began the period, in 1372, when Catherine apparently thought of nothing but the Crusade. She talked of it,

wrote about it, and prayed for it with tears of desire. She
enkindled all her friends with her zeal and they set themselves
to prepare interiorly for the great day of renovation, with
pathetic confidence in its advent. By letter, she rallied all who
were beyond reach of her spoken word. One of many similar
letters is particularly interesting, showing how serenely Catherine
tried to bend to her will minds utterly dissimilar from her own.
It was in those apparently hopeless efforts that she often powerfully prevailed. It is the letter written to William Flete, the
phlegmatic English hermit of Lecceto, known to the Fellowship
as " the Bachelor," from the degree he had acquired at Cambridge. (It will be recalled that it was he who had brought
about the conversion of Matteo Cenni, one of Catherine's oldest
friends.) Flete was a typical Englishman in his sangfroid, his
self-complaisance and his serenely unconscious egotism. In
some respects, though perhaps her most extravagant admirer,
he was the most obtuse of her friends. He had the curious effect
of provoking Catherine to irony and her irony was particularly
subtle and penetrating—as will be seen later on. But did the
Englishman ever taste the salt of it ! Anyhow, Catherine
addressed him as follows about the Crusade :

"Do you not think that I was very glad . . . when I
heard that voice desired by all the Church saying to us :
' Come forth, children, from your lands and from your houses :
follow me, and offer your bodies in sacrifice.' When I reflect
that God has given us the grace to hear this voice and see
such an offering of our lives out of our boundless love of the
Lamb, it seems that at the very thought of it, my soul would
leap from my body. So let us turn then, my sons and brothers
in Christ, offering up our sweet and loving desires, constraining
and beseeching the divine goodness to make us worthy of it
quickly. In this we must not be careless but very solicitous ;
you and the others must urge it on continually. It seems the
time is approaching as there is so much good will everywhere.
I must also tell you that we sent Father James to the Governor
of Arborea with a letter about this crusade ; he answered me

graciously that he wishes to come in person and supply for ten years two galleys, one thousand knights, three thousand foot-soldiers and six hundred crossbow men. Know too that Genoa is all roused, offering goods and men to this same personage . . . "

As early as the 1st July, 1372, a great man in the religious world, Don John of the Cells, entered into the discussion of the Crusade, apparently in opposition to Catherine. He was a hermit, living in Vallombrosa, outside Florence, and was one of the most notable penitents of the day. At an early age he had become a monk and proved an unworthy one. While Superior of the Holy Trinity in Florence, he had even descended to Black Magic and was imprisoned for his crimes. On his release, he became more famous for his self-imposed penances than he had been for his infamy. He retired to the solitude of Vallombrosa, where he led a saintly life. The following extract from a letter of his to a priest-friend, when he began his penances, shows the temper of his mind :

" I used to taste what now, in my wretchedness, I hardly remember. I have fallen and cannot rise by myself ; I strive to return to the man I was but dare not, for my mind is overwhelmed by remorse and confounded by the shame of my sins. Receive me, then, crying to you from the abyss, and begin to build up in me what I have destroyed."

But by this time, Don John's reputation for sanctity had extended far and wide. He was the religious director of a group of Florentine youths, and people everywhere appealed to his counsel. A young nun named Domitilla had taken Catherine's pleading for the Crusade to mean that nuns, too, were to go in person to the Holy Land. Don John wrote to this Domitilla, sternly disapproving the notion. " You have Christ," he said, " in the Sacrament of the Altar." But he had already heard enough about Catherine Benincasa to be able to add this : " Go again to her and ask her how she arrived at such perfection : you shall find it was by silence and prayer, because she kept silence for eight years, according to what is said, and kept to her room always, in prayer." Presently some word of this correspondence reached William Flete in his solitude at Lecceto. Supposing Catherine to have been attacked, he wrote an indignant defence of her to Don John. This led to an exchange of letters between the two hermits. Far from wishing to depreciate Catherine, Don John formally joined her circle as a result of the misunderstanding. In a little while, no other disciple could rival the famous penitent's expressions of enthusiasm in Catherine's regard : " Oh, angelic and divine," he said of her, " she illuminates our hemisphere like the sun." William Flete, as usual, had been too hasty.

Catherine's influence may now be said to have penetrated the very highest ecclesiastical circles in the land. In the year 1372, she confidently addressed a letter to Cardinal d'Estaing, newly appointed Papal Legate at Bologna, a man of outstanding character. She tells him to be " a virile and not a cowardly man, so that you may manfully serve the Spouse of Christ." She wrote also to the Vicar Apostolic in Perugia, the Abbot of Marmoutier, who was detestable in every particular of his public and private life ; one who provided in himself a great handle to the enemies of the Church. He was a nephew of Gregory XI and apparently approached Catherine for advice. In her striking reply, she did not mince words : two evils in the Church must be remedied : nepotism and too much leniency in punishing the guilty.

" To reform the whole, you must destroy right down to the foundations. I beg of you, even if you have to die for it, to tell the Holy Father to remedy all this iniquity and when the time comes to make ministers and cardinals, not to make them for flattery, nor for money, nor for simony. But, with all your power, implore him to look for virtue and good repute in the man, not considering whether he is noble or plebeian ; for it is virtue that makes a man noble and pleasing to God."

Her long letter need not be given in full here. There are phrases in it which must have made the Abbot of Marmoutier wince, brutal cynic though he was. We do not find any record of his having a second time approached her for her opinion.

Catherine having now been admitted to the counsels of the Church, her influence inevitably passed into the sphere of politics also : Into the domain of the Church's perpetual struggle with temporal powers. War was raging in northern Italy between Bernabo Visconti and the Papal Legate. In the late Autumn of 1373 an ambassador from Bernabo Visconti arrived in Siena and made a prolonged stay in the city. While there, he too came to the door so familiar to the Fellowship, seeking an interview with Catherine in the name of Bernabo Visconti, Lord of Milan and of his wife, Beatrice della Scala. This was something new. When Catherine turned to Neri to dictate a reply, she was committed, irrevocably, to taking part henceforth in the confused and shifting world of Italian politics.

Before giving the gist of her reply to the Visconti, it is necessary to explain who and what they were. Hereditary enemies of the Church, first of all. A kind of grim humour ran in the family. When an uncle of this Bernabo, one Archbishop John Visconti, was Lord of Milan, he was summoned by Clement VI to Avignon to answer for his conduct. First, with all manner of imprecations and defiant threats, he refused to go ; then suddenly said he would go. A secretary was sent before him to prepare the accommodation. Every vacant house in Avignon and its environs was rented and immense quantities of food ordered. Hearing of the commotion, the Pope sent for the secretary, to ask in mild surprise how many Visconti counted on bringing in his suite ? He was told : 12,000 knights, 5,000 foot-soldiers and an indefinite number of Milanese gentlemen ! Clement hastily sent word to the magnificent prelate not to trouble to come.

But Archbishop John was a mild lamb compared with this Bernabo, who was a singularly bloody despot. Hunting was his great passion and he indulged it in the spacious way of his family. Five thousand hunting-dogs were quartered upon the citizens, convents and monasteries of the state ; the overbearing keepers of those dogs were more feared than their master. In addition, he burdened his subjects with terrible taxations and game-laws. Two friars once ventured to remonstrate with him and he had them burned alive. The late Pope Urban V had had reason to know him. When simple Abbot, he had been sent with a cardinal to present Bernabo with a bull of excommunication. The tyrant led them to a bridge over the Naviglio in the centre of Milan. " Choose," he said to them suddenly, " whether, before leaving me, you will eat or drink." And, as the astonished legates did not answer, he added with fearful oaths : " Don't think you can go before having either eaten or drunk in such a way that you will remember me." The legates looked around them : they were surrounded by Visconti's guards in the midst of a hostile people. They looked at the murky river beneath them and one of them answered, with an attempt at lightness : " I prefer to eat than to ask to drink near such a river." " Very well," replied Bernabo, " here are your bulls of excommunication. You shall not leave this bridge before you have eaten in my presence the parchment on which they are written, the leaden seals hanging from them and the silk cords which attach them." In the midst of the armed guards and a huge crowd of people, the legates were forced to obey.

This is the fierce despot who now sought Catherine Benincasa's counsel and goodwill. In her reply, she calls him her " dearest brother in Christ," but takes him to task at once for laying hands on priests :

" I tell you that God does not wish you, nor anyone else, to make yourself the executioner of His ministers, for He has reserved this to Himself and committed it to His Vicar. Punish your own subjects when they do wrong ; but never touch those who are the ministers of this glorious and precious Blood, which you can have by no other hands than theirs."

She reminds him of the awful spiritual power of the Pope : " He has the power and the authority and there is no-one who can take it out of his hands, because it was given to him by the first sweet Truth." Then, triumphantly, she leads up to the great opportunity now open to Bernabo for making amends : the Crusade. (What a chance for such as he !) " Get ready, for it befits you to make this sweet atonement ; even as you have gone against him, so now go to his aid when the Holy Father raises on high the banner of the most holy Cross. Be the first to invite and urge the Holy Father to make haste, for it is a great shame and disgrace to Christians to suffer wretched infidels to possess what by right is ours."

Being now a factor, not to be discounted, in the ecclesiastical and political life of Italy, she pushed forward with all her genius the plans for the Crusade. But she was peculiarly solitary. Though surrounded by friends who obeyed her implicitly and hung upon every word of hers, it is enough to review them rapidly again in order to understand the gulf which separated her from them. Lisa, the good housewife ; Cecca, the widowed mother of three Dominican sons, who could lawfully consider her life-work over ; Alessa, though cultured, thoroughly a woman of her age and country—not remotely concerned with achievement ; Father Della Fonte, a really good priest, but neither influential nor learned. Father Bartolomeo, though learned, was still too young to carry weight, (he was only four years older than Catherine.) Neri, the hyper-sensitive poet, who was only learning to distinguish ; Malavolti, the recent convert, not yet dependable ; Father Simone, the shrinking novice ; Father Tantucci (whom they called " the Master "), the re-converted ; William Flete, the slow-moving Englishman ; that other great solitary, Don John of the Cells, all of them eagerly taking guidance from *her*. Then there was Ser Cristofano, the rustic notary ; Father Santi, the aged hermit from the Abruzzi ; Matteo Cenni, also a re-converted, absorbed in his present life of reparation. They all made inordinate demands on Catherine, depending upon her utterly. But she herself stood alone, in a queer circle of solitude. She had no one with whom she could even discuss the problems continually harassing her mind. There were moments when she agonized for the supreme relief of confiding her divine intuitions to a mind capable of testing them. There was no such person in her circle. Above all, there was none among her colleagues with sufficient *influence* in religion or politics to help her materially and every day she perceived more clearly that this need was hampering her efforts. Flung, without any straining on her part, into the very centre of the life of her day, she supremely needed guidance and collaboration.

Providence saw to it, and in the form of a trial. During May, 1374, she was one day perplexed to receive a summons from the Master-General of the Dominican Order, Father Elias of Toulouse, to attend the chapter-general, meeting at Florence at the end of the month. The eyes of the great Order were now fairly levelled on the obscure little tertiary in Siena. This command meant a whole day's journey, riding on a mule through the hills of Tuscany. Alessa, Lisa and Cecca went with her. It was her first journey out of Siena since that fruitless one with her mother to the baths of Vignone twelve years ago. Since the acts of this Chapter have been lost, it is impossible to state definitely the charges laid against her. That she had to answer some accusation, one knows from a Florentine chronicler who tells us she was defended by Father Angiolo Adimari, who had known her as a child in Siena. One can think of many possible charges which could have been urged against her : her fasting continued to give scandal ; she was over-zealous about the Crusade—sufficient to make her religious superiors uneasy ; her enemies liked to quote peculiar examples of her exegesis.

Whatever the charge may have been, Catherine seems to have been exonerated, since her subsequent action was in no way restricted as a result of this citation. But at the annual provincial chapter held immediately after the chapter-general, the new lector appointed to Siena, one Raimondo delle Vigne of Capua, was also officially appointed to be Catherine Benincasa's confessor and director ; this as a safeguard on the part of the Order, for he was one of their most reliable members. Catherine remained in Florence until June 29th. On her return from the chapter-general, her position was immeasurably stronger than it had been before. She was now known to the whole Order and tacitly they had pronounced a " nulla osta " on her work. Some months had to pass, however, before she could fully recognize what the support of her official director meant. Her acquaintance with the newly-appointed lector at Camporeggi was to change her life.

This Father Raimondo delle Vigne of Capua was an aristocrat, first of all : one of his ancestors was that Pietro delle Vigne, Chancellor to Emperor Frederick II, and vindicated for all time by Dante, in his *Inferno*. Raimondo, too, had great learning and had acquired prestige in the Order. At this time, he was some sixteen years older than Catherine, a practical and experienced priest. He had held important offices : as Prior of the Minerva at Rome ; as director of the convent of Dominican nuns of Saint Agnes at Montepulciano. In the delicate work of directing nuns, he was therefore an expert. During the two years spent at this convent, he had written a life of the Blessed Agnes. Thence he had been appointed lector at S. Maria Novella at Florence, and thence now to be lector at St. Dominic's, Siena.

The unquestioned authority of this priest was thenceforward to be used generously by him to protect and further Catherine's work. Their encounter was Providential. In contrast with her ardent, impetuous spirit, he was cool and deliberate. Passionately convinced of her own immediate intuitions, she was impatient of caution. But Delle Vigne never acted on impulse. He weighed every judgment and was cautious, even to the point of timidity. In addition to his learning, he was remarkable for charity and for an exemplary life. The moment he met Catherine, he touched the point of greatness, because he rose immediately to some perception of her possibilities. He was so magnificent in this that the tribute cannot be over-emphasized. In no wise disconcerted by her complete novelty, or by the intrusion of such a phenomenon in the ecclesiastical world, he studied her with interest. Although it was a long time before he was convinced of her divine mission (and then only by miraculous signs), he helped her, pending his decision. One of his first actions was to abolish restrictions on the number of her Holy Communions, insisting that she should

receive as often as she wished. Then he encouraged her to talk
and, it must be confessed, her volubility amazed him. One of
his very first impressions of her, if put into words, would have run
something like this : " Lord, what a talker she is ! " Because
he afterwards naïvely left it on record that he used to fall alseep
at first, while the torrent of her words flowed on. When
Catherine perceived his placid slumbers, not a whit abashed,
she would rouse him relentlessly with : " Oh ! . . . Am I
talking to the walls or to you ? "

But he fully shared her enthusiasm on one point : the Crusade.
And when, in conjunction with her efforts, he began to preach
it with effect, it seemed that between them they would set
Christendom on fire and send Europe marching eastwards again
with the battle cry of victory : " God wills it ! "

Chapter VI

THE DIVINE SEAL

CATHERINE had an amazing faculty of sounding life to its depths wherever she went. During her few weeks' stay in Florence, she had not been contemplating life there from outside drawn curtains and closed doors. She cannot have been a stranger in the city one day, for in her short sojourn there, she formed friendships which endured throughout her life. The group was the usual fantastic medley : Niccolò Soderini, one of the city governors (he was Gonfalonier of Justice in 1371 and later one of the Priors of the Arts) ; Don John of the Cells, the famous penitent, and his group of disciples ; Pietro Bardi, gentleman ; Francesco Pippino, tailor ; Pietro Canigiani, Florentine ambassador on three occasions ; innumerable nuns and priests.

Someone from among this new group of friends in Florence, with sufficient ability and interest, committed to writing a very fine memoir of Catherine. We know not to this day who it was (there are many guesses). But the account was certainly written between May and October, 1374, and the fact is interesting an an indication of her growing fame. With all these people, she discussed the Crusade exhaustively. Through them, she penetrated the civil, political and religious life of their city. Afterwards, she had not merely been to Florence ; she knew it. She had seized the Republic's soul, as it were. Just as she did not write letters because she had too much time on her hands, but rather under great pressure ; so now she travelled under compulsion. Since she had to do it, she did it intelligently and understood what she saw. A complete contrast with that vague somnambulist, the modern traveller.

When she returned to Siena in that June of 1374, the hospitals claimed her again because plague was rife there. Those old enough to remember 1348 saw the same sickening scenes re-enacted. All civic life was at a standstill. In the hot months of June, July and August, the narrow high-walled streets stank with rotting corpses, while the death roll mounted steadily to one-third of the population. All who could do so fled. Efforts for the Crusade were abandoned while the city was so stricken. Catherine threw herself into the work of charity at hand to the exclusion of all else. Carrying a scent-bottle (supreme alleviation to sufferers in that fetid atmosphere) and a small lantern at night, she toiled with the sick unremittingly. She rallied the Fellowship and they too braced themselves to bend close to the livid swollen faces, choking down the nausea of that pestilential odour. Matteo Cenni and all her Dominican friends distinguished themselves ; the neurasthenic Father Simone was among the most courageous.

Even though the plague could hardly be cured, it was the truest charity to remain with the sufferers and help them to die, for their lonely death-beds, especially in the case of children, were the most terrible feature of the epidemic. Nothing could better illustrate this horror of isolation than that last will and testament of Basso della Penna. Popular and applauded always, for he was a notorious jester, when stricken with the disease, he was abandoned by his relations and left with only the flies for company. He succeeded in getting a notary to take his will and dictated :

" That my sons and heirs give yearly, on the Festival of St. James of July, a basket of half-pears to the flies."

Said the notary : " Basso, thou jestest even now."

Said Basso : " Write as I bid you ; because, in this my sickness, I have had neither friend nor kinsman that hath not abandoned me save only the flies alone. Wherefore, being thus beholden to them, I deem not that God would have pity on me if I should fail to render them according to their deserts. And that you may be assured that I jest not and that I speak sooth, write that, if this be not done every year, my sons shall be disinherited . . ."

Many among Catherine's friends suffered grievously. All three Dominican sons of Francesca Gori died. The mortality among children was frightful : Catherine lost six little nieces and nephews and had to bury them with her own hands. She also lost her stepbrother, Bartolomeo (Lisa's husband). Both Monna Lapa and Lisa, being now widows, joined the Dominican tertiaries. So that henceforth all the women with whom Catherine lives wear the white tunic and black cloak of the Third Order. It may be here remarked that a subtle change has come over Monna Lapa in recent years. She no longer cavils at her daughter's way of life, but indeed tries to imitate her. And, out of her large family, she seems to grow every day more pathetically dependent on Catherine's company.

With all their true courage, the Fellowship were not immune. One morning, on his rounds, Father Delle Vigne found the Misericordia Hospital plunged in gloom because Matteo Cenni, the rector, was stricken. He had been carried to his room from Mass and was already incapable of speech. Deeply distressed, Delle Vigne visited him and then left to procure such poor remedies as were, almost hopelessly, applied to the stricken. Meanwhile, Catherine arrived there and learned the news. Never more exasperatingly matter-of-fact than when a miracle might be suspected, she mounted the stairs rapidly, calling out in her gay, ringing voice as she approached the rector's room : " Get up, get up, Matteo, this is no time for you to lie in bed." The rector dragged himself to his feet like a man in a dream ; the plague spots disappeared instantly and strength came back to his limbs. When Delle Vigne dolefully returned from the physician, he found Cenni tranquilly eating his dinner, which (as if to prove the new vigour of his constitution) included even *raw onions*. These people eschewed the dramatic.

No one needed more convincing than Delle Vigne himself where Catherine's miraculous gifts were concerned. As has been said, they were acquainted for a long time before he ceased speculating about her. She knew it well. She often surprised him in a cool, appraising look. It is amusing to notice how slow and deliberate she became when he sought a cure. He told the story afterwards how one night, when about to rise for Office, he was seized with a violent pain in the groin and felt with his hand the fatal swelling. Horror-stricken, he prepared for death and waited impatiently for dawn so that he could acquaint Catherine. His fears increased as the pains in his head became more severe and fever rose. At daybreak, he got a friar to help him down the hill to the Benincasa's. She was already out visiting the sick. Falling on a couch, he begged Monna Lapa to send for her. Catherine came back and put her hand on his forehead without speaking. Then she knelt and began to pray and an hour and a half crawled by, until Delle Vigne began to think she had forgotten all about him. Tremors shook him, like a prelude to the vomitings which usually preceded death. Well he knew every stage of the disease. But Catherine rose nonchalantly and began to prepare some food for him. He took it submissively out of her hands ; slept and, on awakening, found himself completely restored.

By the end of August, the violence of the epidemic had spent itself. Every day there were smaller and smaller numbers of sick to be visited. Those whom the disease had spared began to breathe freely. Trades were resumed. Deserters flocked back to the city. The circle began to meet again. They talked with an ardour enkindled by the enforced dispersal of these months. They took up again, where they had laid it down, the glorious plan of the Crusade and dreamed of its accomplishment. When the first winds of Autumn seemed to cleanse the city of the last miasma of disease, they left the narrow streets for restoring walks in the red and golden woods or through valleys where the vines were a fairy splendour. Accompanied by Delle Vigne, Alessa and one Jeanne, Catherine even went to visit the Dominican convent of Montepulciano, where Delle Vigne had spent two years as director and where he had written the life of the Blessed Agnes, whose body was then preserved there intact. Catherine

had a great devotion to this precocious and original young saint.
It is said that when she bent over the body, it showed life for one
miraculous moment. Girolamo del Pacchia has left a frescoed
representation of that strange scene, with Neri di Landoccio in
the foreground. By this time the grave young poet had been
writing Catherine's letters for her during nearly three years.
He knew her very well. Clad in knee-breeches and doublet,
with an ample cloak flung over his shoulders and a velvet cap
on his long hair, he stands erect and motionless. In contrast
with his impassive bearing all the others present are startled into
expressions of amazement and admiration. But he appears
unmoved and fixes the miracle-worker with an intense and
unwavering regard.

Catherine's efforts for the Crusade spread her fame beyond
Siena. Other Dominican convents besides that of Montepulciano clamoured for a visit from her. Two were particularly
persistent : the Holy Cross and Misericordia convents in Pisa.
Undoubtedly Father Lazzarino must have played a great part
in making her known there. (It will be recalled that he had
retired to Pisa immediately after his conversion.) Anyhow,
following repeated and pressing entreaties, she set out to visit
the great maritime republic at the end of January 1375. She
was accompanied by the usual group of friends and was the guest
of one of the principal Pisan families, the Buonconti. So potent
was the influence of sanctity in the Middle Ages that the mere
breath of her name in the city fanned the flame of a great
religious revival. Fathers Delle Vigne, Della Fonte and Bartolomeo followed her there in a short while to hear the confessions
of the vast throng of re-converted. The priests in Pisa could
not possibly cope with them. In mediaeval Europe, sanctity
was considered by far the highest human achievement : people
ran to see a reputed saint with more curiosity and enthusiasm
than to applaud kingship or any other title to honour. Whenever Catherine appeared on the streets of Pisa, crowds gathered.
They pressed around her to kiss her hand, making the most
extravagant demonstrations of admiration and love. Catherine

never said much on such occasions, but she scrutinized everyone
who approached her with an absorbed and personal interest.
Great artist in life, she was never weary of the human face.
Something in that unfailing attention of hers jarred on Father
Raimondo. He reproached her about it : she should check
this furore of hand-kissing. " But I didn't even *see* how they
saluted me," she protested in amazement. " I was so interested
in them."

Everything in Pisa spoke of the East : the Arabian place-
names, the dromedaries passing through the streets ; the very
soil from the Holy Land in the Campo Santo ; the sea, gateway
to great enterprise, which Catherine now saw for the first time.
In this suggestive spot, she and her companions slaved for the
realization of their dream : the Crusade. Just before leaving
for Pisa, she had been greatly encouraged by a personal message
from the Pope. He had sent Alfonso di Vadaterra (who had
renounced a bishopric through humility and had been confessor
and companion of the famous Bridget of Sweden) with a special
indulgence and a request that she should pray particularly for
the Crusade. Catherine had written Gregory XI a glowing
letter of thanks and praise of " the holy passage," as she called
it. Now, from Pisa, she sent letters all over Italy and beyond
summoning men and women to the heroic adventure.

That persuasive summons to which Cenni had responded from
the gate of death now seemed to ring throughout Europe. One
of her first appeals was to Queen Joanna of Naples, who was
vaguely disturbed by it in her corrupt and gorgeous court. She
had a sinister fame, this woman. Accused by popular voice of
connivance in her first husband's murder, she was now married
for the fourth time. Among her titles was the meaningless one of
Queen of Jerusalem, which caught Catherine's fancy. (Common
report gave the Queen another title, which fitted better :
regina meretrix.) She was at this time past fifty, twenty-three
years older than Catherine, who summoned her as confidently
as she had called to Bernabò Visconti to take this great chance
of redemption, addressing her as :

" Dearest and most reverend Mother and Sister in Christ Jesus, Madame the Queen. . . . Up bravely, sweetest sister. It is no longer time to sleep, because time does not sleep but is always passing like the wind. Raise up in yourself out of love the standard of the most holy cross ; because soon it shall be lifted up in reality since, from what I gather, the Holy Father will raise it against the Turks. And therefore I beseech you so to order that we may all go and die for Christ. Now I pray and implore you on the part of the Crucified to succour the Spouse in her need, in goods, in persons and in counsel ; in every way you possibly can, show that you are a faithful daughter of holy Church. . . . "

Before a reply could be expected, she wrote a second vibrant appeal. The Pope was active in the matter. He had sent Bulls to the Friars Minor, to the Dominican Provincial and to Raimondo Delle Vigne, with instructions for organizing the Crusade. They were to preach it and then take a kind of census of volunteers. Catherine was overjoyed that the plans had reached practical details. She passed on the news to Joanna with a third appeal, this time pressing for an answer : " I beg you humbly, my mother, not to disdain to reply to me, telling me what holy and good will you have put into this sacred work." These letters were a novelty in the Neapolitan court. Joanna was faintly amused ; indeed rather liked herself in the rôle of Crusader. She replied graciously, promising to help. Brimming with exultation, Catherine wrote her again, bidding her inform the Pope of her good will. Thus, step by step, the negotiations went on. Queen Elizabeth of Hungary was approached likewise and many others.

She even wrote to John Hawkwood.

He was the most formidable of all the free-lance captains, bearing out in his character the old proverb : "An Englishman Italianate is the devil incarnate." Born in the county of Essex of good middle-class English parents, he had served in the war with France. After the treaty of Brétigny, not liking to return to civilian life, he had led a company of free-lances south, looking for hire. He had battened ever since on the petty Italian wars. Brave with a savage ferocity, occasionally keeping his word, he was a good leader and his power lay in the discipline of his company. He dominated Italian life for thirty years. He was held in a kind of superstitious horror. One could not do the peninsula a greater kindness than to rid it of him. On this man, too, Catherine tried the persuasion of her written word, calling him her " dearest brother," and reminding him also of the treacherous brevity of time. But she does not ask him to change his nature : " since you delight so much in war and fighting . . . fight the infidels." With some trepidation, Delle Vigne presented this letter to Hawkwood, who was actually touched. He and all his chiefs swore on the Sacrament and gave a declaration in writing, with their individual seals to it, that they would join the Crusade when it was proclaimed.

Things were going very well indeed. Gracious replies poured in on all sides. This visit to Pisa was a happy one. Not merely did Catherine view the sea, but she embarked on the novel highway, visiting the Carthusian monastery on the island of Gorgona. The prior there held her in very high esteem. He got her to speak to the assembled monks and they were delighted. Her glimpse of the vast expanse of water inspired her with a thousand new metaphors which henceforth fill her letters : God is the placid sea in which His creatures may lose themselves ; He is the boundless sea ; the sea of light ; the fathomless sea.

But here, as elsewhere, criticisms of her life were not lacking. She received a poem from one Bianco da Siena, a disciple of Giovanni Colombini, which touched her on a sensitive spot : her fasting. He wanted to know why she could not live like everyone else and preferably a more retired kind of life. As a matter of fact, Catherine came upon Delle Vigne and Bartolomeo reading, in high dudgeon, this curious poem, or " Lauds " (but it was not exactly a song of praise.) The priests had not meant to show it to her. They knew many fine rejoinders they could make this Bianco. But she detested that anyone should take up

the cudgels in her defence.   She wrote back a mild reply.
" You say that I must pray particularly to God to be able to
eat.   And I say to you, Father, in the presence of God, that
in every way I possibly could I have always forced myself to
take food once or twice a day : and I have prayed continually and do pray to God and will pray, that He may
give me grace to live like other creatures in this business of
eating, if it is His will, because it is mine . . . "
Just this also she had to say : " I pray you, too, not to judge
lightly if you are not well enlightened before God."

But pugnacious critics dogged her.   Two Pisan doctors came
to her one day : Master Giovanni Gutalebraccia, doctor in
medicine, and Count Pietro degli Albizzi da Vico, doctor in
law.   They despised what they knew of her and righteously
wanted to show her up.   Their visit made Father Lazzarino and
Master Giovanni Tantucci very uncomfortable.   The two
doctors tried to confuse her with clever questions, like : " Has
God a mouth and a tongue ? " " No." " Then how did He
create the world by a word ? " The Fellowship were really
getting hardened to this kind of fooling.   But it was always a
great trial to Catherine's patience and bitter waste of time when
mighty enterprises were afoot.

Behind all this movement, this persistent letter-writing and
the prolonged discussions inevitable in the organization of such
a vast campaign, Catherine lived securely the ordered life she
had devised for herself years ago in her little room in Fontebranda.   Every day she seemed to pray more intensely, to
meditate with profounder effect and to emerge from those hours
of solitude with more knowledge and strength.

None knew better than she the apparent hopelessness of the
project.   She was well aware of the real character of Bernabò
Visconti, John Hawkwood and Joanna of Naples, the queer
captains of her dream-army.   Little as was to be hoped from
them, less could be expected from the rank and file.   They
resisted higher inspirations as stubbornly as wet straw resists
fire.   But Catherine spoke of the Crusade as though the Pope had

only to give the signal. Her optimism was not from human sources.

One morning after Mass, on the 1st April, 1375, in the Church of Santa Cristina on the Lung' Arno, not far from the Buonconti house where she was staying, she made an unusually prolonged thanksgiving, Alessa, Lisa, Cecca and others were kneeling behind her, waiting ; Delle Vigne was at the end of the church, also saying his thanksgiving, for he had celebrated the Mass. Suddenly he noticed Catherine look up at the Crucifix painted on the wall nearby. (The representation is preserved to this day : a queer unmoved Crucified, almost sleek ; a strange conception, inspiring fear.) Then her eyes closed ; she knelt upright abruptly, her face flushing, and flung out her arms. She remained so a few seconds, while all those in the church watched her uneasily. Two of the women were just rising to go to her, when she collapsed into utter inertness. They hastened to support her, and one would have said life was extinct. Summoned by their anxious, backward looks, Father Delle Vigne went to her. With barely moving lips, she told him that she had received the marks of Christ's Passion in her body. The pains were so violent, she believed she was dying. They carried her back to her room in the Buonconti palace and for days she seemed to be sinking. A difficult patient, because all food was insupportable. She could take only water ; even sugar mixed with it made it unendurable. They tried bathing her wrists with a rare wine, to impart nourishment. The friend who supplied this wine said it flowed miraculously from a cask he knew to be empty. The fame of this fact spread around the city and Catherine was very angry when she heard of it. She recovered and the stigmata were no longer so painful. They were invisible but she was sensible of them, occasionally acutely so, to the end of her life. She described her experience to Delle Vigne. Meditating on the Passion, she had been blinded by blood-red rays darting down upon her from the Five Wounds of the Crucified. Her heart, feet and hands were pierced with fiery pain and, seizing the mystery, she had cried out, as she fell : "Ah, Lord, let those marks be hidden."

She returned to Siena in June, Delle Vigne remaining in Pisa to carry on the work. At home, she found the burning topic of discussion was the case of Niccolò di Toldo. A young Perugian aristocrat, he had been arrested and condemned to death merely for speaking lightly of the Sienese government. The Papal Legate of Perugia intervened on his behalf, but in vain. It was a savage sentence, but Siena and Perugia had been at war in 1358 and relations were strained ever since. No one felt very squeamish about it. This Toldo was a foreigner. Had not a Sienese been executed for giving a public banquet to which he had not invited a single member of the government? Rulers had to be stern to protect themselves. Young Toldo's despair was terrible. Raging powerlessly in his dungeon, he refused to prepare for death and repulsed with fierce blasphemies the priests who approached him. Since he had to die, religious Siena thought it a pity that he should die like a dog. Catherine Benincasa returned to the city at this juncture. She was asked to go to him. She did so and prevailed. When the execution was over, she wrote an account of the affair to Father Delle Vigne, the most vivid document in all her amazing correspondence :

" I went to visit him of whom you know ; whereby he was so comforted and consoled that he confessed and prepared himself right well. And he made me promise for the love of God that, when the time of execution came, I would be with him. And so I promised and did. Then, in the morning, before the bell tolled, I went to him ; and he was very glad. I took him to hear Mass ; and he received Holy Communion, which he was never to receive again. His will was attuned and subjected to the will of God ; and there alone remained a fear of not being brave at the last moment. But the boundless and flaming goodness of God surpassed his expectation, inspiring him with such great love and desire of God, that he could not remain without Him, and he said to me : ' Stay with me and do not leave me. And so I cannot be other than well ; and I die content.' And he laid his head upon my breast. Then the desire increased in my soul and feeling his fear, I said : 'Be comforted, my sweet brother ; for soon we shall come to the nuptials. You shall go there, bathed in the Blood of the Son of God, in the sweet name of Jesus, which I never wish to leave your memory. And I will wait for you at the place of execution.' Now, think, Father, his heart then lost all fear, and his face was transformed from sadness to joy ; he rejoiced, exulted and said : ' Whence comes so much grace to me that the sweetness of my soul will await me at the holy place of execution ? ' You see what light he had received when he called the place of execution holy ! And he said, ' I shall go there all joyous and strong ; and it will seem a thousand years to me before I reach it, when I think that you are waiting for me there.' And he uttered words of such sweetness about the goodness of God, that one could scarce endure it.

" I waited for him therefore at the place of execution ; and I waited there with continual prayer and in the presence of Mary and of Catherine, virgin and martyr. I besought and implored Mary for this grace : that he might have light and peace of heart at the last moment and that I might see him return to God. My soul became then so filled through the sweet promise made to me that though there was a multitude of people there, I could not see a single creature.

" Then he came, like a meek lamb and, seeing me, he laughed ; and he asked me to make the sign of the Cross for him. I did so and said, ' Up to the nuptials, my sweet brother ! for soon you shall be in everlasting life.' He knelt down with great meekness ; and I stretched out his neck and bent down over him, reminding him of the Blood of the Lamb. His lips said nought save Jesus and Catherine. And, so saying, I received his head into my hands, closing my eyes in the Divine Goodness and saying, ' I will.'

" Then I saw God-and-Man, as one sees the clarity of the sun, receiving that soul in the fire of His divine charity. Oh, how ineffably sweet it was to see the goodness of God ! With what gentleness and love He waited for that soul as it left the body. . . .

" But Niccolò did a gracious act that would draw a thousand hearts. And I do not wonder at it ; because he already tasted the divine sweetness. He turned back like a spouse who has reached the threshold of her new home, who looks round and bows to those who accompanied her, showing her gratitude by that sign.

" Having had the reply, my soul reposed in peace and quietness, in such fragrance of blood, that I could not bear to have removed from my garments the blood that had fallen on them.

" Wretched and miserable that I am ! I say no more. I remained on the earth with the greatest envy."

Chapter VII

THE TUSCAN LEAGUE

THE work of organizing the Crusade was now interrupted by something worse than the Plague. A moral disorder was spreading through Italy more rapidly than the disease. Not immediately (in this June of 1375) did the Fellowship relinquish their efforts. They carried on for some weeks longer, but with failing vehemence, like men who know they are fighting a losing battle. The new obstacle that had arisen had first to be removed. Catherine did not abandon the great plan. She put it aside while she doctored men's souls in preparation, very much as she had doctored their bodies.

Papal Legates of the inglorious stamp of Gerard du Puy, Abbot of Marmoutier, had helped greatly to brew the mischief. Italy was at one in detesting the usually incompetent and often arrogant rule of the French Legates. In justice to them, it must be said that theirs was by no means the worst form of government the peninsula had known. But they were strangers to their subjects because of the barrier of race and language. In any case the communes seemed to be chronically dissatisfied with every method of rule. When the plague left Florence with an aftermath of famine, she had begged corn from Bologna and was refused, although the Legate there had received contrary instructions from Avignon. On the 4th of June, a year's truce had been signed in Bologna between the Church and the Visconti. In this quarrel, the formidable John Hawkwood had been in the pay of the Church. He was now free. At the end of June, he appeared in Florentine territory, burning such harvest as they had. Florence chose to see in this an act of aggression on

87

the part of the Church and declared war shortly afterwards. In July, she entered into an alliance with Bernabò Visconti. Orators (and they were exceptionally good ones) were sent round to all the Papal States, inciting them to revolt not so much against the Church as against French dominion in Italy. The reward was in most cases a new tyrant for the old one, but anyhow a red banner with the word *Libertas* written across it in white letters and the pledged support of Florence.

The response was overwhelming. Within ten days eighty towns or castles had revolted against the Church. There was a great exchanging of ambassadors, much fervid oratory, excited dispatch and reception of the streaming banner of freedom, general commotion. At first Siena, Pisa and Lucca remained neutral, a most necessary counterpoise on the side of the Church. Of her own republic, Catherine could feel sure. It seemed terribly necessary to steady Pisa and Lucca if the whole country were not to precipitate itself into ruin. This war put an end to her hope of any immediate great achievement. Being Italy against the Church, it was particularly painful to her. She worked feverishly against the tide, crying for peace by word, by letters, in long solitary hours in her room, sweating prayers for miracles to happen. All Italy was now aware of her, standing out against this rush of revolution : sublimely foolish, like a woman trying to dam a flood with outstretched arms.

She went to Lucca in August, accompanied by the usual group : Alessa, Lisa, Cecca, Neri, Father Bartolomeo and one or two more. On August 10th, the Pope had written to the government of Lucca, aiming to preserve their loyalty. The Fellowship worked there for the same purpose.

It is the irony of her life that in this harassed moment she was singled out for a little more clerical persecution. One day, when she was too ill to go to Mass, a priest who doubted her genuineness, brought her an unconsecrated host with all the solemnity of lighted candles and swinging censer. It was a favourite mediaeval test of discernment. The trick was tried on a valiant little saint almost a contemporary, Lydwine of

Schiedam, whose body was a pyre of physical suffering. She had endured the imposture with tears of anguish starting from under her closed eyelids, not knowing what to do. Catherine reacted differently. She sprang up indignantly with, "Aren't you ashamed of yourself, Father, to bring me common bread and try to make me commit idolatry?" The priest's reply is not recorded, nor with what bearing he withdrew. For one of her companions, Lucca remained a happy memory. It was there that, profoundly touched by one of Neri's unfortunate fits of dejection, Catherine assured him that his ultimate salvation was assured and he knew that she touched the edge of prophecy. Hence he, of all others, liked to recall this journey.

From Lucca, the pilgrims for peace proceeded to Pisa. This time Catherine put up at a hostel near the Dominican Church. She was at the centre of influence. When there was question of her return to Siena the Archbishop asked the Dominican general's permission to detain her in Pisa a few days longer. Catherine explained this in a letter to Della Fonte, giving us, indirectly, much light on the position she had attained. Bad news battered on them every day. Florence seemed possessed of the Seven Furies, so prodigious was its activity. In October, Donato Barbadori, the best Florentine orator, arrived in Pisa to persuade that city to break with the Holy See. He did not then succeed, but it was really only a question of how long Pisa could hold out. On November 27th, Siena joined the Tuscan League. Before the end of December, Montefiascone, Viterbo, Città di Castello, Narni and Perugia had risen. It was Delle Vigne who brought this latter news to Catherine and it is nothing to the discredit of this priest, who prided himself on his coolness, that he was actually in tears over it. Perugia was the last straw. All Italy was now in arms against the Church. The Crusade was doomed. Alas, for their dreams of a great Christian army assembling! Of what use now were the thousand knights led in person by the Governor of Arborea, or his three thousand foot-soldiers, six hundred cross-bowmen and two galleys? All their joyous plans, all that had seemed the fruit of their joint prayer, preaching and writing, were wrecked by this calamity. First the plague had frustrated them, now this. And one might as well try to stop the plague as this onrush of war.

Catherine listened unmoved. She reserved all her tears for the seasoning of her prayers. In the dispatch of her daily life, she was so unemotional as to seem hard. By way of comfort, she said to him : " This is milk and honey compared to what will follow." And, at his exclamation, she added positively, with sombre eyes : " The clergy themselves will rebel and divide the Church." Delle Vigne did not pay much attention to this at the moment, but three years later, he started when it recurred to him.

The one gleam of hope now was that Gregory did not altogether abandon the rallying of Crusaders. Also, it was rumoured more and more persistently that he intended to confirm Rome's allegiance by returning there in person. As early as 1372 (over three years ago), he had announced this intention in full consistory. Catherine always believed that, if the Holy See were restored to Rome, the Pope would have all Italy at his feet. It would remove the abuses in Government and bring peace to the whole peninsula. Then the whole face of Italian politics would change and a new era would dawn.

The Archbishop of Pisa released her finally in December and the group returned to Siena. The first news she heard on her return was that nine new cardinals had been nominated in Avignon. She asked for their names in a kind of panic. So much depended on the choice. It was disappointing. Seven of the nine were French, one was Italian and the other Spanish. Three of the Frenchmen were the Pope's near relatives, of whom one was the detestable Abbot of Marmoutier, definitely unworthy of the honour and at that moment besieged in the fortress of Perugia by his exasperated subjects.

Another factor which distressed her was that Pisa and Lucca, while being harried every moment by the Tuscan League to join in, were receiving no encouragement whatever from the Holy See for their difficult loyalty. Either Gregory was a very poor organizer, or he was hopelessly misinformed about the urgency of affairs.

All this led Catherine to dictate her second letter to the Pope. The tone of it is staggering. This woman of twenty-nine (who was not mad) could never have sent it unless she had had clear proof already, in their brief direct intercourse, that her words carried tremendous weight with the Head of the Church. She tells him now that temporal things are failing him because he had abandoned the care of spiritual things, and then goes on :

" I have been to Pisa and Lucca until now, urging them as much as I could not to join the League with rotten members who rebel against you. But they are greatly perplexed, because they have no encouragement from you and are being continually urged and threatened by the other side to join it. But, up to the present, they have not quite given in. I beseech you also to write strongly to Misser Pietro Gambacorti about this and do it immediately without any delay. I have heard that you have created cardinals. I believe that it would be more to the honour of God and better for yourself if you would always take care to choose virtuous men. When the contrary is done, it is a great insult to God and disaster to Holy Church. We must not be surprised afterwards if God sends us His chastisements and scourges, for it is but just. I beseech you, do what you have to do manfully and with the fear of God. I have heard that you are going to promote the Master of our Order to other work. Therefore I beg of you, for the love of Christ Crucified, that if it be so, you see to giving us a good and virtuous vicar ; because the Order needs one, being too full of weeds. You can discuss this with Misser Niccolò da Osimo and with the Archbishop of Tronto. And I will write to them about it."

The stream of conversions which seemed to spring up in her footsteps flowed steadily on around her. One of the most interesting cases was Nanni di Ser Vanni : a surprising genius but a very queer fellow. He was rich and seemed to batten on family feuds, secretly fanning the flames while disclaiming all responsibility : an urbane hypocrite. He made the game his intellectual amusement. William Flete managed to get hold of him and extracted a promise that he would visit Catherine. This was the Fellowship's favourite method : " Only see her once ; that is all I ask." And most people fell into the trap because it seemed a simple request to grant, if somewhat stupid : to spend a few minutes with a foolish little nun. But Vanni was seen leaving the interview with his face marred by most unusual emotion. He re-ordered his life. One of the first things that happened to him subsequently was that he was thrown into prison and set free only on payment of enormous fines.

Nevertheless, all the venom had gone out of him. He gave Catherine a handsome present, at least distantly worthy of her. By legal deed of gift, he made over to her a half-ruined castle belonging to him, called Belcaro. It stood on a magnificent site about three miles from Siena, approached by a narrow road winding tortuously through the hills. Shaded with oaks or lined with cypresses, it was a lovely road in every season. The castle stood on a hill and it had a singular rampart of glorious ilexes. The view from it was superb : Siena's group of towers and spires (luminous under that clear sky) seemed within hailing distance ; almost underneath it was the blue-green mass of Leccetto wood, the home of William Flete and the other Augustinian hermits, around which the air seemed to slumber. Siena now saw Catherine in the rôle of landed proprietor. She decided to turn the place into a convent for tertiaries and call it Saint Mary of the Angels. But for that, permission was required both from the Pope and from the Commune and meanwhile other affairs were more pressing.

On the 6th of January, 1376, Gregory sent messages to Italy that he intended to return to Rome and " live and die among the Romans." The breach between Italy and the Holy See widened every day. The defection of Perugia was followed by that of Assisi, Spoleto, Ascoli, Città Vecchia, Forlì and Ravenna. Within two months, almost all the States of the Church were in rebellion and Florence harried with letters and embassies such few as remained neutral. There was consternation in the Papal Court. Gregory made peace overtures which were rejected by Florence, arrogant because strong. Though timid by nature, the Pope could be implacable when roused. On the 11th February, 1376, he drew up a terrific indictment of Florence in which all the commune's crimes were set out at length and the leading citizens cited by name to appear in Avignon to defend themselves. When Catherine heard this, she wrote trying to placate the Pope. One of the penalties of her intelligence was that she saw so clearly the faults on both sides of the quarrel :

" I beseech you on the part of Christ Crucified to show me this mercy : overcome their malice by your kindness. We are yours, O Father. I know that they all realize they have done wrong ; even if there is no excuse for wrong-doing, nevertheless, on account of the wrongs, injustices and iniquities they had to endure from bad pastors and rulers, it seemed to them they could not do otherwise. For when they perceived the bad odour of the lives of many rectors (who are demons incarnate, you know), they fell into such wretched fear that they acted like Pilate, who not to lose office, killed Christ ; they did the same ; in order not to lose their state they persecuted you. Therefore, Father, I implore mercy for them. I tell you, sweet Christ on earth, on the part of Christ in heaven, that if you act thus, without quarrel or tempest, they will all come and put their heads in your lap, with sorrow for their offences. Then you shall rejoice and we too, because you shall have lovingly restored the wandering lamb to the sheepfold of Holy Church. And then, my sweet babbo, your holy desire and the will of God shall be fulfilled in making the great Crusade. Raise up quickly the gonfalon of the most holy cross and you shall see the wolves become lambs. Peace, Peace, Peace ! So that the war may not delay this sweet time."

She concludes with a passionate appeal to him to come to Rome. Nothing else mattered half so much.

" Oh Father, I die of sorrow and cannot die. Come, come

and resist no longer the will of God who is calling you and the hungry sheep who look to you to take and hold the place of your predecessor and example, the Apostle Peter. Because you, as Vicar of Christ, should repose in your own place. Come, therefore, come and delay no longer.."

She wrote at the same time to Niccolò Soderini, her influential friend in Florence, begging him to labour for peace. It is a striking letter : " Can we dare," she asks him, " despise the Blood of Christ ? And if you say to me : ' I do not despise the Blood,' I reply that is not true. He who despises this sweet Vicar, despises the Blood, because he who strikes one, strikes the other, since they are bound together. How can you say to me that if you hurt a body, you do not hurt the blood that is in that body ? Do you not know that the Church holds in itself the Blood of Christ ? "

The story of the war must be continued because it was the lurid and shifting background to all Catherine's thoughts during these months. She followed the news closely and every event was to her like a cruel personal experience. The Abbot of Marmoutier, Gerard du Puy, had received the red hat while besieged in a castle by the long-suffering Perugians. He succeeded in making a treaty with them and was suffered to depart to the camp of the pontifical troops (John Hawkwood and his men, again in the Church's pay). He had to go out empty-handed and his baggage was handed over later. One Thornbury, for the English soldiers, and the Perugian delegates met in the cloister of San Martino and made a hurried inventory of the new cardinal's belongings. Not edifying : he had very costly effects ; several women's dresses ; of books only a breviary and a volume of songs. His things were packed again very hastily, the episcopal mitre and rosary beads being rammed into the same valise as his riding boots and stockings.

March was a terrible month : on the 12th, Pisa and Lucca took the step which was clearly inevitable since Christmas. Despite all Catherine's efforts to hold them back, they joined the League. On the 19th, Bologna declared for the rebels.

Ten days later, John Hawkwood and his men took Faenza in the name of the Church. With cries of " Evviva la Chiesa," they butchered all the inhabitants. During the sack, Hawkwood came upon two of his soldiers fighting with arms for the possession of an unfortunate nun, who was crying on Mary to help her. Yelling, with ferocious justice, " Half each ! " he slashed her dead with his sword.

The time-limit for the Florentine leaders of the rebellion to present themselves in Avignon was March 31st. Although the League seemed to be winning, they were uneasy. The Pope had hardly stirred yet. It was rumoured that he was mobilizing a great army in France ; he had terrible spiritual weapons in his armoury which could paralyze commerce. Working as he always did with Catherine, Father Delle Vigne was preaching peace and got into touch with the government of Florence. They asked him to go to the Pope in her name (having heard of her influence with him) and smooth the way for their ambassadors who had to be in Avignon on the 31st. The Dominican obtained permission at once and set out.

This event brought the Fellowship with a run into the very thick of the dispute. Delle Vigne left for Avignon near the end of the month, accompanied by the " Master " (that is, Giovanni Tantucci), and several others. He carried with him Catherine's fourth letter to the Pope. In it she repeats her appeal for peace, but now in terms so poignant as almost to shock. It is like looking on the bare human heart quivering. She calls Gregory, " Holiest and dearest and sweetest Father " and implores him to use his power to three ends : First, remove from office unworthy priests, " who in the garden of Holy Church are evil-smelling flowers, full of uncleanness and cupidity, swollen with pride. They poison and rot the garden." Second, come to Rome, and *then* organize the Crusade.

" Do not for any reason whatever delay your coming. Come immediately. Respond to the Holy Spirit who is calling you. I say to you : Come, come and do not wait for time because time does not wait for you. Be manly and not fearful.

Answer God who is calling you to take possession of the place of the glorious shepherd, Saint Peter, whom you represent. Restore to Holy Church the heart of burning charity which she has lost : she is all pale because iniquitous men have drained her blood. Come, Father ! I, wretched woman that I am, can wait no longer : living, I seem painfully to die. . . . Come ! "

Delle Vigne presented the Latin version of this letter and furthered its effect with his persuasive tongue. On the 31st March, two Florentine ambassadors (of whom one was the famous Donato Barbadori) appeared in Avignon to defend their Commune against the papal indictment. The citizens whom Gregory had cited to appear could not obey because they were in prison (being out of favour with the present rulers). This annoyed the Pope. Then the defence was arrogant. Barbadori justified Florence by a crude description of the crimes of French Papal Legates in Italy. Gregory was irritated. He was preparing to use force against his enemies : galleys were being prepared in the Rhône and Breton mercenaries were assembling under the papal flag. Now he drew out his last and most formidable weapon. In his final interview with Barbadori, he read a sentence on Florence, which would be terrible if put into effect. All the leaders of the war were excommunicated with dreadful anathemas, which descended to their children ; all Florentine territory was placed under interdict ; the goods and person of every Florentine in the world were declared the free possession of anyone who cared to seize them. Henceforth no person, community or prince could have any dealings with them under pain of a similar penalty. One could not sell a Florentine even firewood, or the necessities of existence. The arms of all Christendom were invoked upon them. In short, the Florentines were stripped of every religious and civil right and made the pariahs of the Christian world. A Crucifix hung at the end of the long hall in which the decree was solemnly read. Barbadori turned from the Pope and appealed to it dramatically. Falling on his knees, he cried, in the words of the Psalmist :

" Look upon me, O God of my salvation and be Thou my helper ; do not Thou forsake me for my father and my mother have forsaken me." That was the end of the embassy. Five days later, Charles IV put Florence under the ban of the Empire, but *he* was such a joke that everyone laughed at that.

Catherine waited restlessly in Siena for better news which never came. She had given Delle Vigne a verbal message to the Pope, suggesting that she too should come to Avignon. She believed (and her phenomenal life may excuse her) that if she could but *see* the Pope, she could persuade him to anything. In one of the first letters she wrote the little group at court, she said : " Tell Christ on earth not to make me wait any longer. And when I see him, I shall sing with that sweet old man, Simeon : *Nunc dimittis servum tuum, Domine, secundum verbum tuum in pace.*"

In a further letter, she asked Delle Vigne whether he approved of Neri going to Avignon. The next best thing to a personal visit was to send Neri. He was now so thoroughly permeated with her thoughts that she could make him her spokesman with implicit confidence. Delle Vigne approved and Neri set out on his three weeks' journey. It is an instance of Catherine's superhuman activity that while he was yet only at Pisa waiting to embark, he received a letter from her, heartening him for his enterprise. She had spread out the little army she had trained and, like an efficient general, she kept closely in touch with them. In this simple action and in the letter itself, there is all the shining light of the Fellowship. She sends affectionate, intimate messages to all her friends at Pisa. Malavolti, who wrote the letter, adds a joke and a personal word. However the winds might blow, the school had created a little world of their own in which they were happy. Neri, smiling over the letter at Pisa, forgot the weight of his embassy and his loneliness. With that piece of parchment in his pocket, he could look upon life with a " sure, glad and indifferent soul." He carried much in his head that could not be trusted to paper. He also carried another letter from Catherine to the Pope, saying : " Peace, peace, peace, my sweet Babbo and no more war ! I would

rather say all this by word of mouth than by letter because I
believe I would better express my soul. Now I can do no more."

Just at this juncture she found another "son" in Stefano
Maconi, who happened along most conveniently to replace
Neri. He was exactly her own age : twenty-nine. A scion of
one of the lesser noble families, one of the city's darlings, he was
an unusually complete fellow. Handsome, dashing, always
splendidly accoutred and mounted, he was also cultured, sweet-
tempered and pure in his life. Every aristocratic house in
Siena had a feud with someone or other : so had the Maconi
naturally. They were at deadly enmity with the Rinaldini and
the Tolomei. (It all began with a question of precedence at
some social affair !) Stefano took up these two quarrels on
behalf of his family with great zest and earnestness. It was a
point of honour ; the normal thing to do. He liked leading
his retainers out at a gallop and thundering down the narrow
paved streets. He enjoyed the sudden clash of arms to his cry
of "A Maconi ! " The daily excitement of this left no room for
other ideas in his mind. But his mother grew weary of it and
wanted peace made. She suggested Catherine Benincasa as an
arbitrator, but Stefano scoffed at the notion. He had heard of
her, of course, but had never met her : was not interested.
" Tell her to go to church and say the Rosary," he said.

However, friends continued to press him and finally he went
along to Fontebranda, divided between disdain and embarrassment. He expected to be met with the prim and vinegary
sweetness of the traditional old maid. But Catherine greeted
him with that casual intimacy reserved for old friends. She
read his face with an intentness that was disconcerting. He
began to tell her the great story of the quarrels, the dire offence
to his family name and so on. As he talked, he had a most
unusual sensation : he felt a fool. It all suddenly seemed so
stupid, like the mouthing of an idiot. He had an intuition that
Catherine had heard thousands of similar yarns. She listened
with a slight air of weariness and her comments were brief.
But later when she talked of other things (and her head was full

of a possible journey to Avignon), her face lighted up and he thought he had never seen such a countenance.

This Maconi was impressionable and felt himself seized with an indefinable anguish : he saw visions which shook his self-complacency. He had never thought of " Siena " as the corporate commune ; still less as a *Civitas Dei* at peace within and without. He hardly knew what " Italy " and the " Italians " meant ; he had not suspected it was so important whether the Pope stayed in France or not and as for this Crusade they were planning ! If one could not say of him that he never saw beyond his nose before, he had certainly never seen beyond the Tolomei and the Rinaldini. Catherine, with a compassionate smile, had moved these things away from him as though they were a child's puppets and, looking up, he saw an incredible landscape. When he went down the hill again, the world seemed to have turned topsy-turvy and he walked as in a dream. A quarter of an hour ago, the name of Tolomei made his hand fly to his sword-hilt ; now it made him yawn. In brief, the feud was settled and Stefano joined the singular club of Fontebranda. He, too, wrote Catherine's letters for her and every time he did so, his heart burned and his education progressed. The street urchins who used to admire him so mightily, whistled " Caterinato " after him, too, in great disgust.

Meanwhile Spring advanced in Siena and Easter was at hand. Outside the city, the valleys were veiled in cherry and plum blossom. The warm air was full of the pungent scent of cyclamens. Catherine was out of tune with the gladness of the vivid landscape. The war oppressed her like a nightmare and there was no prospect of peace. About the middle of April she wrote to the Lords of Florence, offering to negotiate the peace for them. Once more, she puts the position before them unrelentingly : " Even if the clergy and the Pope were demons incarnate (whereas the latter is a good and benign father), we should be subject and obedient to them, not for their own sakes, but out of obedience to God, since the Pope is the Vicar of Christ."

Florence was experiencing some dismay as a result of the

interdict. It had already been put into effect in Avignon, where all Florentine citizens were despoiled of their possessions. Protests from other quarters were reaching the government every day. If the terrible sentence were promulgated in full, it would ruin their commerce. They therefore welcomed Catherine's suggestion and, as a result of their reply, she left Siena for Florence at the beginning of May. Maconi accompanied her and the usual group of women.

They found that Florence was scrupulously observing the interdict. As frequently happens, the deprivation of Mass and the Sacraments provoked a passionate religious revival. The people stood in throngs all day round the deserted altars singing psalms of entreaty. Relics were carried through the streets by weeping processions. New confraternities were formed. Everyone received fresh impetus to live a decent Christian life. Yet Florence had never been so united politically. They were all one in affirming the Republic's rights against the supposed or real Papal aggression. Catherine remained there only a few weeks. Then she was asked by the Peace Party to proceed to Avignon and plead with the Pope for the second Florentine embassy leaving shortly. Her mission was purely unofficial. It is not clear that the Florentines expected great things from it. They were, above all, anxious to gain time, being disturbed by rumours that a formidable army was about to leave Avignon. Catherine thought their attitude sufficiently repentant and humble. About the middle of May, she wrote to Gregory :

" It seems to me that God in His goodness is turning the great wolves into lambs. I am now coming to you at once, to lay them humbled in your lap. I am certain that you will receive them like a father, notwithstanding how they have injured and persecuted you. Now that your lost sheep is found again, you will take it on the shoulder of love and put it into the sheepfold of Holy Church. Keep back those soldiers whom you have hired to come here and do not allow them to come ; for they would ruin everything, rather than set things right. You ask me about your coming and I answer that you must come as soon as you can. Come before September if you can do so ; in any case do not delay beyond September. And do not heed any opposition you may meet ; but come like a virile man who does not fear. Take heed, as you value your life, not to come with armed men, but with the Cross in your hand like a meek lamb. Come, Come."

Shortly after the despatch of this letter, she set out on her three weeks' journey to Avignon, *via* Bologna and the Riviera to Marseilles, where she took ship for Avignon. She was with a large party : Maconi, Alessa, Cecca, Lisa, Father Bartolomeo, three friars from Pisa and a number of other men and women : they were twenty-three in all. Her prayer to hold back the Papal army either did not prevail or reached Gregory too late. At any rate, on May 27th, six thousand Breton foot soldiers and four thousand horse left Avignon under the command of Cardinal Robert of Geneva, carrying orders to march upon Florence. Three weeks later, on June 18th, Father Delle Vigne, Neri and the " Master " were waiting in a little group at the landing stage of Avignon, their eyes on the hurrying waters of the Rhône. Presently the galley bearing the travellers from Italy turned into sight from the sea and pulled slowly alongside. The disembarkment was joyous. Bare and forbidding, the colossal brown palace of the Popes frowned down on them from the Doms Rock. Its very air of a fortress was suggestive. There was nothing hallowed in the atmosphere of Avignon. No martyrs had consecrated it. But the " bella brigata " (as they jokingly called themselves) were in high spirits at their reunion. They were comfortably housed all together, at the Pope's expense, in a mansion with a fine private chapel on the first floor. As soon as they arrived there, Catherine went up alone to the chapel to pray.

Chapter VIII

IN EXITU ISRAEL

GREGORY XI had made a brilliant career in the Church. The favourite nephew of his uncle, Clement VI (they bore the same name, Peter Roger de Beaufort), he had been created Cardinal at the age of eighteen and elected Pope at forty. He was ordained priest the day before he was crowned Pope. He was a scholar, with very nearly all the learning of his magnificent uncle, Clement. His health was always poor. In appearance he was small, slim and pallid. He was a good man, but not firm. Conscious of his own irresolution, he varied it with an unreasonable obstinacy which did not impress but dismayed the Curia.

Two days after her arrival in Avignon, Catherine was presented by Father Delle Vigne to this Pontiff. She had already written to him six times in an intolerably dictatorial tone, a little sweetened with expressions of her perfect Christian deference. It is greatly to Gregory's credit and typical of the age that he answered her mildly and even sought her opinion. These two now examined each other's countenance. They could not converse, because Catherine spoke only the Tuscan form of Italian, of which Gregory was ignorant. Delle Vigne therefore remained to interpret in Latin. Kneeling before the Pope, Catherine had nothing to ask but the three requests which were the subject of all her letters : peace with Florence, the return to Rome, the Crusade.

Instead of reading her words, doubly chilled of their fervour by translation, the Pope now listened to that nervously fluent talk, looked at her interesting face and was swayed by her appealing gestures. He liked her and the interview was a great success. He said he would willingly confide to her the negotiations for peace with Florence, " only be careful of the honour of the Church." He had definitely decided to take the Curia to Rome in September. As for the Crusade, he would organize it as soon as there was peace in Christendom. They debated this point. Apparently Gregory's enthusiasm had cooled during recent troubles. She begged him not to wait for peace because the Crusade itself would bring that about. It was all so clear to her. Three good things indeed would result : peace among Christians, a chance of atonement would be offered the freelance soldiers and a chance of salvation extended to the Saracens.

Catherine felt at peace after this audience. For the moment there was nothing to do but wait for the arrival of the Florentine ambassadors, who, she understood, were to follow her immediately. Meanwhile the French cardinals (who were in the majority in the Sacred College) were horrified at the idea of going to Rome and therefore disposed to exaggerate the trouble with Florence. They made much of a rumour that new heavy taxes had been imposed on the clergy there. Catherine waited restlessly for a week and then wrote to the War administration (the Eight of War) :

' I protest strongly to you if it is true what is said here that you have imposed a levy on the clergy. I beg of you not to resist the grace of the Holy Spirit which (though you do not deserve it) our sweet Christ on earth is willing in his kindness to give you. Do not put me to shame and reproach. What could result but disgrace and confusion if I tell him one thing and you do the opposite ? I implore you not to let it happen again. But strive in word and deed to show that you want peace and not war. I have spoken to the Holy Father. He listened graciously and—through God's goodness and his own— was affectionately willing to make peace like a good father. After a long conversation, he said at the end that if what I said about you is true, he is ready to receive you as his children and act in the affair as I thought best. It did not seem to the Holy Father that he should give any more definite answer until your ambassadors arrive. I am amazed that they have not yet come. As soon as they arrive, I shall see them and then go to the Holy Father ; and I will write to you how things are going. But you, with your levies and innovations, are spoiling my work."

June and half July dragged out in this anxious atmosphere of daily expectation. No news came. Gregory began to get restive. He said the Florentines had deceived her : either the ambassadors would not come, or they would arrive without the necessary mandate. Perplexed and disappointed, she continued to assure him of their good faith.

In the meantime, one had to endure Avignon. The women there were awful. Every Cardinal had a niece, or a sister, or some " in-law," or perhaps a mistress. Fluttering incessantly round the Curia, it was terrible how much they counted. They dressed in the richest silks and brocade, carried quantities of jewels and were heavily perfumed. Toilette was the great business of life and food the absorbing topic of conversation. Catherine had heard of this type, but she had never met them until now. She never before had to brace herself so much for any encounter. They examined her dress with lazy amusement. They visited her in queues, just as they pressed to every diversion that promised to colour their vacant days.

She might have borne it if they had not wanted to talk to her about the soul. They became an affliction at that point. It is pitiful to remark how sharp her replies become under the strain. Once she turned her back on a woman and refused to say another word. Some of them were vindictive hussies, as for example Lady Elys de Turenne (wife of the Pope's nephew ; therefore one who counted at court). She with some others came to see Catherine receive Communion one morning. Having heard that she became rigid in ecstasy at the moment of receiving, they wanted to see. Lady Elys was sure the Italian woman was only pretending and determined to prove it (like that young Dominican in Siena years ago). Feigning great devotion, she stooped over Catherine's feet as though to kiss them and stabbed viciously through the sandals with a sharp instrument. The feet did not even twitch and she went off in disgust. Long afterwards, when Catherine recovered consciousness, she found she could not walk because of the wounds in her feet. It was only then that Alessa and the others discovered what had been done.

Behind such cruelty as this, there was the oppressive weight of an atmosphere of callous indifference ; that frame of mind against which Petrarch had reacted with such explosive violence. It is sufficiently expressed in that famous argument a cardinal used to the poet against restoring the Holy See to Rome : " But we could not get French wines in Italy."

After over a month's delay, the Florentine ambassadors arrived at last. Catherine sent for them eagerly. She was rudely told that they had had no mandate whatever to transact any negotiations through her. They refused to treat with her and she was made to look a fool. She knew well what a number at court were hostile towards her. Her only excuse for being in Avignon was her mission. But now that her credentials were denied by the city that had given them, her position was painful in the extreme. There would be a reality about the jeers. It was one of those strange junctures in life when we look at a man furtively to see what he will do next. The circle looked at her in dismay. Her action was brilliant because she did nothing. She resorted to none of the prosaic things one would expect, like breaking out into denunciations, or sending couriers racing to Florence, or shaking the dust of Avignon forever from her feet. She who was always urging, compelling, even harrying people into action, now affirmed her solitary and single greatness by doing nothing. The Florentines had merely used her as a pawn to gain time. She gave no hint of retiring, but used her favour with the Pope to urge him to be kind to them. However, the embassy was a failure. The Pope would not interview them. After some delay he appointed two Cardinals to do so, giving them peace terms so rigorous that nothing could be done. When the cardinals proposed some modifications he said : " Either I shall destroy Florence, or Florence will destroy Holy Church."

The envoys kicked their heels in Avignon for more than six weeks and then departed no better off than when they had come. Catherine expressed her mind in a letter to a personal friend in Florence : Buonaccorso di Lapo, a man of weight in Government circles :

"Alas, alas, dearest brother ! I grieve at the methods adopted in asking peace from the most holy Father ; there have been more words than deeds. I say this to you, because when I came to Florence to you and to your lords, they showed in their words that they were repentant for the fault committed and it seemed that they would humble themselves and beg mercy from the Holy Father ; for when I said to them : ' See, my lords, if you really intend to use all humility in deed as well as word and that I should offer you up to your Father like sons that were dead, I will labour in this to the utmost of your wish. In any other way I would not go.' They answered me that they were content. Alas, alas, dearest brothers, this was the way and the gate by which it befitted you to enter ; and there is no other ; and if you had followed this way in deed as in your words, you would have had the most glorious peace that ever any one had. I say not this without reason, for I know what the Holy Father's disposition was ; but since you left that way, following a policy of astuteness, putting into effect something quite different from what was first professed in words, you have given the Holy Father cause for more anger, instead of peace. For when your ambassadors came here, they did not adopt the right method suggested to them by true friends. You have gone on in your own way ; and I was never able to confer with them, although when I asked for the letter of credentials you told me you would tell them we should confer together about everything. Your humble words were inspired more by fear and necessity than from the spirit of love and virtue. But do you realize what evil has come from your obstinacy ? So I say to you in the name of Christ crucified that, as often as you are spurned by our father, Christ on earth, so often must you fly back to him. Trust in him, for he is right. And now he is coming to his spouse, to the place of St. Peter and St. Paul. See that you run to him at once, with true humility of heart and amendment of your faults, following the holy beginning with which you began. If you do so, you will have spiritual and bodily peace ; but, if you act in any other way, our forefathers never had such great woes as we shall have ; for we shall be calling the anger of God upon us and shall not partake of the Blood of the Lamb. I say no more. Be as zealous as you can, now that the Holy Father will be in Rome. I have done and will do all that I can, even to death, for the honour of God and for your peace and in order that this obstacle may be taken away, for it impedes the sweet and holy crusade. If no other evil came from it, we should be worthy of a thousand hells."

Gregory indeed was saying very firmly for the hundredth time that he meant to go to Rome quite soon. He repeated it so often that the French Cardinals began to get uneasy in case he meant it. The French Government also heard of the decision and began to wonder if he meant it. In July a number of officials left Avignon to prepare the way : a fitting reception was to meet the Pope at some port near Rome on September 20th. Seven galleys and seven smaller ships were being prepared at Marseilles. It was thought significant when Louis, Duke of Anjou, brother of the French King, arrived at the Papal Court and it was rumoured he had come on the part of the King of France to dissuade Gregory. This prince met Catherine and was tremendously impressed. He invited her to his castle at Villeneuve to meet his wife.

Catherine accepted and remained at Villeneuve three days. They talked over the whole political situation of Europe. Louis told her all about his brother, Charles V, called " the Wise " ; who was so frail he could not wield a lance and who liked best to shut himself up in the Louvre where he had 900 precious manuscripts stored. Louis pressed her to come to Paris, believing that if she did so she could settle the war between England and France. But Catherine refused to take this on. (Avignon had a more significant interest for her.) They also discussed the Crusade and the Duke so seized her ideas about it that he promised to raise and lead an army himself, when it was proclaimed. He was a man of facile and short-lived enthusiasms.

One of Gregory's objections to an immediate proclamation of the Crusade was that he had no leader. Catherine now countered this by urging the name of Louis d'Anjou. She also wrote to the King of France, beseeching him to make peace with England, that the Crusade might be mobilized. " Your quarrel (*la briga vostra*—so she dismisses the Hundred Years' War) has prevented and is preventing the mystery of the holy passage." For all his book-lore, she practically tells the King that he is asleep. " Sleep no longer in this little time that is left to us, because time is brief and you must die and you do not know when."

But this was all above the heads of the Avignonese. What stuck in their minds was that she had come upon an embassy from Florence and then when the official ambassadors came, they would have nothing to do with her. Obviously she was a fraud ; perhaps she was a witch. So at Avignon, too, she had to pass through the same inquisition she had endured at Siena, Florence, Pisa and Lucca. One day three pompous prelates of the Curia knocked at her door, armed with the Pope's permission to examine her in doctrine. Maconi answered the knock and ushered them in. They were very offensive : " Couldn't the Florentines find a man to send instead of a wretched little woman like you ? " They passed from politics to theology and their examination was very thorough ; indeed, lasted all day. The circle listened for hours, exchanging glances. As evening drew on, Father Tantucci could not stand it any longer and ventured to interpose. (It was this man's penance to have to assist at such interrogations. It will be recalled he had begun his acquaintance with Catherine by a similar attack.) Now he offered a solution of one of the problems she was wearily solving. The other prelates turned on him fiercely and said one of her replies was far better than all his explanations. In a word, they went away at last satisfied in a glum fashion. Next day all Avignon was talking about it and the interview was given a sinister aspect by a remark the Pope's physician made to Maconi : " I can tell you if they had not found her solidly grounded, she would never have made a more unfortunate journey."

Louis d'Anjou had not succeeded in dissuading Gregory ; rather he had been won over to the contrary view by Catherine. But there were others not so easily convinced. Only one member of the Sacred College favoured the move : that was the Spaniard, Pedro de Luna. The French cardinals and the Pope's own father and brothers, resident in Avignon, were bitterly opposed to the change. All August passed away and September set in, while Gregory still wavered and could not determine the date of his departure. Obviously now he could not be met at a port near Rome on September 20th. Catherine thought every day he spent in Avignon was like a battle lost. The situation in Italy was growing hourly more acute. The Cardinal of Geneva and his Bretons had pushed south to the territory of Bologna and were burning and killing as they went. There was intense exasperation on both sides. It would be splendid of the Pope to go to Rome now, and such action might win over the people. But the reason she most insisted on was this : he had said so often he was going that not to go, was to make himself a laughing-stock. And it was a pity to destroy in men's hearts the ideal of a perfect Father of Christendom ; an ideal which persisted strongly despite all the rebellion and despite all the Papacy's lost prestige. In short, Gregory must go *now*.

The struggle of wills closed in around the irresolute Pontiff and became the bitterest and strangest in all history : as though, from the vast camps of good and evil the cosmic forces had issued and were massing and deploying with intolerable tension round the Palace of the Doms. Catherine wrote almost daily to the Pope and he replied in short notes or by messages, because their interviews were rare. The cardinals were active, too, in devising arguments. Here is the seventh letter Catherine wrote him :

" I learn from the note you sent me that the cardinals

maintain that Pope Clement IV would never take action without the advice of his brother cardinals. And even if often he thought his own opinion better than theirs, nevertheless he followed theirs. Alas, most holy Father, they quote Pope Clement IV but they do not quote Pope Urban V. When he was in doubt about whether to act in a certain way or not, then he asked counsel ; but when he was certain and sure of some action, as you are about your departure (you are certain of it), then he did not wait for their counsel, but followed his own and he did not care whether they were all against him. I implore you on the part of Christ Crucified to make haste. Use a holy deceit ; that is, appear to defer the day and then go quickly and soon and you shall escape the sooner from this anguish and travail. Let us go quickly, my sweet Babbo, without any fear. If God is with you, no one else shall be against you. It is God who moves you : therefore he is with you. Go quickly to your Spouse, who is all pale waiting for you to bring her colour back. I do not want to burden you with more words because I would have much to say. Pardon my presumption. I humbly ask your blessing." The Papal fleet at Marseilles was all ready.

Then the cardinals heard of rumours that a plot was formed to kill the Pope en route. He was warned to look out for his life. Catherine had to begin all over again.

"According to what I understand, they want to make you afraid in order to prevent you from coming, through fear, saying : ' You shall be killed.' And I tell you on the part of Christ Crucified not to fear for anything whatever. Come securely. Up like a man, father ! I tell you there is no need to fear. You are bound to come : come then. Come sweetly without any fear. Take comfort and have no fear ; there is no need for it. Father Raimondo told me, on your behalf, to pray to God and find out if there be any obstacle. I have already prayed, before and after Holy Communion and I saw neither death nor any peril whatever."

The next thing was an anonymous letter to the Pope, pur-

porting to come from a very holy man, warning him that poison
was prepared for him in Rome and that he would do better to go
among the Saracens than among the Italians. This letter was
passed on to Catherine for her opinion and when she replies,
weariness makes her words faintly pungent with irony. She
dismisses the document as a forgery. It was not the kind of thing
a saint would write.

"According to what I can see and understand, I do not
believe it to be written by a holy man ; he is not that by
the sound of his words ; it is a fraud. But the writer of it
does not know his art well. He should therefore go to school
because he really knows less than a child. It seems that this
man of poison on the one hand commends your coming, saying
that it is good and holy ; and on the other hand he says
that poison is prepared there for you. He advises you to send
trustworthy men in advance who shall find it on the tables
in bottles, so that it can be administered temperately, daily,
or monthly, or yearly. Wherefore indeed I assure you that
poison like that can be found on the tables in Avignon and
in other cities, just as in Rome ; it can be had like that
temperately, by month or year, or copiously, just as the buyer
likes : and it is found everywhere. I judge that the letter
sent you was not sent by that servant of God named by you,
but it was written not very far away ; quite near in fact and
by servants of the Demon, who little fear God. I pray His
infinite goodness for this grace : that soon I may see you put
your foot across the threshold, with peace, repose and quiet
of body and of soul. I pray you, sweet father, to give me an
audience as soon as it pleases your Holiness ; because I would
like to see you before I go. The time is short so that, if it may
please you, I would wish it to be soon."

She had the desired audience and won her final victory.
Gregory followed her advice in the matter of a " holy deceit."
He gave hardly any notice of his departure but, pale and shaken,
walked down the staircase of the Palace attended by his suite,
on the 13th of September 1376. The exodus was not as reposeful

as Catherine could have wished. Omens darkly thronged about them and were hailed as divine warnings to turn back. The very date was inauspicious. The Pope's father, Count William de Beaufort, an old man, came running to the door, imploring his son not to go. Being firmly repulsed, he flung himself across the threshold, saying Gregory should not leave save over his grey hairs. It was an unpleasant scene. Quoting the verse : " Thou shalt trample upon the asp and the basilisk," the Pope stepped across the prostrate body of his father. Then his mule shied, backed, and could not be made to move. Another mule had to be brought, while murmurs arose from the mournful knot of people gathered to watch. Six cardinals remained in Avignon. All the others accompanied the Pope, who proceeded in easy stages to Marseilles.

Catherine left Avignon the same day, with her company, taking another route by land. The brief comment she made on her work in France was this : " Mysterious, and very fruitful." She had not accomplished what she had intended but, on the other hand, she had done far more than she had ever dreamed of. Her embassy on behalf of Florence had been a complete failure. Yet that republic's treacherous withdrawal of her credentials— which should have been a cruel humiliation—had hardly cost her a thought. The fact is, the moment she got into personal contact with Gregory, gauging perfectly at a glance the full measure of his irresolution and of the opposition ranged against him, she had understood that the restoration of the Holy See to Rome was the most imperative need of all. Beside that, everything else paled in significance. On that supremely necessary move therefore, she had concentrated all her energies. Exultingly, she had seen the difficult thing accomplished. Now her face shone when she thought of the Pope travelling southwards, steadily nearing Rome. Her hopes soared so high, even a thousand Tuscan leagues could not dash them.

Altogether the Fellowship had reason to rejoice. The Pope had given Delle Vigne one hundred florins for the expenses of the return journey. (One can read the little entry to-day in the register of the pontifical treasury under the date of 12th September.)   Louis d'Anjou had given them a similar sum.   They were almost thirty in number returning : quite a battalion, mounted on mules.   Gregory had given Catherine several other privileges :   she was allowed a portable altar-stone, upon which she could have Mass celebrated anywhere at any time, even before dawn.   Three confessors had been designated with faculties to absolve anywhere any penitents she would bring them : Father Delle Vigne, Father John Tantucci, and one other at her choice from one of the mendicant orders.   Delle Vigne had been confirmed in his office of directing her ; she was authorised to work for the Crusade.   She had also received permission for the opening of the new convent : Saint Mary of the Angels. The company travelled rapidly (much faster than the papal procession) by way of Toulon and Varazze, and reached Genoa early in October.   Here they were received by an aristocratic lady, Monna Orietta Scotti.   They intended to accept her hospitality only a brief while but, in fact, remained with her one month, detained by illness.

They arrived exhausted by travel.   They had passed through several plague-infected districts on the way, and were hardly landed in Genoa when Neri was found to be desperately ill.   He had such severe internal pains, he could not endure to remain in any position, but crawled about his apartment on his hands and knees.   Others suffered from various indispositions.   Monna Scotti was a notable hostess.   She looked after them all like a mother and had two physicians attending the sick daily.   They all recovered except Neri, whose case was very serious.   By this time Stefano and Neri were welded together in a friendship closer than any bond of blood.   Stefano's bright clear vision was the perfect complement to Neri's tenuous and often tortuous imaginings.   When one was in pain, they both suffered.   So Stefano came to Catherine in deep distress, begging her to work a miracle.   She was very unwilling, showing that curious detachment which is so like hardness, but is really wisdom. In their queer debate on the case, she reproached Maconi for being so much afraid of death. She knew very well that, if she happened to die before Neri, he would make a very bad shift of life. But Stefano went on imploring and in the end she gave in. She prayed and the poet recovered. Then Maconi himself fell sick, worn out from nursing the others. He naïvely related afterwards that when Catherine visited him on her rounds, he was so pleased to see her he could not remember what ailed him. In his case, she merely joked with him and he got better quickly.

The Pope and his court did not move so fast. They did not actually leave France until October 2nd. The embarcation at Marseilles was miserable. A great crowd had gathered on the quay, sobbing and wailing. The cardinals were visibly affected. The tears were running down Gregory's own face. Indeed his heart was wrung. A Frenchman beloved of his people, he found his own country a very pleasant place. The future in Rome was full of hazard and gloom. And still the portents pursued them. The moment they left port, they were buffetted by a storm which battered them all along the Riviera. It was the 18th of October before they made Genoa.

Thus, by mere coincidence, the Pope and the Curia, Catherine and her company were all in Genoa at the same time.

During the voyage from Marseilles, the Pope had been continually harried by the cardinals with new and excellent reasons for abandoning his foolhardy plan. Moreover, he was unnerved by the storm at sea, by the novelty of his surroundings, by the barbarous dialects sounding in his ears in place of his pleasant Provençal. A cordial enough reception met him in the port, but the news from the rest of the country was very bad. During the troubled days he spent in Genoa, it is related that he visited Catherine once, incognito, dressed as a simple priest. He kept this interview a secret from the Curia. He entered unannounced and, at a glance, she recognized him and knelt down. They talked for a long time alone. Immediately afterwards, he gave orders to proceed and the fleet put to sea again on October 29th.

At the same time she received a characteristic letter from her mother. Monna Lapa complained bitterly about her daughter's long absence and said she would die if she did not hear from her at once. Patiently, Catherine tried to mollify her. She had just been heartening the Pope to carry out an enterprise upon which hung the whole subsequent history of Christendom. But she had to excuse herself to her mother like the merest truant :

" *Dearest Mother :* You know that I must obey the will of God ; and I know that you wish me to do so. It was His will that I should set out on this journey, which has not been without mystery nor without great fruit. You, like a good and gentle mother, should be content and not distressed at bearing all burdens for the honour of God and your salvation and mine. Remember that you did this for the sake of temporal goods, when your sons left you in order to acquire temporal riches ; but now, to acquire life eternal, it seems to you such a burden that you say you will die if I do not send you a reply at once. Now be comforted and do not think yourself abandoned either by God or by me. We shall be back soon by the grace of God."

Maconi's patrician mother was also on the warpath. (In fact the couriers from Siena had brought a disagreeable bundle of letters.) Catherine had to write, too, to Monna Maconi :

" Be patient and do not be troubled because I have kept Stefano so long ; for I have taken good care of him. Through love I have become one thing with him and therefore I have taken yours as though it were my own."

They got away from Genoa at last early in November, taking the sea route to Leghorn and thence to Pisa. They, too, encountered bad seas and barely escaped shipwreck. Monna Lapa (unable to contain herself) met the group at Pisa, accompanied by Father Della Fonte and others. Stefano's mother would not be put off any longer ; so, to his chagrin, he had to go on immediately to Siena, carrying messages and letters

to a number of people from Catherine. The others remained
in Pisa for a month.

Although separated from the glowing heart of the Fellowship
for only a short time, Maconi could not endure life in Siena.
Everything was terribly insipid after the adventure of Avignon.
Nothing could illustrate the young chevalier's transmutation
better than his behaviour during this month of waiting. He
did nothing but write letters to Neri : like this :

" *Dearest Brother :* We arrived here in Siena safe and
sound the Friday following, although we were very much
afraid because the road we took from Pecciole is a very
dubious one on account of bandits. Just at that time too
certain bad things happened there. If I had known it, I
would never have taken that road and I tell you this so that
you may take a prudent route. I have given the letters to Sano
and all those things you sent by me and I have distributed all
the other letters and have carried out the commissions given
me. All the sons and daughters of our Mamma were greatly
consoled and we are all longing for your return. It seems to
me you are delaying too long. Hasten as much as you possibly
can for if I see you staying too long, I believe I shall repent
having come back. Give my love to our sweet Mamma and
remind her of what I told you when I was leaving. And
remember me to Father Raimondo, the Master, Father
Tommaso, Father Bartolomeo, Father Felice, Monna Lapa,
Monna Cecca, Monna Alessa and Monna Lisa, asking them
to pray for me, wretch that I am—God knows it ! If hope
that the time will be brief did not console me, I do not know
what I would do with myself."

He wrote the above letter on the 29th November ; two long
letters on December 5th and another long one on December
8th. In every letter, he repeats the injunction : " Come back
quickly : we are longing to see you all."

This longing was not appeased until just before Christmas,
when the travellers finally arrived in Siena. Catherine had
been absent nearly eight months. For the few who, like Stefano,

counted every hour until her return, there were many who greeted her reappearance with sneers. They said : " The Queen of Fontebranda and her ' caterinati ' are back again ! " Stupid and shallow people, who could seize only the appearance of things, they thought she was enjoying life too much. They understood nothing, except that she came and went, always with eager companions whose faces were too bright and whose steps too alert, while they remained at their insignificant tasks. So they stood at their doors and said what a queer tertiary she was to go careering round the country like that. It would be better for her to mind her home. Look at the state her poor mother had been in. All really holy people live retired and humble lives. So on. They had found even a better stick than the fasting. Catherine was never in her life known to deviate from her course for fear of what people would say. But this prolonged rain of little barbed arrows made her hesitate for a moment the next time the call for action came to her.

Meanwhile the Pope's journey from Genoa on had hardly prospered. He was shaken by storms at sea and dismayed by bad news in every port he touched. There were tumults in Rome. Queen Joanna of Naples had taken up arms for the Church, but was meeting with little success. Finally, the papal fleet was driven on to the island of Elba. No lives were lost and after intense, prolonged hardship, they reached Corneto, in the Papal States, on December 5th. Here Gregory remained over a month negotiating with his subjects in Rome. Here he received a Christmas letter from Catherine, in which she talks to him of strength and patience ; she implores him again to conclude peace and to go as soon as possible to " his place, that of the glorious apostles Peter and Paul."

Just before Christmas, Rome made a comulete submission to Gregory, giving him the same dominion of the city as Urban V had enjoyed in his brief sojourn there. On January 13th the battered little fleet sailed out of Corneto on the last stage of their portentous voyage. At last the weather smiled on them and, on January 16th, they sailed joyously up the Tiber to St. Paul

Outside the Walls. Here the Governors of the city laid their banners at the Pope's feet. Next day, he rode into Rome in triumph, on a white mule. It was a great day. The city was richly decorated and bronze trumpets announced the start of the splendid cortege. One thousand musicians dressed in white preceded it. All Rome was out-doors, the people dancing in the streets for joy. Flowers were flung from every window, balcony and roof until the road was carpeted with blossoms. The Romans are emotional. People were seen kneeling along the route, their arms stretched out to the Pope, crying for gladness. St. Peter's was reached only at dusk, but eight hundred torches lighted the way in the vast square. When Gregory rode in to this place of " glorious memories," the history of the Christian world also came to a turning-point. He was not happy, being spent with fatigue and full of fears. But he had one consolation : it was the reassurance he had heard so often from Catherine : " Go manfully ; it is God who moves you."

Chapter IX

THE PEACE-MAKER

ALL Catherine's friends had welcomed her back to Siena except one, whose visit was missed : Francesco Malavolti. During the absence of the Fellowship (the steadying factor in his life), he had lapsed back into some of his old ways. It is to his credit that he did not feel fit to associate with them and therefore avoided them rigidly. In the midst of her other preoccupations, Catherine grieved about him. She detested spoiled friendships (those lugubrious monuments which mark all our passing years). She enquired for him, sent repeated verbal messages, but he failed to appear. Finally, she wrote to him :

"*Carissimo e sopracarissimo :* I, a wretched mother, go about seeking and sending for you. Alas, alas, where are now your noble desires ? Comfort my soul and do not be so cruel to your own salvation in making your visits so rare. Do not allow yourself to be deceived by the devil through timidity or shame. Break this knot ; come, come, dearest son. I may well call you dear : you are costing me so much in tears and sweat and much bitterness. Come now, and take shelter in the fold. I excuse myself before God that I can do no more. And if you but come and remain, I ask nothing more of you except that you do the will of God."

When Malavolti received this, he sought her out. She welcomed him as though he had never strayed away. But Alessa could not forbear reproaching him, and Catherine had to intervene. "Never mind," she said, laughingly, "one day I will cast such a noose around his neck that he shall never escape from me any more."

Belcaro now absorbed her attention. On January 25th (being already furnished with Papal permission for the foundation), she had had presented to the Commune of Siena a petition for leave to build a convent on the site of the half-ruined castle. As was customary, this petition was put to the vote and granted by 333 affirmatives to 65 negatives. The work was put in hand at once and consecrated with great solemnity. The Abbot of Sant' Antimo presided at the ceremony, representing the Pope, and the Augustinian, Father William Flete, said the first Mass there. While this was going on, Catherine did not forget the war for a moment. During January, she wrote to the Pope again, begging him to make peace and remove at the same time the cause of all war with the Church : " pastors who are puffed up with pride and unclean, like leaves turning in the wind of their own wealth and worldly vanity."

But the following month one such pastor, by his action, made peace recede again like an unattainable mirage. It will be remembered that the Cardinal Robert of Geneva had left Avignon the previous July at the head of the Breton lances (he was more soldier than prelate ; a polished man of the world, with little of the priest about him). He had quartered the troops for the winter at Cesena, a large town in the Romagna, loyal to the Church. There was some inevitable friction between the inhabitants and the soldiers, who commandeered supplies with provocative brutality. At last, early in February, there was an armed rising of the citizens in which a few hundred Bretons were killed. The cardinal, in his citadel, came to terms with the people who, in token of submission, deposited their arms with him. (They were people very devoted to the Church.) But meanwhile he had summoned to his aid Hawkwood and his English mercenaries. These entered the city by night and received orders to massacre the people. What followed is too disgusting to relate in detail : it was the most horrible episode in the whole war. Having trustfully laid down their arms in the citadel, the citizens had no chance. Between men, women and children, at least four thousand were butchered in cold blood ;

fifteen thousand escaped out of the shambles and tried to get to neighbouring towns for protection, but most of these, too, died of cold and hunger on the way. Even religious who tried to succour the fugitives were murdered with the rest. This wantonness repelled even the most loyal supporters of the Church. Florence promptly made the most of it, writing to all the states of Italy to point out how this horror justified the policy of the League.

By April, part of Belcaro was habitable and Catherine went to live there. This new convent of hers, St. Mary of the Angels, was the realization of an old dream. Belcaro is lovely in Spring, when the landscape around it is clothed with a thousand different greens and sparkles with the foliage of the olive. But, already wretched over the war, Cesena struck her sharply like a cruel personal experience. She wrote again to the Pope :

" Have mercy upon so many souls and bodies that are perishing. O pastor and keeper of the cellar of the Blood of the Lamb, let not trouble nor shame nor the abuse that you might think to receive draw you back, nor servile fear, nor the perverse counsellors of the devil, who counsel you to naught save war and misery. O most holy Father of ours, I beg you for the love of Christ crucified to follow in His footsteps. Alas, peace, peace, for the love of God ! "

There is pathos in the conclusion of this letter, showing that, were it not for Cesena, she might have been happy. She dates it : " Written at our new monastery, which you granted me, called Saint Mary of the Angels."

Siena had its own domestic troubles in the feud which now broke out between the two branches of the Salimbeni family. Of the five great houses which made up the Sienese aristocracy, the Salimbeni were the richest and most powerful. There had always been a Salimbeni in Siena from the misty beginning of her history. They had led in every great enterprise : in the Crusades, it was a Salimbeni who first scaled the wall of Antioch ; another of the name, Bishop of Siena, had celebrated this deed in a Latin poem, and so on. Besides prowess and culture, they were very astute merchants indeed. They were bankers too. They had more money than the Republic, which was once obliged to borrow 20,000 florins from them and pay back the debt in castles. Conscious of their power, they were turbulent, a perpetual thorn in the commune's side. In this year, 1377, the two representatives of the family, Cione and Angiolino, were fighting about a castle which they both claimed. They were convulsing the whole countryside with their ambushes, encounters and skirmishings. The women in the families sent to Catherine, asking her to arbitrate the question and make peace. She assented and, since the disputants were living in a state of siege, she had to visit them separately. This involved considerable travel in mountainous regions. The reconciliation was not an easy one to bring about. It took the best part of a year to do it.

The majority of the Fellowship left Siena with her : Alessa, Cecca, Lisa, Monna Lapa (determined not to be left behind again), Stefano, Neri, Francesco Malavolti (whom it was just as well not to leave behind) ; at least five priests went : Fathers Delle Vigne, Della Fonte, Bartolomeo, Matteo Tolomei, the " Saint." These were to assist in the peace negotiations and hear the confessions of the reconverted, who seemed to spring up out of the ground wherever Catherine went. The group proceeded first to the Dominican convent of Montepulciano, where Cecca had a daughter a novice. She and Monna Lapa remained there, while the others went on to Castiglione d'Orcia, the stronghold of one of the contending war-lords, Cione Salimbeni. Here the history of the feud was examined : a most wearisome business. When a basis of agreement was arrived at, they proceeded to the other castle, Rocca d'Orcia, belonging to Angiolino Salimbeni. The mother and wife of the two cousins respectively were good and grateful hostesses. The parleys were spread out over some months and, in the process, the group got scattered over the whole countryside.

Meanwhile, there was a truce to the fighting in Val d'Orcia and plenty of other work to be done. Catherine was pursued. It was a district notorious for religious laxity, but Christian fervour flamed up everywhere at her appearance. Sometimes more than a thousand people, between men and women, were seen descending the mountains together, making their way laboriously to the castle " as though summoned by invisible trumpets." She had no need to speak to those curious pilgrims. The moment they looked at her, they clamoured for the Sacraments. Malavolti, who never left Catherine during these months, was an amazed witness of this miraculous apostolate. He has left us the best account of it. Seven priests were not sufficient to hear the confessions, though they worked all day and part of the night, often fasting until vespers. Numbers of the penitents had not been to confession for forty years.

The headquarters of most of this activity was Rocca d'Orcia, a castle-fortress on a height, at the foot of the last ascent to Monte Amiata, in a wild and desolate region. From this fortress, Catherine had to write continually in every direction to justify her absence. First, to her mother, waiting for her impatiently at Montepulciano :

" I beg of you, if it seems to you that I am staying here too long, to be content ; because I cannot do otherwise. I believe that, if you knew the case, you yourself would send me here. I am trying to remedy a great scandal, if I can. It is not, however, the Countess's fault ; and so all of you pray to God and Our Lady to send us good results."

And to friends in Siena, who bewailed her long absence and implored her to come back :

" I know that my presence is a great consolation to you. But why do you grieve so excessively over things that have to be done ? Oh, what shall we do when great things have to be done, if we get so faint over the little things ? You are in Siena and Cecca and the Nonna are at Montepulciano. Father Bartolomeo and Father Matteo have been there and are going there again. Alessa and Monna Bruna are at Monte Giovi, eighteen miles from Montepulciano, with the countess and Madame Isa. Father Delle Vigne, Father Della Fonte, Monna Tomma, Lisa and I are at the Rocca—among scoundrels. There is work here for a good price. We shall come back as soon as possible according as may please the divine goodness."

Then the government of Siena got suspicious. (They were always uneasy where the Salimbeni were concerned.) What was she doing so long in that territory? Plots were only too frequent. She had great names among her companions. The famous theologian, Delle Vigne, was with her. There were not wanting in Siena those who could give every assurance that Catherine was only a political intriguer. If she were *really* working for peace, they could give her plenty of work like that at home. They sent her a message of recall, to which she replied :

"*Dearest Brothers and Lords :* I reply to the letter I received on your part from Tommaso di Guelfaccio. I thank you for the charity I see you bear towards your citizens, seeking their peace and quiet, and towards me, a wretch not worthy that you should desire my coming. I always put the will of God before that of men. And therefore I do not see how I can come in the very near future, as there are some things I must do for the monastery of Saint Agnes and for the nephews of Misser Spinello for peace with Lorenzo's sons. You know that a long time ago you began to negotiate this peace, but it was never concluded. Therefore I should not wish it to be left again, through my carelessness or through going away at once ; because I should be afraid of being reproved by God. I shall conclude it as soon as I can, according as God gives me the grace. And you and the others have patience ; and do not let your minds and hearts be filled with evil thoughts and fancies, which come from the devil to impede the honour of God and the salvation of souls and your own peace and quiet. I am sorry for the toil and fatigue my citizens are going to, in thinking and talking about me. It seems they have nothing else to do but throw missiles at me and at my company. They are right about me, because I am full of defects ; not so the others. But we, through enduring, shall win ; because patience is never conquered, but is always the victor."

Friends in Siena warned her of what was being said : even some members of the Fellowship had fallen so low as to join in the campaign of slander. She replied in the same tone of spirited resignation :

" I confide in Our Lord Jesus Christ and not in men. I shall do this. And if they give me infamy and persecution, I shall give tears and continual prayer, as God gives me grace. Whether the devil likes it or no, I will use my life for the honour of God and the salvation of all souls in the world, especially in my own city. It is a great shame for the citizens of Siena to think or believe that we are making plots in the territory of the Salimbeni, or anywhere else in the world. We are plotting to overthrow the devil and wrest from him his dominion over man in mortal sin. These are the plots we are weaving. Poor calumniated Father Delle Vigne asks you to pray for him that he may be good and patient."

She was, however, forced to write a second time to the Governors of Siena :

" I have heard that the Archpriest of Montalcino, or someone else, has incited you to suspect us ; this he does to cover up his own wickedness towards the Abbot of Saint' Antimo, who is the greatest and most perfect priest that has been in these parts for a very long time. So that if you had any light at all, you would not only not suspect him in the least, but you would greatly revere him. I beg you therefore for the love of Christ crucified not to impede him but assist and support him as much as he needs. You are complaining every day that the priests and other clergy are not corrected : and now when someone would correct them, you make obstacles and you still complain.

"According to what I hear, you have also received complaints about my coming here with my family and you have grown suspicious. I do not know, however, whether this be true. But if you cost yourselves as much as you cost me and them, neither you nor the other citizens would have such thoughts and passions roused so easily. And you would close your ears so as not to hear. I love you more than you love yourselves. I love a peaceful state and your conservation as much as you do. Then do not believe that either I or any member of my family would do anything against it. I came for no other reason but to eat and taste souls and draw them from the hands of demons. I would give my life for this, if I had a thousand lives. And for this reason I shall go and I shall stay according as the Holy Spirit directs."

The Sienese government had executed a man for giving a public banquet without inviting one of their number ; they had executed the Perugian, Niccolò di Toldo, for speaking slightingly of them. Now, Catherine Benincasa gave them just ground for uneasiness by making a prolonged stay in enemy territory. They ordered her out of it and she calmly replied : " I shall go and I shall stay according as the Holy Spirit guides me ! "

Yet all this pother about nothing was what she would have described as " fatti piccioli." During this time, she was thinking far more about Gregory's unfortunate position in Rome than about the Salimbeni tangle, or the dark suspicions of the Lords of Siena. When Sienese ambassadors left for Rome, she wrote to the Pope recommending them : " If there are any people in the world who can be taken with love, it is these. And so I beseech you to take them with this love." Then she sent Father Delle Vigne from the Rocca to Rome, " with certain proposals, good for the Holy Church of God, if they had been understood." It is assumed that these proposals concerned peace with Florence, but their exact nature is not known. However, when Delle Vigne got to Rome, a bolt fell from the blue. The Master General of the Order reappointed him Prior of the Minerva there. This news was profoundly afflicting to Catherine. It was perplexing, because the Pope had confirmed him as her director. There was no one in the world whose opinion she valued more than his. When he had gone, she said : " I have no one with whom to give vent." Left alone so unexpectedly, she struggled against a feeling of helplessness with all her violent energy.

Meanwhile, there seemed no hope of making peace. The Florentines were arrogant and the Pope intransigent. He was furious with the League and would not yield an iota of his demands for indemnities. The Sienese embassy was a failure. A Florentine embassy came to nothing. In the Autumn of 1377, things took an uglier turn. Florence decided to pursue the war until a better peace could be forced from the Pope and, pending this, to cease the observation of the interdict. The clergy who left the Republic's territory were compelled to return and the people made to hear Mass. It was piling offence upon offence.

The last letter we possess from Catherine to Gregory was hardly soothing at such a juncture. It was probably inspired by the fact that he had never publicly condemned the outrage of Cesena. And the great handle for enemies of the Church remained : unworthy prelates. No attempt had been made at reform. She now tells him that it would be better for him to lay down his authority than not use it. She adjures him it is God's will he should make peace with Tuscany and give the needful authority to those who were clamouring for a Crusade. Gregory seems to have been annoyed and ceased communicating with her. Delle Vigne and his proposals were very coldly received. This was bad news indeed. Catherine wrote to Delle Vigne, trying to encourage him, and half-way through the letter, she breaks off in a passionate appeal to the Pope :

" Most holy Father, mitigate your anger against me with the light of reason and with truth, not for my punishment, but so as not to be unreasonable. To whom shall I turn, if you abandon me ? Who would succour me ? To whom can I fly, if you drive me away ? The persecutors are tormenting me and I fly to you and to the other sons and servants of God. And if you abandon me, with displeasure and indignation, I will hide myself in the wounds of Christ crucified, whose vicar you are ; and I know that He will receive me because He wills not the death of the sinner. And if I am received by Him, you will not drive me away ; nay, we shall stay in our place to fight manfully with the arms of virtue for the sweet Spouse of Christ. In her am I fain to end my life, with tears, with sweat and with sighs and to give my blood and the marrow of my bones. And if all the world should drive me away, I will not care, for I shall find rest, with weeping and with much enduring, on the breast of that sweet Spouse. Pardon me, most Holy Father for all my ignorance and for the offence I have committed against God and against your Holiness. Let the truth excuse me and set me free : Truth eternal. I humbly ask your blessing."

It seems that the stupid always choose such moments of tragedy to pester the great. Monna Tolomei now swept on the scene. Years ago, this woman had appealed to Catherine about her terrible children. Her eldest son was twice a murderer, a ferocious bully, with whom one could no more reason than with a wild animal. Her two daughters were ridiculously vain and silly, with a tendency to worse things. Catherine went to this patrician woman's dreadful home and worked until she had Christianized it. The eldest son married and settled down as a decent citizen ; the two daughters became tertiaries ; but her triumph was with the younger son, Matteo.

He was then a mere boy, who caught fire at her look. He entered the Dominican order and she helped him through the noviciate with her wise and gentle letters. After his ordination, he did everything he could for her and now he was assisting Father Bartolomeo with the confessions in Val d'Orcia. But Monna Tolomei got wind of the gossip in Siena about plots with the Salimbeni. Her son was a Tolomei ; that is, hereditary enemy of that house. He must come home at once, *under pain of her curse*. She made the excuse that her daughter Francesca was very ill. The pretext was transparent. Already there were not sufficient priests in Val d'Orcia and Delle Vigne had had to go. Yet Catherine's restraint is admirable. She says nothing about gratitude (first consideration that springs to the ordinary mind). Instead she wrote to the infuriated mother a patient little treatise of spiritual progress, and concludes :

" You sent saying that Francesca is very ill and that therefore you want Father Matteo to come, without fail ; and if he does not come, you will curse him : saying, if he cannot do anything else, he must get a peasant to accompany him back. I tell you you cannot deny your folly and stupidity. Leaving aside that it is not according to God ; yet even according to that little common sense Nature gives us, if you had that much, you would not have written as you did. If you yourself wanted Father Matteo to come, or to please your daughter, you would have sent two friars out, one to accompany him back and the other to replace him here. You know very well that neither one nor the other can come or remain alone. But you talk away like a person in a passion, whose ears are full of gossip. All this comes because you have not raised your face from the earth, or you would desire only that your son should seek the honour of God and the salvation of souls. With this desire you and the others would stop up your ears and cut out your tongues, rather than hear the things that are said to you, or repeat them."

Advent thus closed in at the Rocca and " among scoundrels," as she casually expressed it, Catherine savoured the salt of solitude. From the projecting terrace of the castle, the " sprone " where she was accustomed to pray, a stupendous view stretched away on every side. (She was an unusual figure on those grim ramparts : ethereal in her white tunic, with burning, thoughtful eyes in a wasted face.) The wind whistled and roared about the fortress constantly. It was called the " Island " from its isolated position and because, in certain weather, when clouds drifted below it, one had the illusion there of being lost in a grey sea. Lisa, Neri, Father Bartolomeo and Malavolti were among the few who remained with her.

This was the fitting theatre for what was surely the most intimate tragedy of her life : one in which she would willingly have given a thousand lives to have had no share. The reader will not have forgotten that unhappy member of the Fellowship who, after his disgrace, passed into their language as " that other." Some of them charitably kept in touch with him. He never went back to his order, but sank into a more wretched state as the months passed. Here, at Isola della Rocca, Neri received two letters from him which must be quoted in full, as they express all that cold despair of which the later Middle Ages were capable :

" *Dearest Brother :* I received news of you through Gabriele, who came to me with comforting messages from you. I therefore write to you, not because I wish to write, but because of your great importunity in sending me greetings so often. I am very much surprised that you remember a wretch like me, since I have become a vessel of contumely, perceiving no longer the fragrance in which I was nurtured. I am beyond all good. But know that if I lived again in the sweet time that is past, I could not keep myself from writing to you often. You must know that at present, when I think of my misery, I am too ashamed to write to you, or to any friend of God. May God keep you in His grace, both you and your Mamma. F.S." Given at the Rocca. To Neri di Landoccio.

The second letter shows an aggravation of the evil :

" *Neri, dearest Brother of all the Friends and Servants of God :* You have sent to me several times, consoling and greeting me. I was once your very dear brother, both in savouring the same food and in true love and charity. But now for a long time, I find myself broken, dismissed, and can-celled from the book in which I was so sweetly taught. For that reason I do not now consider myself a brother to you or to your dear friends. Do not wonder that I have not written you, or indeed if I do not write you again, until I return to gather the fruit of true obedience, patience and true humility. But it is so long since I left the right way, that I believe it almost impossible for me ever to find or taste again that food, or reach a place of repose. And this has come upon me because

I kept the eye of my understanding closed in darkness and banished the light from my soul. I have been driven away from the table, because I was clothed in darkness. I no longer hunger or have appetite for what is good. I put no beginning or end to the present letter, because it is not in me. I do not add my name, because I know not if I have a name. God give you grace and perseverance and a good end." Given to Neri di Landoccio. At the Rocca.

The next news they had of the writer was that he had committed suicide by hanging himself. It was an act in harmony with the sullen skies over Catherine and the dripping November weather. She never offered any explanation of the mystery : why this man whose aspirations were so much above the ordinary, should have ended so wretchedly ; or why she, who had converted thousands, should have failed with him. Indeed, they buried the episode in a decent silence. But instead of getting any comfort from her immediate circle, it was she who had to rally them. Neri, especially, was overwhelmed. For long afterwards, he was tortured by the obsession that he himself would end up in some such calamity. And Catherine had to reassure him repeatedly : " Have no fear that God will permit in you what He permitted in ' that other.' "

There was perhaps only one member of the circle who could penetrate her state of mind and that was Alessa Saracini. She wrote anxiously to Catherine, begging personal news. This is part of the reply she received :

" You write that God seems compelling you to pray for me. Thanks be to the Divine Goodness, who shows such ineffable love of my miserable soul. You ask me to tell you whether I am suffering and whether I have my usual infirmities at this time. I answer that God has most wonderfully provided within and without. Apparently the Eternal Truth wished to make a very sweet and thorough trial of me, within and without, by suffering which can be seen and by suffering which is hidden (much greater—immeasurably so—than what is seen). But He has so gently cared for me, while testing me,

that my tongue cannot explain it.   Therefore I wish suffering
to be my food, tears my drink, sweat my ointment.   Let
suffering fatten me, suffering heal me, suffering give me light,
suffering give me wisdom, suffering clothe my nakedness,
suffering divest me of all self-love, spiritual and temporal.
The pain of being deprived of the consolation of every creature
made me discover my little virtue and recognize my own
imperfection.   I beg of you not to cease praying ; indeed,
redouble it (because I have greater need of it than you can
know).   Our Saviour has placed me upon the Island and the
winds beat upon me from every side."

.   .   .   .   .

Peace was concluded at last with the Salimbeni and Catherine
returned to Siena in the New Year.   The sky had brightened
a little, because she was re-instated in the Pope's favour.   He
was writing to her again.   She had hardly got home when she
received an order from him, through Delle Vigne, to go to
Florence and she obeyed immediately.   Negotiations for peace
were in progress again and she was to use all her moral influence
to further them.   They were in danger of being frustrated by a
faction in power who did not want peace.   The Pope was in a
desperate way.   He had not sufficient money to pay the soldiers
he had hired and there was disaffection in the army.   Half the
peninsula was in anarchy.   Rome was giving him great trouble.
His best supporter, the Queen of Naples, showed signs of wavering
in her allegiance.   As anti-clerical feeling was running very
high in Florence just then, no priests went with Catherine, except
the old hermit whom they called " the Saint."   Lisa, Neri and
Maconi also accompanied her.   She was at first the guest of
Niccolò Soderini.   Later, another influential friend, Pietro
Canigiani, collected money from his party and had a house
built for her at the foot of St. George
    Briefly, the position in Florence was this : the majority of
the people longed for peace with the Holy See but were prevented by the ruling party, who preferred utterly to break the

Church's temporal power before treating again. Catherine urged an immediate peace. (She vowed to herself she would not leave the city again until it was concluded.) Niccolò Soderini brought her to speak to the officials of his party more than once and she favoured depriving of office the rulers who were deliberately prolonging the war. Now, the system of " admonishment " was a most convenient way of depriving men of office. It consisted in getting the captains of the party to vote an adherent as suspect ; he was then formally denounced and was obliged to retire. He could not interfere in public affairs again. Catherine supported the use of this easy weapon to get the obstructionists out of office and thus secure peace. But really it was dangerous to sanction any move in that boiling cauldron of contending factions which was Florence. The admonishing was carried to excess in a short while, every man having his private enemy admonished without the slightest reference either to peace or truth. The worst of it was that Catherine's name was used as a party catchword to justify the evil. She protested strongly, but to no avail.

Among her best friends at Florence during this visit were the Canigiani family : Pietro Canigiani and his two sons, Ristoro and Barduccio. The first held office as Captain of the Guelph Party during this Spring of 1378. The second, Barduccio, was only a boy, very delicate in health, with aspirations above the welter of politics. He was a friend of Don John of the Cells. He clung to the Fellowship, becoming the Benjamin of the group. Being cultured, he could do for Catherine the same kind of work as Neri and Stefano. She became warmly attached to him, because he was as pure-minded as an angel.

Despite the growing scandal of the admonishments, there was yet reason to hope for peace with the Church. Early in the New Year (1378), the Pope had appealed to Bernabò Visconti to preside at a peace conference and Sarzana was chosen as site. Representatives of the Curia, of France, Venice, Naples and the League attended. Otto of Brunswick (husband of the Queen of Naples) was there in person. The delegates very quickly

agreed to the amount of indemnity which should be paid the
Church.   The other terms were being discussed, when a hasty
message reached the Council, the most unexpected and depressing news of all : the Pope was dead.

Gregory XI had been ailing, more or less, all the Winter, but
as he was still a comparatively young man, there had been no
alarm on his account.   He had only a few days' serious illness
when he died, in the evening of March 27th, 1378.   Catherine
was overwhelmed.   Happily the estrangement between them,
whatever it was, had ended in loving reconciliation some months
previously.   In one of her letters to Delle Vigne in Rome, she
says she had been " consoled " by a letter from the Pope.   The
supreme mark of her restoration to favour was that he had sent
her to Florence.   But how grateful it would have been to her
to have sent him the traditional olive-branch.   He had died
with peace almost within reach.

During one of Gregory's last difficult days, the *Banderesi*,
or Governors of Rome, had practically forced their way into his
room to have a look at him.   On leaving, they were heard to
remark that he could not last long and that it was time for them
to be good Romans and see to having a Pope of their own.
The city was convulsed and the air full of menace.   Almost
with his last breath, Gregory adjured the cardinals to proceed
at once to the election of his successor as the least delay would be
dangerous.   Meanwhile, the council of Sarzana broke up.

Catherine's company would then have been glad to return to
Siena and there await developments, but she would not hear of it.
She had come to Florence to make peace between the Tuscan
League and the Church and in Florence she would remain until
that was done.   With very little delay, a new pope was elected
on April 8th.   There had been a most exciting conclave and
some confusion at first in the news that reached Florence.   The
first courier said the Roman Cardinal Tebaldeschi had been
elected.   This was shortly afterwards officially contradicted :
the new Pope was Bartolomeo Prignano, formerly Archbishop
of Bari, who had taken the name of Urban VI.   Catherine had

met him at Avignon. She remembered him perfectly : a man under middle height, solidly built, with a sallow complexion. He had been hostile towards her at first, but very cordial in the end. He had a brusque manner, but was of good repute generally. His private life was honourable. He had been assistant to the Vice-Chancellor of the Holy See in Avignon, had accompanied Gregory to Rome and had then been promoted to the Archbishopric of Bari. It remained to be seen how he would figure as Pope.

The feature of the Florentine affair which most distressed Catherine was the violation of the interdict. From the moment of her arrival, she laboured to have the Church's ban observed. The lords governors who took up office on May 1st were anxious to propitiate the new Pope and with them her efforts prevailed. The interdict was re-observed in the city in May and eight ambassadors were sent to Rome to greet Urban ; four of them were given powers to conclude peace if possible. Catherine's hopes rose again. She wrote joyfully to William Flete that " the first light of dawn is appearing." She wrote in the same strain to Alessa, asking her to get special prayers said for peace, " so that God may have mercy upon us, and that I may not return without it ; and for me, that He may give me grace to be always a lover and proclaimer of the truth and to die for that truth."

But within the city, discontent was chronic. The tide of the *ammoniti* (men excluded from office without rhyme or reason) swelled daily during March and April. Catherine's unpopularity was increasing for having sanctioned this high-handed proceeding. The truth is that she was daily protesting against the abuse of " admonishing." On April 22nd, one of the Eight of War was admonished ; on the 30th, one of the Priors and one of the Lords Twelve. There was no stability of rule because no one felt secure in office. An attempt was made to check the evil by decreeing that no name should be put to the vote for admonishing more than three times. But a few weeks later, voting was repeated twenty-two times in succession in order to force an " admonishment." The murmurings and excitement increased all during May. On June 22nd, the reaction broke out. The lowest classes of the people, the poorest artisans and the unemployed, rose in arms at the instigation of those who had been thrust out of office. They ran through the city, looting and burning the houses of all the leaders of the Guelph party, including those of Niccolò and Tommaso Soderini, Pietro and Ristoro Canigiani, all particular friends of Catherine. Then the mob went on to worse excesses, as is usual. The gaols were broken open and all prisoners released. A monastery to which the citizens had hastily carried their possessions for safety was broken into and looted. Two lay brothers on guard over the goods were killed. Finally, towards evening, the Governors sent out soldiers to seize and hang five rioters from each quarter of the city as a warning. This was done and the insurrection was quelled by nightfall.

That June day Catherine was in the garden of the house the Canigiani had given her. By this time Maconi had been obliged to go back to Siena on family business, but the rustic notary, Ser Cristofano, had replaced him in Florence. There were also in the garden Lisa, Neri and Barduccio, listening to the uproar in the city and watching the fires blaze up in the sky. Suddenly a number of armed roughs came running up the hill, shouting : " Down with that hypocrite Niccolò and his blessed Catherine." They swore with fearful oaths that they would burn the witch, or cut her up, and burst into the garden in search of her.

She was that day in the very mood of martyrdom. No peace she had ever tried to bring about had proved as difficult as this one. Already she had been struggling with it for a year. It seemed *she was not able to do* what God had clearly sent her to do and such mystery dismayed her. She had no idea of what had happened in the city ; except she knew that her friends must have suffered, especially the Canigiani (and Barduccio was standing rigidly beside her). When the gate burst open and she grasped what the cries meant, she sprang up with the face of one who has discovered a secret. Death would explain everything. If she could die for the peace . . . and she ran down the garden, crying, " Here I am ! " It is doubtful whether the roughs with raised weapons had ever seen her before. They stopped in confusion, glaring at her and at the statuesque group behind her, turning away from her ardent eyes. Then they retreated hastily, still foolishly muttering threats. It is quite certain that even young Canigiani laughed. Catherine sat down and cried heartbrokenly. In her next letter to Delle Vigne, she said :

" The Eternal Bridegroom played a fine joke on me, as Cristofano will tell you fully in person. I am right in weeping, because I am not worthy that my blood should give life, nor light to darkened minds, nor peace between father and son, nor that it should wall up a stone in the mystical body of Holy Church. Indeed it seemed as if the hands of him who tried to kill me were tied. And when I said : ' I am she : take me and let the others alone,' my words were like knives that pierced his heart."

She was still in danger though. The circle implored her to go back to Siena, but she would not think of it. She repeated doggedly that she would not leave Florence until there was peace. Some good man, whose name is not known, finally took her into his house with every precaution of secrecy for a few days. Then she retired to a hermitage outside the city, where she remained until the disturbance had subsided.

In Rome, Delle Vigne had found favour with the new Pope, Urban VI. Through the Dominican, Catherine began to send him messages, always to the tune of imploring peace. Then, encouraged, she wrote him directly, giving him the name she used to give Gregory : *dolce babbo mio.* "Alas, I wish to remain here no longer. Do with me afterwards what you will. Grant this grace and mercy to me, wretched and miserable, knocking at your door. My Father, do not deny me the crumbs I am begging for your children."

Meanwhile the ambassadors in Rome were working strenuously too for the same end and reporting favourably. Urban was not anxious to continue his predecessor's war. The great day of peace arrived at last. On July 18th, a courier from Rome came riding into Florence, carrying the symbolic olive-branch and letters announcing that the peace had been concluded. All the bells of the city rang out as the olive was fastened in a window of the Town Hall where everyone could see it. The streets were thronged immediately with rejoicing crowds. The state notary read out the agreement from the palace balcony, but hardly anyone heard anything, the applause was so terrific. It was a great relief. That night the city was illuminated and no one went to bed. Catherine wrote off joyously to her friends in Siena, enclosing some olive-leaves in the letter :

"*O dearest Children* : God has heard the cry and the voice of His servants, who have been pleading so long, and the wailing they have raised over dead children. Now they have risen again : from death they have come to life, and from blindness to light. O dearest children, the lame walk, the deaf hear, the blind see, and the dumb speak, crying in a great voice : Peace, peace, peace ! The cloud has passed away and the serene weather come. Rejoice, rejoice ! Exult in Christ sweet Jesus ; let our hearts burst at the sight of the largess of the infinite goodness of God. The olive arrived on Saturday at one o'clock at night ; to-day at vespers, the second one arrived."

She was now free in conscience, but it was not possible to leave Florence immediately. Two days after the rejoicing, there was a second and far more terrible uprising of the lowest stratum of the people : the Ciompi, unskilled artisans who had no political rights. Their grievances were mostly questions of trade but the uproar was fearful. There was more sacking, looting, burning and indiscriminate knighting in the name of the People. A wool-carder, Michele di Lando, was popularly acclaimed Chief Lord of Florence. He proved a good fellow, who saved the city. Yet another set of magistrates entered into office and by August 1st all was quiet again. On that day, too, a message arrived that the peace with the Holy See had been formally ratified on July 28th.

Catherine and her friends then got away. It was not judged safe for her to visit the government before leaving, so she sent them a dignified letter of farewell :

"I did not expect to have to write to you, for I thought, by word of mouth and face to face to say these things to you, and to rejoice with you at the holy peace, for which I have laboured so long in all that I was able. Now it seems that the demon has set hearts so unjustly against me, that I have not wished that sin should be added to sin. I go away consoled, as that is accomplished which I set before my heart when I entered this city, never to leave it, though I should have to die for it, until I saw you reconciled with your father ; but I go away grieving and with sorrow, since I leave the city in such great bitterness."

She had, therefore, not been overwhelmed with thanks by the commune for whose welfare she had spent herself so generously. The little group riding back to Siena (which included Barduccio Canigiani) were thoughtful. They were glad to escape from the turmoil, but Catherine had a stricken expression. By now she had heard all about that tumultuous conclave in Rome and Delle Vigne's recent news was terrible. There seemed to be a doom over the Christian world.

Chapter X

THE MYSTERY OF FAILURE

The shortest way of describing the famous Conclave of 1378 is to say that the Romans went mad. They had not had a conclave there within living memory : not for seventy-five years and it went to their heads like wine. Excitement rose when it was rumoured Gregory was dying and it continued to rise like a tidal wave until the Sacred College assembled, when it burst around and into the Vatican. The mountaineers and all the countryfolk poured into Rome. The streets were thronged. Deputations waited upon the cardinals, urging them to elect a Roman. The general opinion was that the Papacy should be forced to remain in Rome now and that a Roman Pope would see to that.

Meanwhile the cardinals, sixteen in number, of whom ten were French and four Italian, were split into three factions and seemed unable to find a basis of agreement. The government of Rome undertook to protect the Conclave. Yet, when it opened, the mob broke into the Vatican cellars " to taste the Pope's good wine " and became increasingly vocal as they got drunk. The catch-cry was " We want a Roman " (*Romano lo volemo*), and it roared incessantly in the cardinals' ears like an angry sea. It was a mob with a sinister repute, capable of anything. Everyone remembered what they had done to Cola di Rienzi, that " tragic actor." Less than twenty-five years ago, when they were weary of his rule, they had vented their savage fury on him, dragging through the streets the headless body that was wounded in a thousand places, and finally hanging it up in a butcher's shop.   That yelling, threatening throng *was* a thing to be feared.

But it is not clear that the cardinals were desperately afraid. They did not fortify themselves—as they could have done—in Sant' Angelo ; they summoned no armed assistance, though there were nearly a thousand Bretons within easy reach of Rome. The Conclave, however, was certainly agitated and very hurried, one of the shortest in history. On April 8th, Bartolomeo Prignano, Archbishop of Bari, was elected Pope and he took the name of Urban VI. A subject of the Queen of Naples, he had lived for years at Avignon and had acquired French ways, so that the French cardinals looked upon him as one of themselves. His experience had made him practised in Church administration. Those who hated nepotism were comforted by the thought that he had no kindred. Those who prayed for reform in the Church were consoled by knowing that he was the avowed enemy of simoniacs and pure in his life.

There was a terrible uproar at the conclusion of the Conclave. The air was filled with the deafening clamour of bells, ringing *a stormo*. All the citizens were running to arms, not knowing clearly why. Some of the cardinals announced the election from a window of the Vatican and there were yells of execration from the swaying mob, who hopelessly misunderstood the name. Men burst in and ran through the halls, brandishing axes and yelling : " We want a Roman."   In a panic, the cardinals forced the Papal ornaments on the aged and protesting Roman cardinal, Tebaldeschi, and stood around him, intoning the Te Deum. Then they got away while the people pressed round for the supposed new Pontiff's blessing (in reality the poor old man was nearly raving—a most unwilling party to the deception). Next morning there was perfect calm in Rome and the ruse was explained. The city accepted the Neapolitan Pope without murmuring ; satisfied that he was at least an Italian. He was officially assured by the cardinals that he was validly elected. He was robed in the Papal vestments and enthroned on the altar. Again the Te Deum was sung, while the doors were opened for clergy and laity to pay him homage. Nine days after, that is, on Easter Sunday, April 18th, he was crowned before St. Peter's with all due solemnity. Then he led the Sacred College in the customary procession on white horses to take over the Lateran. The Emperor and Europe in general were informed of the election. The cardinals asked from the Pope, and were granted, temporal and spiritual favours. The Church seemed to have entered upon a new and peaceful era.

Urban began his pontificate with a zeal for reform which was formidable. In supreme command, his brusqueness became domineering rudeness. It was vastly uncomfortable for everyone. Only a few days after his election, he told some bishops sojourning in Rome that they were perjurers not to be attending to their sees. The cardinals liked good fare and were accustomed to it. Being determined to check ecclesiastical luxury, he cut them down to one dish on the table, he himself setting the sour example. Not content with enforcing regulations against simony, he said he would excommunicate prelates who accepted presents and he would not grant an audience to anyone he suspected of that sin. The Frenchmen were longing to go back to Avignon and far from dreaming of transporting the Holy See there again, he told them they would have to stay in Rome even all the Summer. In fact, whenever they opposed him, he threatened to create sufficient Italian cardinals to make them preponderate in the Sacred College. On one such occasion, the Cardinal of Geneva went white with anger and walked out of the room. The consistories were stormy affairs. The Pope would interrupt a cardinal's speech with : " Stop that foolish chatter," or " You have said enough," or " You don't know what you're talking about." He called one a blockhead and told another he had stolen the Church's money. " You lie ! " the latter retorted. Things could hardly continue like that. The cardinals became embittered by the insufferable edge of Urban's temper. They themselves were of haughty and arrogant bearing ; not men who practised either humility or patience. They began to wonder why they had ever elected him. They regretted it.

This news filtered through gradually to Catherine. The letter to her from the Prior of Gorgona, about this time, is an instance of how information was constantly reaching her :

" I must tell you, my Mother in Christ, that Andrea Gambacorti came back to Pisa last Sunday. According to what he says, this holy Father of ours is a terrible man and terrifies everyone by his actions and words. Many things are said about him which are not necessary to write here. He shows that he has great confidence in God and therefore is not afraid of any man in the world. He openly declares that he will destroy the simony and the great pomp reigning in the Church of God. And he shows by his own example how to live modestly at court."

Already at Florence, she was profoundly uneasy. True, the most urgent need of the day was thorough Church reform. But it was a tremendous and delicate undertaking, which had to be worked very prudently. She knew well the mettle of the French cardinals and the danger of alienating them. In her first letter to this reforming Pontiff, she said : "Justice without mercy is clouded with cruelty."

Then some of her circle happened to go to Rome : the "Master" and Father Bartolomeo. The latter was interrogated in an audience with the Pope, and not giving satisfaction, learned for himself what Urban's outbursts were like. Catherine wrote to apologize for him :

" When an ignorant son offends you like this, correct him in his ignorance, without irritation on your part. According to what the Master and Father Bartolomeo told me, the latter, by his defects and scrupulous conscience gave you pain and made you angry, whereby we all suffered, thinking to have offended your Holiness. Have patience and bear with his defects and mine."

What was much more serious was the cardinals' attitude. She knew they were not likely to take things as meekly as her friends. The Frenchmen were a tremendous majority and a counterpoise should be secured. She points this out to Urban :

" Truly, most holy Father, I do not see how any reform can be accomplished if you do not choose a number of holy men, who are virtuous and do not fear death.   And do you not look to greatness, but to seeing that they zealously govern their little sheep.   And get a number of good cardinals, who shall be real pillars of strength to you, helping you to bear the weight of many burdens, with the divine assistance."

It would have saved Urban much anguish if he had created new cardinals immediately.   He made the greatest mistake of his unhappy pontificate when he ignored this advice, or deferred acting upon it until it was too late.

But there was one member of the Sacred College in whom Catherine greatly hoped.   He was the Spaniard, Pedro de Luna, who had helped Gregory XI in the transfer from Avignon, where she had met him.   In Rome, Delle Vigne had become friendly with him.   He was a man of profound scholarship, austere life, remarkable charity ;   a fine personality with great courage ; over-ambitious perhaps.   When Gregory gave him the Red Hat, he warned him :   " Take heed lest thy moon (luna) be eclipsed."   From Florence, Catherine wrote to him on devotion to the truth :   " Truth is silent when it is time to be silent, but when silent, it cries out with the cry of patience."   When the first news of dissensions at court reached her, she appealed to him to work for good :

" Be a strong pillar in the garden of Holy Church.   I have heard that discord is arising between Christ on earth and his disciples :   at which news I suffer intolerably, solely from the dread I have of schism, which I greatly fear may come because of my sins.

" So I beseech you by that glorious and precious Blood, shed with such great fire of love, never to sever yourself from virtue and from your head.   I implore you to beg the Pope persistently to make peace quickly (because it would be too terrible to have to combat within and without), so that he can attend to cutting off this danger.   Tell him to make strong pillars now by creating cardinals out of virile men, who would be willing to die for the love of truth and the reformation of Holy Church. Alas, alas, delay no longer ; do not defer finding a remedy until the rock falls on our head. Alas, my wretched soul ! For all things else, war, dishonour, and other tribulations are less than a straw or a shadow compared with this. Think of it ! I tremble at the thought of it. I tell you my heart and my life seem to leave my body through grief."

During May, when the first heat came to Rome, the sixteen French cardinals retired gradually to Anagni, the summer residence for the Curia chosen by Gregory XI. Most of the Court officials followed them, including the chamberlain, Peter de Cros, who carried with him the papal tiara and ornaments. Pedro de Luna hesitated in Rome a month longer and then joined them.

Rumours spread that they had broken with Urban ; he seemed the last to hear the reports. He had allowed the cardinals to go, intending to join them himself at Anagni later on. When he heard they were plotting against him, he sent the three Italian cardinals to reason with them, but to no effect. On June 27th, he went to Tivoli, accompanied by the good old Cardinal Tebaldeschi, and there he summoned the French cardinals to appear before him within a certain time. Instead of obeying, they assembled a small army of mercenaries for their defence. On July 20th, they called on the Italian cardinals to join them within five days. These did not consent, but in order to remain neutral, removed to Palestrina. When Urban had signed the peace with Florence, he returned to Rome from Tivoli, still with only the aged Tebaldeschi for company.

This was the news that soured all the joy of the peace for Catherine. One week after her return to Siena, on August 9th, the French cardinals declared the Holy See vacant and the Archbishop of Bari an intruder, whom they had pretended to elect to escape death. It is said that when Urban received this declaration, he took horse and galloped out for a long, solitary ride, wandering at dusk round all the city gates. On August

27th, the cardinals removed to Fondi, where they intended to hold another conclave under the protection of the Count of Fondi, with whom Urban had most conveniently (for them) quarrelled. Other powerful secular protection was afforded by Charles V, who was galled from the outset by Urban's independent attitude. The French King secretly encouraged the cardinals all through this period. On September 6th, Cardinal Tebaldeschi died. The other three Italian cardinals, who had been wavering between the two sides, joined their colleagues at Fondi about the same time. Urban was now alone, without a single member of the Sacred College to support him. He then had reason to remember Catherine's prayer to create new and trustworthy cardinals while there was yet time.

From Siena, she was still making desperate efforts to avert the calamity. She *realised* what schism would mean. She wrote to the Count of Fondi adjuring him to withdraw his protection from the rebellious cardinals. She tells him they are all acting out of pride and resentment, the plain truth being that Urban VI is the true Pontiff. She assures him he knows it in his secret heart. But the white heat of her anger is reserved for the three Italian cardinals, whose conduct she cannot excuse. To them she wrote a letter of scorching denunciation, branding them with infamy and harrying them with her implacable logic :

" What proves to me that you are ungrateful, coarse and mercenary ? The way in which you and the others persecute the Spouse, at the moment when you should be shielding her from blows. *You* know well the truth, that Urban VI is the valid Pope, the Sovereign Pontiff, chosen with orderly election and not influenced by fear, elected more through divine inspiration than through your human co-operation. So you informed us and your words were true. Now you have turned your backs on him like craven and miserable knights, afraid of your own shadow. What is the cause of it ? Self-love which poisons the world ! That is what has made you, who should be pillars, weaker than straw. Instead of flowers giving forth perfume, you corrupt the whole world. Instead

of being lamps placed on high to shed the faith, you hide the
light from us. Instead of being angels in human form,
you have taken on the office of demons. This is not the
blindness of ignorance. No : you *know* the truth ; it was you
who announced it to us, not we to you. Oh, what madmen
you are ! You give us the truth and taste a lie yourselves.
Now you want to deny this truth and make us believe the
opposite, saying that you elected Pope Urban out of fear.
It is not so ; whoever says it, lies on his own head (not speaking
to you with reverence, because you have deprived yourselves
of reverence). It is quite evident to anyone who wishes to
know, that he whom you pretended to elect through fear was
Cardinal Tebaldeschi. You may say to me : Why do you
not believe us ; we who elected him know the truth better
than you do ? But I answer you that you yourselves have
shown me how you depart from the truth. If I turn to your
past lives, I do not find them so good and holy as to convince
me that you would retract a lie through conscience. How
do I know that Lord Bartolomeo, Archbishop of Bari, was
elected canonically and is to-day Pope Urban VI in very
truth ? The solemnity of his coronation proved this to me.
I know that the solemnity was carried out in good faith by the
homage you paid him, and by the favours you begged and
obtained from him, which afterwards you fully used. You
cannot deny this truth except by lies. Fools that you are,
worthy of a thousand deaths ! You are so blind that you do
not see your own shame. If what you say were as true as it is
false, did you not lie then when you announced that Urban
VI was the lawful Pope ? Were you not simoniacs if you
asked and received favours from one whose authority you
deny ? Yes, indeed. The truth is you could not endure to be
corrected : not merely correction in fact, but even a sharp
word of rebuke made you lift up your heads in rebellion.
This is the reason why you changed : this is the truth : before
Christ on earth began to bite you with words, you confessed
and revered him as the Vicar of Christ, which he is in truth."

She wrote to the Pope, too, to encourage him in his solitary struggle :

"Alas, alas, alas, my sweet Father ! With pain and sorrow and great bitterness and tears I write this. Wherever I turn, I cannot find where to rest my head. If I turn to you (and where Christ is, life eternal should be), I find around you, Christ on earth, a hell of iniquity, and the poison of self-love which made them turn against you when your Holiness could not endure them to live in their misery. Do not give up, though. Although you see yourself abandoned by those who should be pillars, do not falter."

She advises him to take counsel from holy men and adds :

" I wish for no more words, but to find myself on the battle-field, enduring pain, and fighting beside you for the truth unto death, for the glory and praise of the name of God and for the reforming of Holy Church."

Her tears and prayers and vehemence were all in vain. On the 18th September (too late !), Urban nominated twenty-nine new cardinals, of whom six refused the honour. Two days later, at Fondi, the French cardinals held a conclave and elected a rival Pope. Their choice of Robert of Geneva was determined by the fact that he was a kinsman of the King of France (whose support they relied on), *and because he meant to live in Avignon*. But Italy was mortally offended by the nomination, because that prelate had acquired a sinister fame as the " butcher of Cesena." He took the name of Clement VII, and now it seemed to men as if the " abomination of desolation " were already standing in the holy place. When Catherine heard the news, she wrote again to Urban, telling him (in words that seem to falter) that " nothing great is ever done without much enduring."

" I have heard that those demons in human form have elected an anti-Christ against you. Now, forward most holy Father ! Go into this battle without fear. I and all those whom God gave me to cherish with special love and care for their salvation, are ready to give our lives for the truth ; we are ready to obey your holiness and endure unto death ; we

shall help you with the weapon of holy prayer and by pro-
claiming the truth wherever pleases the sweet will of God and
your Holiness. I shall never rest in peace until I am in your
presence, speaking to you with the living voice, because I
wish (although not worthy) to shed my blood and give my
life and distil the very marrow of my bones for Holy Church.
I pray the infinite goodness of God to make us all worthy
now, who are offering ourselves. It is the time for the flowers
of holy desires to open and show who will be a lover of himself
or of the truth. Tell me your will that I may obey in everything until God shall send me the grace to die."

The above letter was written on the 5th of October. Catherine
had no doubt what Urban's reply would be. She knew she
would have to go to Rome to help him personally. She looked
around Siena like one who is taking final leave of a place that is
dear. She had offered her friends as well as herself to die for
the truth. The supreme moment had arrived for the Fellowship ; she was going to test their years of training. She considered those men and women now with that mixture of
calculation and compassion with which a humane captain
reckons up the chances of his little army. She gave them
their final preparation. For her circle, this month of October
in Siena had all the character of a young chevalier's last night
of vigil, when he kneels with his sword before the altar in prayer,
before being armed in the morning.

She set her affairs in order with significant finality. Having
provided for the administration of Belcaro, she had nothing
else to dispose of except what was in her head. Between the
9th and the 13th of October, she kept Maconi, Neri and Barduccio writing in turns all day, while she dictated to them her
great religious philosophy of life. They worked in the hermitage
of that good priest whom they called the " Saint," probably
leaving the city in order to be free from interruption. Those
ideas which she had broadcasted in over four hundred letters
up and down Europe, through every stratum of society, were
now condensed and clarified in a book. Her method of dictation

was always an amazing performance. She often, for instance, dictated three letters simultaneously to three scribes, without falling into the slightest confusion. Once it happened that all three writers noticed they had written the same sentence and stopped in some bewilderment to interrogate her. She laughed and said it fitted into each letter and they found that it did. They took the dictation of the book in turns ; she never stopped speaking. She would begin, walking up and down, or sit with folded arms, or with her face hidden in her hands. But always the intensity of her feeling overcame her in a few seconds and she would become rigid in ecstasy, insensible to all seeming, except that the words continued to pour from her mouth in a torrent.

When the book was finished, Ser Cristofano described it as about the size of a Missal. It purported to be a dialogue between God and the human soul (but an intelligent, exquisitely sensitive and passionate soul, Catherine's in fact). Its title was as singular as its manner of composition : " The Book of Divine Doctrine, given by the Person of God the Father, speaking to the intellect of . . . . ." " It is hardly a thing to be believed," wrote the good Cristofano in his Memoirs some years later, " but those who heard and wrote it know it for a fact and I am one of those."

The dialogue concerned the whole scheme of redemption. Catherine made no plan of the book, yet it fell naturally into treatises as it proceeded : an introductory treatise which is really a table of contents ; a treatise of Discernment, of Prayer, of Tears, of Divine Providence, of Obedience. First, she drew a great picture of the universe, which staggers the imagination : God the Son is the bridge stretching from earth to Heaven ; mankind either proceed by that Bridge in stages, past the Feet, the Heart, the Mouth, or they disregard it and are lost. Then she analyzed the state of the pilgrim soul who sets out by the bridge, ascending gradually until she reaches those subtle sins that look like sanctity (those last rags of selfishness to which the soul clings so desperately) : serving God only as long as the service affords personal consolation and delight ; ignoring our neighbour's needs lest we forego our peace of mind (the most damnably deceptive of all temptations against charity). Catherine put into this work all her experience of life and all the wisdom she had won from God. The Treatise of Tears is the most pitiless analysis of human misery that was ever penned : she explains the absolute futility of all worldly sorrow, " tears that proceed from the disordinate self-love of the heart." The Divine Teacher seems almost implacable : "And that which I gave you for life, you have received unto death, with the same measure of grief that I had of love in giving it." (When the intellect is really tempered and keen, it seems cold and hard, like the brilliance of a diamond : this is the Catherine who debated so long with Stefano at Genoa about whether Neri's death would not be preferable to his cure.) She dictated sublime passages on the Blessed Eucharist and on the dignity of the priesthood. Then, with effective transition, describes the clerical corruption she met at Avignon and elsewhere : dark and terrible pages, which confirm—but are far more impressive than—the tales of that coarse sniggerer, Boccaccio. Catherine was no stylist straining after effects. She wanted to be useful rather than artistic. Yet she achieves unconscious marvels with a phrase, such as this : " They who murmur *persecute* God with their great impatience." In the last treatise, that of Obedience, she explains how the perfect Christian community is balanced by an interchange of responsibility. One final excerpt must be given, because it is like a footnote to her whole life. It is the idea which bound her and the Fellowship together ; the motive of all her wild vaga-bondage. God explains to the soul how He is perfectly loved :

" I require that you should love me with the same love with which I love you. This indeed you cannot do, because I loved you without being loved. All the love which you have for me you owe to me, so that it is not of grace that you love me, but because you ought to do so. While I love you of grace, and not because I owe you my love. *Therefore to me in person, you cannot repay the love which I require of you and I have placed you in the midst of your fellows, that you may do to them that which you cannot do to me, that is to say, that you may love them of free grace, without expecting any return,* and what you do for them I count as done to me."

With this work, Catherine cheated the fevered days of waiting for a reply from Rome. She referred to it afterwards as : " the book in which I found some recreation." But if she was interested, her secretaries were absorbed. After five hundred and fifty years, one cannot read it without perceiving its vibrant reality : " The Eternal Truth seized and drew more strongly to Himself her desire . . . allowed Himself to be constrained by her tears . . . replied with lamentation . . ."

But what of Maconi, Neri, Barduccio and Cristofano who sat around her in that leafy solitude, their parchments on their knees, writing and resting in turn, and silently putting the sheets together in order ? They *witnessed* what still beats under the cold print : the fierce straining of that valiant soul through the shell of her consumed body. They heard her panting with desire ; witnessed her agony over an unheeded world ; saw her gestures of supplication, her tears, all interspersed through the rapid flow of speech which went on for four days. When they wrote "Amen " to the incredible colloquy, they knew at least what prayer meant.

On October 31st, Clement VII was crowned Pope and the schism was complete. One of his first actions was the creation of nine new cardinals. There were now two Popes claiming allegiance, two Curias disputing every detail of administration, and the dark confusion that spread throughout Christendom was simply indescribable. The Clementines called the Urbanists' Mass a blasphemy ; the Urbanists reprobated the Clementines' worship : in many places the Mass was discontinued.

The nations grouped themselves slowly under the rival standards, the grouping being mostly determined by political motives, but in no country was one obedience complete. The split in authority widened until the whole ecclesiastical fabric was rent and not one little entity within the great unity remained entire. Religious orders divided on the question and elected rival heads, an Urbanist and a Clementine, who made permanent the division. Even local monasteries could not agree. Two bishops would be seen contending for one See, two Abbots for one Abbey, even two curates for one vacancy. The very families of Christendom were sundered by it. It was spectacular. If it is difficult to-day to determine the facts after the clarifying effect of centuries and with all the evidence accessible : it was impossible at the moment. The conflict of evidence was too overwhelming. The fact that all those concerned in the election afterwards repudiated it made the perplexity extreme. Groups of the laity began to split off and form conventicles. New sects were spawned and swarmed in the darkness. Strange new prophecies were given credence. If ever the Church proved that the principle of divine life was within her, it was in working herself out of this calamity. Quite certainly no human institution could have survived such a shattering blow.

It was the finishing stroke to all Catherine's great hopes. She had thought all her life of a Crusade, organizing it, praying for it, dreaming of it : this great regeneration of Europe. She had written letters about it that amounted to volumes ; she had gladly travelled hundreds of miles to bring it to pass. Nothing would deflect her from this purpose : not plague, not Italy's war with the Church, not the incurable enmity between France and England, not the hostility between Genoa and Venice (maritime republics whose help was indispensable), not the appalling characters of the people she rallied to it, not even the death of the Pontiff who preached it. She rode through all this with pennons streaming, but the schism was like the opening of a dark abyss before which even her courage was daunted. She never lost hope, until now. Everything was superable, except this. A woman wrote her about the Crusade during this month and her reply is the most poignant thing in her whole correspondence. She says : " In answer to your message about going to the Holy Land, *this is not the time to think of it.* Pray for Christ on earth and for me that I may get the grace to die for His sweet truth." This is the first time in six years of most exceeding difficulty that she abandoned hope. These few phrases, dismissing the superhuman and dogged labour of years, express the whole tragedy.

Now a man's sour discontent with his condition is curiously sweetened by the failure of others and therefore, for his greater assuagement, he is unconsciously eager to magnify and complete that failure. It was not enough for Catherine's contemporaries that her prolonged and generous efforts for the Crusade had been so much labour wasted. They said she *prophesied* the great event and therefore she was a false prophet. It was easy so to misinterpret her confident appeals for the expedition. But it was a lie, and the slander added to her suffering.

The second great idea for which she had lived was Church reform : prudent and determined, penetrating down from the highest offices to the lowest. She had been striving for it by letter and the spoken word since she entered public life six years ago. In her first message to the Pope (through the Abbot of Marmoutier), she had said : " If you want to build, you must destroy right down to the foundations." Despite all her efforts, nothing had ever been done. Urban indeed had set out as a reformer, but with what a brutally mistaken method and dire consequences. Now, reform was utterly out of the question. With discipline so impaired, all the evils that had crept into clerical life were multiplied a hundredfold. If there were any sincere minds, who had occasionally jibbed at Church authority as being arbitrary—even tyrannical, they were learning now with anguish what the lack of it meant. Here again, it is not surprising that discipline broke in the *débacle*. What staggers the imagination is that *any* order persisted in ecclesiastical affairs. That there was a boundary line beyond which the disorder did not go ; that the old sanctions *were* observed in the main during all the fearful confusion, is again overwhelming proof of the divine life within the Church. But, for Catherine, the plan of reform had failed.

Under this dark cloud of failure, all her political work was blackly mysterious. She had been to Pisa twice : on Crusade work and to hold them back from joining the Tuscan League ; both enterprises had come to nought. She had gone to Lucca to prevent them from joining the League : they had joined, so with them, too, she had failed. She had consented to be the ambassador of Florence at Avignon and then that Republic had repudiated her. Gregory sent her to them again on a peace mission and he had died before anything could be concluded. The Florentine government had made their peace independently of her. They regarded her with such disfavour that, on leaving their city, she dared not even bid them farewell.

Concerned exclusively with her material failure, one prescinds here of course from the spiritual results of her work. They were incalculable. Wherever she went, hosts of the re-converted sprang up around her. She who soared so frequently into prophecy and communicated with unseen forces, could perhaps make a just estimate of that invisible throng, finding therein the consoling fruit of her labour.

But to her contemporaries, ordinary short-sighted people, prejudiced moreover as to the value of her interference, not concerned with her spiritual harvesting, her position seemed unenviable. To such observers, humanly speaking, she was an absolute failure. Any contemporary speculating on her political action would see all the threads of her life tangled and twisted into a most ignominious pattern of failure. Her work did not make sense. She had already begun to realize this in her grey days of solitude at the Rocca. Now the night of schism swallowed up everything. Until now, one star had gleamed in the darkness of her universal frustration : she had helped to restore the Papacy to Rome—helped to bind the Holy See again to the place of Peter and Paul.

But now even that light had gone out and she was utterly discredited. Horrified at the present position, men were saying it would not have come to pass if the Papacy had remained in Avignon. It must be repeated, it had been there a lifetime : a position to which Catherine's generation were accustomed and indifferent. At least now, the obvious conclusion was that the transfer had been most inopportune. It had provoked the schism, and better a Pope in exile than two Popes. Those who knew the part Catherine had played in bringing about that change against all odds were appalled at the results. All except her closest friends were looking at her curiously. Immense evil to souls seemed the dead-sea fruit of that brief triumph. Her enemies pointed her out as having counselled the false move. Look at the results of it ! It had been the counsel of the devil. What of her sanctity now ? Can a saint give the devil's counsel ?

This is the explanation of the curious curtain of silence which descends henceforth, among her disciples, regarding her action in Avignon. While the schism was inflaming minds and blinding judgment, the supreme achievement of her life would not bear talking about. In their loyalty to Catherine, they tended to hush it up rather than attempt to expound it.

Meanwhile, Catherine had one relief from the burden of her thoughts : action. To check the horror before it spread ; to heal the sickening breach in unity before it had become irrevocable. Therefore she and her friends were counting the days until the Pope's reply could be expected from Rome.

END OF PART I

PART TWO

SCHISM

*Haec dicit Dominus Deus . . . Sicut visitat pastor gregem suum
. . . sic visitabo oves meas, et liberabo eas de omnibus locis, in quibus
dispersae fuerant in die nubis, et caliginis.*—EZECH. XXXIV, 11-12.

Chapter I

IN DIE NUBIS ET CALIGINIS

Clement VII having been crowned Pope at Fondi on October 31st (with the tiara which Peter de Cros had carried off from the Vatican), the schism was ratified. Day after day, all those great names upon which Catherine's hopes were based passed over to his camp : the Master-General of the Dominican Order, Father Elias ; the Master of the Sacred Palace, Father Nicholas, O.P. (who was later created Cardinal by Clement). Indeed the Dominican order was one of the first religious bodies to be divided on the question, so giving Catherine's adherence to Urban the character of religious disobedience. (Her enemies could say of her that she knew better than the Master-General.) Those who, at Urban's election, were heartened by the thought that he had no kinsmen to promote were quickly disillusioned by the appearance of a nephew : Francesco Prignano. He was not merely obtrusive at an unhappy juncture, but a thoroughly worthless fellow. Plans for this nephew's advancement happened to conflict with some projects of the Queen of Naples and this induced Urban to insult the Neapolitan ambassador, Spinelli, and even the Queen's husband, Otto of Brunswick. Urban had a genius for alienating people from his cause, as this anecdote shows : At a state dinner, Prince Otto of Brunswick offered to fill the Pope's glass (kneeling, as was customary). Urban pretended not to see him and continued to retain his glass in his hand, thus keeping the Prince in an awkward position. The cardinals at table were ashamed and, to end the painful situation, were obliged to say to him : " Your Holiness, it is time to drink."

Towards the end of October, the Pope's reply came to Catherine, through Delle Vigne, bidding her come to Rome. She was not satisfied with the way the summons came, because it gave a handle to the critics who said that she was interfering in Papal affairs again. She therefore wrote Father Delle Vigne to send her the Pope's order in writing, with his signature, so that it would be clear to all that she travelled under obedience. She explained that she did not want to be a further cause of scandal to those who objected that her constant journeys accorded ill with a life of penitence and prayer. This hesitation is worth considering. Since Urban's election, she had been longing to go to Rome and her desire increased as the trouble down there increased. The delay she imposed upon herself was like a penance. It proves that malignant criticism of her was such that it could not be ignored. It also shows that her material failure had broken some buoyant quality in her soul. This is not the Catherine who gave her only cloak to a beggar and was, in consequence, serenely prepared to be mistaken for a courtesan on the streets of Siena. This unusual regard for public opinion is ominous. It is like a sign of the end.

Meanwhile, she made all preparations and informed her friends that she was going. In every direction, she implored prayers for her enterprise. Her letter of the 4th November to her tailor-friend in Florence and to his wife is typical of this rallying. She says :

" By the great goodness of God and by command of the Holy Father, I believe I am going to Rome about the middle of this month, more or less as pleases God and we shall go by land. So I am informing you, as I promised. Pray God that we may accomplish His will. I beg of you, Francesco, for the love of Christ crucified, to take pains to deliver immediately the letters I am sending with this, for the honour of God and to please me. Go, too, to Monna Paula and tell her if she has not received from court what she wanted, to write to me and I will do for her as for my mother. Tell her to pray and get all her daughters to pray for us. Find out Niccolò, the poor

man from Romagna, and tell him that I am about to go to
Rome and that he must take heart and pray to God for us.
Above all, I beg you to give the letter for Leonardo Fresco-
baldi into his own hands as soon as possible and also that for
Father Leonardo ; take it to him if he is not with you. Barduccio asks you to give a letter from him to his father and
brothers and tell them to give you anything they have to send
him ; and if they give you anything, have it sent to us, or
bring it if you come here."

Barduccio had apparently decided to go with her from the outset and was saying good-bye to his people in Florence. Indeed
there was excitement in the Fellowship. Everyone wanted to
go to Rome. They closed in around her pathetically. There
was a nervous tension, a heavy finality about this parting, which
they had not felt before. Maconi, to his great chagrin, could not
go because his mother wanted him in Siena to attend to family
affairs. But he promised to follow as soon as he could get away.
Catherine had to make a choice among the others and prohibit
numbers from coming. In the end it was decided that Alessa,
Cecca, Lisa and Jeanne di Capo should go among the women ;
the priests were Father Bartolomeo, the " Saint," the " Master " ;
Neri, Barduccio and Gabriele Piccolomini also accompanied
her. Like Stefano, Monna Lapa was to follow later.

The Pope's written command being duly received, the unusual
little cavalcade galloped out through the southern gate of
Siena one morning in November. The horses' hooves rang on
the road to Rome. There was an element of danger in the
journey because the whole country was swarming with mercenaries. But they hardly thought of that. Their hearts were
swelling with a different emotion as they rode silently beside
Catherine, who was carrying her heroic testimony to the great
tribunal where hosts innumerable had witnessed in blood. She
glanced up at Belcaro as she rode through the valley : her ideal
home on the wooded height, whose repose she had hardly tasted.
They looked back at the towers of Siena before they fell away
in the distance. Two of the party never saw them again.

The journey down was quite peaceful and uneventful, but it was the end of the month before they reached Rome. Father Delle Vigne met the pilgrims and Catherine was conducted at once to an audience with the Pope. He received her, surrounded by the new cardinals he had created. This time, she had no need of an interpreter, because all who listened to her were Italians. She offered herself and her friends to work for him until death. They were impressed by her courage and conviction ; indeed Urban remarked that she put them to shame.

Her native city had news of her as quickly as courier could take it. There was at that time in Rome a Sienese ambassador named Misser Lando di Francesco Ungaro, who was working there for the restitution of the port of Talamone to Siena. He wrote to his government on November 30th :

" Catherine, daughter of Monna Lapa, has arrived here, and our lord the Pope saw her very willingly and heard her. What he asked her is not known, only that he saw her very willingly. Castello Sant' Angelo is still holding out and the Romans are bombarding it daily."

Indeed the travellers from Siena found themselves on a real battlefield, amidst the dust and noise of war. Castello Sant' Angelo was held by Breton soldiers, under two French captains, on behalf of Clement VII. The Romans were subjecting it to a vigorous siege. Urban's communication with the sea was choked by Clement's armed galleys at the mouth of the Tiber. The very gates of Rome were threatened. Both Pope and anti-Pope were collecting troops all over the country. The day after Catherine's arrival, on November 29th, Urban excommunicated Clement and all leaders who were assisting him. The three Italian cardinals and Pedro de Luna were spared for the moment. Although the Italians had been present at the Fondi election, they had not voted and retired afterwards to a place called Tagliacozzo, from which neutral position they appealed to a Council to settle the matter.

Catherine and the Fellowship were lodged in a house indicated by the Pope in the Rione della Colonna. They had no money, but they were given abundant alms. They had a simple, but efficient, way of keeping house. One of the women took it in turns weekly, thus leaving all the others free to pray, or write, or make pilgrimages. There was one rule : Catherine had to be notified the previous day what food was needed on the morrow, in order that she might provide. Little sufficed, because they all fasted and took only one meal daily. Offerings were sent them from Siena and elsewhere, but when none was forthcoming, one of them begged alms on the street. Catherine herself did this occasionally so that her guests should not starve, but mostly she was absorbed in her audiences with the Pope and in dictating letters. By Christmas, Monna Lapa and a number of others from Siena had joined her (Stefano was not among them). The stable number of the little community was then eight women and sixteen men, between priests and laymen. But all pilgrims from Siena found their way to her house and often she provided for thirty and even forty people.

The first news Father Delle Vigne told Catherine was that he had to leave Rome almost immediately. On November 8th, Urban had given him a Bull charging him to preach a crusade against Clement. A week before Catherine's arrival, the Pope had further given him a letter of credentials to the King of France, whom Delle Vigne was to try to persuade to the Urbanist cause. Probably the Dominican had waited only to see Catherine before setting out. They had only a few days in which to say much. As Prior of the Minerva, he was very well informed of events in Rome during the previous year. One of his subordinates there, Father Gonsalvo, was the confessor of Cardinal Pedro de Luna, who had hesitated longest before deserting Urban. In her conversations with Delle Vigne, Catherine completed her information and apparently strengthened all her previous convictions as to what was the real truth about that Conclave last April.

Queen Joanna of Naples had declared her allegiance to Clement on the 20th November and had paid to him her usual tribute to the Holy See. This was Urban's greatest worry when

Catherine got to Rome, and he thought of sending her to that Queen to win back her support. As he was a Neapolitan himself, her adherence was invaluable to him. Catherine readily agreed to go. She thought such an embassy profoundly interesting. All through her public life, she had expressed a curious tenderness for this sensual Queen.

Now there was in Rome at this time one Princess Catherine (or Karin) of Sweden, reputed to be a saint. She was the daughter of that dead Saint Bridget of Sweden. It was suggested to send the two Catherines to the Queen of Naples. But Karin recoiled in horror from the idea. Nothing would induce her to go, because she was well acquainted with that sovereign and her gay and dreadful court. Six years previously, she had been a guest there with her mother and brother, Charles, when they were on their way to the Holy Land. Charles was married and had left his wife in Sweden. So was the Queen married— for the third time—and she was nearly twice Charles' age, but she fell in love with the blonde young Scandinavian. Her passion was reciprocated and the two decided to marry despite all impediments. It was an abominable beginning to the pilgrimage. Karin knew what her mother had suffered and how they had both prayed and prayed for the intervention of God. As the arrangements for the marriage were being completed, Charles was stricken with fever and died in a few days. They buried him down there at Naples, with thanksgiving for his deliverance. It is not strange that Karin of Sweden shrank at the thought of visiting that terrible court again. But Catherine Benincasa felt differently about it and was bitterly disappointed when, in the end, Urban decided not to send her. She continued to plead to go. They told her that the route was infested with mercenary soldiers ; that Joanna would afford her no protection : she was the kind of woman who would laugh if a nun were violated.

But all these objections Catherine waived. It was curious how she seemed to thirst for this woman's conversion. She was weary of writing to her. She wanted to see her, to overwhelm

her with the blinding blaze of her personality (well she knew its
effect), to look into those seductive, cynical eyes ; to caress her
with words until she won her from evil and possessing her,
reformed her in grace. She knew her power to do this thing and
chafed at being frustrated. Father Delle Vigne sided with the
Pope in forbidding it and this was a double disappointment.
Catherine thought her friend should have understood her and
burst out indignantly against his " human prudence." Anyhow,
she had to be content with another letter to Joanna, in which
she tried to express her soul. Just before leaving Siena, she had
written her not to support Clement, repeating then about the
cardinals concerned in the election what she had written them
personally. With admirable instinct, she discovered an argument
that might appeal to the haughty and perverse Queen. She
did not insist so much on the sinfulness of supporting Clement as
on its stupidity. It would be just like a woman to make such
an idiotic mistake : a feminine touch to be so unstable and
unenlightened in judgment. She knew well that though Joanna
would not hesitate at crime, she would detest a blunder. In
this second letter, she finds another good argument. She points
out that the majority of Joanna's subjects are in favour of Urban
(the Neapolitan) ; that by disowning his cause, she would
provoke rebellion in her kingdom. Even politically speaking,
it would have been just as well for the Queen if she had considered
this point.

Father Delle Vigne had to leave early in December on his
embassy to the King of France. Although it had been definitely
settled before Catherine got to Rome, he seemed to need a tremendous lot of heartening when it came to the point. They had
several long talks, during which she screwed him up to the
enterprise. As a matter of fact, personally, she hated to see him
go. One of her consolations in coming to Rome was that he
was there. But she discounted personal feeling in her gladness
that he had been honoured with such an embassy. She thought
his mission glorious : to convince France of the truth, and,
through France, all Christendom.

The day came for Delle Vigne's departure.   His plan was to
row down the Tiber and sail from the mouth of it to Pisa,
dodging through enemy galleys as well as he could.   At the
moment of parting, Catherine broke down badly and her grief
was painful to witness.   Now that he was really leaving her,
there rushed in upon her mind an acute sense of isolation in that
battlefield of a city, her implied responsibility for the Schism,
the exceeding difficulty of Urban's character.   In that nightmare
through which they were living, Delle Vigne was one of the few
she could revere consistently for his integrity, his great charity,
and his unfailing wise counsel.   Then they were linked together
by such an unusual experience of life, shared in common : in
Siena, Avignon, Val d'Orcia.   They had a last long talk of
several hours.   She walked down to the river with him and said :
" We shall never again talk like that."   They blessed each
other.   The tears were running down her face as he stepped into
the boat.   It drew away and she (who was never dramatic)
knelt down at the riverside and prayed heartbrokenly.

December passed away and Catherine saw Urban very
frequently, reinforcing the effect of their interviews with numerous
letters.   In these letters, one has always the impression that she
was infinitely careful of what she said to him.   Their tone is
strikingly different from the tone of her letters to Gregory XI.
She is very cautious with Urban and asks little of him, beyond
trying to sweeten the bitter asperity of his nature.

In considering the relationship between Catherine Benincasa
and this gloomy, choleric man who was Pope Urban VI, one is
reminded of those marvellous lines of Racine describing Agrip-
pina's first intuition of the monster in the eyes of Nero, though
he was yet reigning justly.   How much of the real Urban did
Catherine know ?   His mental progression is profoundly interesting.   To the end of his days, he lived simply and austerely
and abhorred simony.   But he turned out as much a nepotist
as any of the French Popes and gradually he became submerged
in the troubles of his reign, losing his wide glance and all appetite
for reform.   His brusqueness became domineering brutality and

then cold cruelty. He suspected everyone. He was the Pope who read his breviary aloud while his ears were filled with the cries of his cardinals, who were being tortured to wring a confession of plots from them. Later, he dragged those cardinals around with him, loaded with chains, and they all—save one—perished miserably and mysteriously. He became impossible. From a trusted subordinate and revered Archbishop, he developed into one of the most cordially hated Pontiffs who ever sat in Peter's chair. He died in absolute abandonment, reputed insane, detested by the most fervent champions of the justice of his cause. Most probably his mind did give way under the weight of his multiplied misfortunes. Catherine never saw the beginning of his progress downwards. All through her life, men respected him. But how much of his capacity for cruelty did she divine? She had marvellous intuition and the prophetic spirit. It must have been no small part of her final martyrdom to know the real character of the Pope, whom she believed and proclaimed to be truly the Vicar of Christ, and on whom the hopes of Christendom were centred.

Chapter II

DISILLUSIONMENT

IN the letters Catherine wrote to the Pope before coming to Rome, she had urged him to surround himself with holy men, seeking and following their advice : " Choose a band of very holy men, who are virtuous and do not fear death." " Fortify yourself with the prayers and company of the just. I would like to see them by your side, so that they may be your refresh- ment in the trials of this life. Besides divine aid, seek to have the help of His servants, who shall advise you with faith and candour, not partially, nor corrupted in their counsel by self-love." " Get good and virtuous ministers and have holy men by your side."

Still more, since coming to Rome and observing his daily conduct of affairs, did she urge this course upon him. She saw him very frequently, as we learn from that useful Sienese ambas- sador previously quoted. On the 27th of December, he reported to his government :

" Catherine, daughter of Monna Lapa, is here. The Holy Father has spoken to her several times and has sent for her very often. . . . He is convoking here many holy people, those of Leccetto and many others. . . . "

In fact, in the middle of December, Urban took her advice and endeavoured to rally to Rome a little brigade of the just. He wrote a letter to Catherine's friend, the Prior of Gorgona (in whom she had great confidence), and what he says might well have been inspired by her :

" In this dreadful tempest that threatens the Church with shipwreck, we believe and hope that we shall be divinely

helped by the prayers and tears of the just, rather than by the arms of soldiers and by human prudence. Therefore, with Peter, who when he was sinking in the sea besought aid from the Lord, and was immediately helped by His loving hand, we earnestly and devoutly summon to our assistance the holy tears and assiduous prayers of the just children of the Church, that they may humbly and fervently assail the ears of the Lord, and He may the sooner bend to have compassion upon us."
Instructions were given at the same time for special prayers and Masses to be said throughout the country. The Pope called to Rome the Prior of Gorgona, Don John of the Cells, Father William Flete and others of religious fame.

Most of the names were suggested by Catherine. It was the Fellowship's great moment. She was going to prove them now. She herself sent the Papal Bull to the Prior of Gorgona, writing simultaneously to all her friends who had been summoned and calling to Rome many others also who had not been named in the Bull.

" Now is the time to show who is a lover of the truth. We must rise from sleep and hold up the Blood of Christ before our eyes to hearten us for the battle. Our sweet holy Father, Pope Urban VI, true Supreme Pontiff, wants to use the remedy necessary for reforming Holy Church. He wishes to have the servants of God by his side and to guide himself and Holy Church by their counsels. Therefore he sends you this bull, ordering you to summon all those named therein. Do it zealously and quickly, without any loss of time, for the Church of God can brook no delay. Set aside everything else, be it what it may, and urge on the others to get here quickly. For the love of God, do not delay, do not delay. Come into this garden to labour here. Father Delle Vigne has gone north to work, for the Holy Father has sent him to the King of France. Pray for him that he may be a true sower of the truth, giving his life for it, if there be need."
To William Flete and Father Antonio, her two friends at Lecceto, she said :

" Now I shall see if you are truly in love with the reformation of Holy Church ; because if you are so in truth, you will follow the will of God and of His vicar. You will leave the wood and come to enter the battlefield. Therefore I beseech you for the love of Christ crucified to come immediately at the Holy Father's request and make no delay. Up, dearest sons ! Sleep no more : it is the hour of vigil."

To the hermits of Spoleto, she said :

" Was the Church ever in such need, when those who should help her, strike her ; and those who should light up the way for us, lead us into darkness ? "

Then, in case they should look upon the journey to Rome as something too much like a pleasure trip, she adds :

" You need not fear delights or great consolations. You are coming to endure and to find no joy, save the joy of the Cross. Come, come, and do not delay waiting for time, because time does not wait for us."

To Don John of the Cells, she said :

" Enter this battlefield with a virile heart, with true and cordial humility. Let all the just go forth and come here to proclaim the truth and endure for it ; now is their time."

From the moment of Delle Vigne's departure, she thought of him constantly and of his particularly weighty embassy. He bore briefs to the King of France, to the University of Paris, to the Duke of Anjou, to Cardinal de Grimoard and to various French bishops. He was accompanied by one other ambassador : Jacopo di Ceva, Marshal of the Roman Curia. The journey was fraught with great physical danger and she collected prayers for him assiduously. When he reached Pisa, she had him met by a letter from her (just as she had previously heartened Neri at the same stage to go on to Avignon). She invoked on him the " true and most perfect light of God," saying :

" This is the light which makes the soul faithful, which cuts it off from the lie of its own sensuality, which makes the heart mature and the tongue discreet. It is no longer time to sleep, but to wake up from our carelessness, to rise out of our blind ignorance, to proclaim the truth and prepare to die for it. Now, be silent my soul, and say no more. Dearest father, I do not want to begin saying what pen cannot write nor tongue speak ; my silence expresses what I want to say."

She also wrote to Maconi, telling him to help Delle Vigne on his way if he could, doing for him what he would do for her.

She particularly wanted Maconi to come to Rome, imploring him not to wait to unloosen the ties keeping him in Siena, but to cut them, " because unloosening takes time and you are not sure of having it ; it is passing by you rapidly."

In Rome, where she seemed to be walking on the warm blood of the martyrs, the whims of Maconi's patrician mother seemed negligible.

" Be a man ; make haste ; respond to Mary who is calling you with such great love. The bodies of those glorious martyrs are buried here in Rome ; but their blood, which they shed with such fire of love in giving their lives for Life, their blood boils up, inviting you and the others to come and endure for the glory of God and Holy Church. Say this also to Pietro and tell him, if he can come, to seek us out for anything he needs."

Catherine sent all these letters off during her first weeks in Rome. Then she waited confidently for the response. With all the spiritual strength of Italy backing Urban, she believed he would prevail. She thought with tender reminiscence of their ardent talks in Tuscany on Church reform. How high their ardour used to flame ! Now, by Divine Providence, it seemed to be put into their hands. While she waited, she spent herself in prayer, arduous and prolonged. "One hour of it," said Barduccio, "exhausted her more than two days continual devotions would weaken another person."

.   .   .   .   .

The New Year (1379) opened while she waited and then the response from the Fellowship came filtering in and her heart seemed to die within her.

First, about Father Delle Vigne : he had threaded his way successfully through the enemy galleys as far as Pisa and thence by sea again to Genoa. Here he disembarked and proceeded by land to Ventimiglia. At the frontier, Jacopo di Ceva, his colleague, was seized by Clementine's soldiers and imprisoned. (He was not released until he became a partisan of theirs.) Delle Vigne received definite information that an ambuscade was waiting for him, too, and that death was certain if he went on. The route was impossible, blocked on all sides. He made his way back to Genoa and reported to Urban, who ordered him to stay in Genoa and preach there against the Clementines. The Pope was satisfied that he had done his best, but Catherine did not think he had distinguished himself. He should have tried all ways of getting into France. What was the use of talking so much of their readiness to die for the truth if they were to scurry back from danger ? She wrote him her opinion :

" You were not yet worthy to stay in the battle, but you were hunted back like a child ; and you fled gladly and you were thankful to God for the concession to your weakness. Bad little father ! How blessed your soul and mine would have been if you had walled up with your blood one stone in Holy Church for love of the Blood ! Truly we have cause for tears to see that our little virtue does not merit so much good."

Poor Father Delle Vigne was hardly consoled at the measure of her disappointment in him. He wrote back very sadly, defending his action and saying that he was afraid she had lost her affection for him.

Some months later, when prospects had considerably brightened, Urban resolved to make another attempt to win over the King of France and once more confided the embassy to Delle Vigne. On this occasion, he wished the Dominican to go by way of Spain and sent a brief to the King of Aragon, recommending Delle Vigne to him for a safe-conduct. But the Spanish cardinal, Pedro de Luna (in whom Catherine had hoped so much), had already gone to the King of Aragon as Clement's legate. Urban's ambassadors had been imprisoned through this prelate's influence. Therefore Delle Vigne could not expect much consideration. He seems not to have tried to go, but reported to the Pope his knowledge of the state of affairs.

To Catherine, this second failure seemed the last straw. She refused to believe that there was *no way* open into France. Delle Vigne had simply shirked trying. She wrote to him again in indignant terms, answering at the same time his letter in which he had reproached her for losing affection :

" Our faith in God has bound us together with a close and special love, above the ordinary. This love expresses our faith and it never alters, not through what people say, nor through the devil's illusions, nor through change of place. It seems from your letter that you think you were given a greater burden than you could bear. And you thought that I was judging you by my own standard and that my love for you had diminished. But you do not perceive that it is you who are losing affection. I love you as I love myself, with great faith that what you lack, God in His Goodness will supply. But this did not happen ; because you found a way of throwing your burden to earth. And you have many excuses to cloak your faithless fragility, but not so many that I do not see through them clearly enough. I shall think it a good thing if others besides myself do not see through them too. So that I show how my love for you has increased rather than lessened. But what shall I say that your ignorance should have given rise to the least of such thoughts ? How could you ever believe that I wish other than the life of your soul ? Where is the faith that you always had and should have ? And the certainty you had that, before a thing is done, it is seen and determined in the sight of God : not so much this, which is a big thing, but every least thing ? *If you had kept faith, you would not have wavered so much, nor fallen in doubt of God and me. But, like a faithful son, ready to obey, you would have gone and done what was possible. If you could not walk there, you would have crawled ; if you could not go as a friar, you would have gone as a pilgrim ; if you had no money, you would have begged your way there.*

This faithful obedience would have wrought more in the sight of God and in the hearts of men than all your human prudence. I have been working day and night on other matters, which all came to nothing because of the little zeal of those concerned, but especially through my sins, which prevent every good. And thus, alas, we see ourselves drowning and the sins against God increase to our torture. I am living in agony. May God in His mercy take me quickly out of this dark life. Do not give me any more cause for tears, nor to be ashamed of myself in the sight of God. As you are a man in promising to labour and endure for the honour of God, do not be like a woman when it comes to the point. See that that does not happen to you which happened to the Abbot of Sant' Antimo who, out of fear and under cover of not tempting God, left Siena and came to Rome. He thought to have escaped imprisonment and to be safe. But he was put into prison, with what penalty you know. Thus pusillanimous hearts are served ! "

Nothing precise is known about this act of cowardice on the part of the Abbot of Sant' Antimo, to whose punishment Catherine refers so sternly. His failure, too, must have been dramatic enough. It will be remembered that it was he who had opened her new convent at Belcaro. He had been a loved friend. A year ago, she had written to the Government of Siena, praising this man and his zeal for reform, describing him as " the greatest and most perfect priest that has been in these parts for a very long time ; one to be greatly revered and assisted." He was another poor soul whom the Schism sent reeling from his poise.

Then came the disillusionment in Father William Flete. Apart from intuition and the prophetic spirit, Catherine should have felt absolutely sure of him. His devotion to her was so embarrassingly intense. This is what Ser Cristofano tells us about the Englishman's attitude to her :

" He revered her so much that he made it a point to touch her garment and he touched it with such reverence and devotion as though it were a sacred thing. He used to say to us : ' You do not know her. You do not realize what she is. The Pope should think it an honour to be among her sons ; truly the Holy Spirit is in her.' "

But when she entreated him to come to Rome in this hour of the Church's great need, he was far from recognizing the call of the Holy Spirit. He flatly refused. It was not so much his refusal as the *way* he refused that crushed her spirits. He had been named in the Papal Bull of convocation. It was his Christian duty either to obey, or to ask the Pope directly for permission to remain in Lecceto. But he ignored Urban, like the veriest Clementine. He wrote instead to Catherine, answering for himself and for Father Antonio, saying that both she and the Pope were mistaken in asking such a thing : it was an illusion of the devil to make the hermits abandon their quiet and consolations. They would lose all unction in Rome ; they could pray only in their wood. It will be remembered that Father William Flete and Father Antonio were Augustinians and that Catherine had with her in Rome at that time an Augustinian of great fame, the " Master," Father Tantucci. This precedent seems to have troubled Flete's cocksureness and he hinted that Tantucci had gone there to get promotion. To Catherine, it seemed like the end of the world to hear her friends talking like that. This is one of the few letters she received during her life to which she never replied. She was too overcome.

But she wrote to Father Antonio (Flete's friend and identified with him in this action), her opinion of their behaviour :

"According to the letter Father William wrote me, it seems neither he nor you mean to come : but I am very sorry he is so simple. If he does not want to come through humility and fear of losing his peace of mind, he should use that virtue of humility. He should mildly and humbly ask permission from the Vicar of Christ, begging his Holiness to be good enough to allow him stay in his wood for his greater peace ; resigning himself nevertheless to the Pope's will, like one truly obedient. This would be more pleasing to God and more profitable to himself. But he did just the opposite, claiming that he who is bound by divine obedience, need not obey creatures. Of other creatures I would care little, but to include among them the Vicar of Christ grieves me greatly, seeing him so forgetful of the truth. He says also that if you and the others came, you would lose your life of the spirit and so you would not be able to help with prayer, nor remain in spirit with the Holy Father. Too lightly is the spirit held if it is lost through change of place ! Is God then an accepter of places, found only in the wood and not elsewhere in time of necessity ? If at least he spoke for himself and not of other holy people ! Whoever comes here comes to endure ; not for promotion but for the dignity of much labour, tears, vigil and continual prayer. I am amazed (because I know the contrary) that the Master, Giovanni, should be judged to have come only to gain preferment. With all my heart I feel intolerable grief at this, seeing God so much offended under cover of virtue ; for the intention of a creature neither can nor ought to be judged."

It is not known whether Don John of the Cells obeyed the Papal summons. There is no record of his active assistance in Rome. In any case, if he went there, he remained only a short time, because he was certainly in Florence at the end of the year. His attitude to contemporary affairs cannot have comforted Catherine greatly. We know, through his letters, that he was ultimately deceived by one of the innumerable false prophecies that pullulated out of the schism. He inclined to the Joachim theory : that it marked the end of the world. Such a state of resignation does not usually result in vigorous action.

Maconi's younger brother, Battista, had been very ill and Stefano had not liked to leave his mother. But Battista recovered and still Stefano could not come to Rome. He and Pietro di Venture wrote that they were longing to come, but . . . there was always something. Catherine answered them in a joint letter :

" I shall easily prove whether you desire to leave your homes and come here ; because if you really have that desire, then

you will zealously bring to an end all the affairs that are keeping you back. Come quickly."

But the whole year passed away and Stefano never came. The
poor fellow left his own palatial home and took a room in the
Misericordia Hospital in order to be with Matteo Cenni and to
lead something like the life he aspired to. All through the year.
he wrote constantly to the group in Rome, sending messages
through Neri to our " *dolcissima Mamma*," " *benignissima
Mamma*," " *venerabile, dolce e gioconda Mamma nostra*." But still
he did not come. Pietro ceased writing. Then some Abbot
wrote to Catherine that Maconi was going to enter his order
and she was hurt and bewildered that he had not told her first.
It was what she wanted him to do, but so unexpected that he
should do it then, without consulting her. (As a matter of fact,
the good Abbot was mistaken and Maconi had no such intention.)
This stupid misunderstanding arose, one would say, to press
down the measure of her cup of bitterness. In her letter to
Stefano about this, Catherine adds a message to Pietro (in the
sound of which one hears her weariness) :

" Say to Pietro that if I told him God delights in deeds
rather than words, I did not thereby mean to impose silence
on him, or that he should not speak and write to me about
what may be to his peace and consolation. Indeed, I have
often marvelled that he has not written."

During those distressing months in Rome, when the progress
of the schism did not leave her a moment's repose, what thoughts
were Catherine's. . . . Delle Vigne so disappointing and
estranged ; the Abbot of Sant' Antimo in prison ; William Flete
ignoring and disobeying the Pope in his hour of direst need ;
Stefano unwilling or unable to come to her assistance ; Pietro
silent, and how many others ? The bugle-call to battle had
sounded, but it came too soon for the Fellowship. When
Catherine sprang into action, they seemed to scatter on every
side in panic. Yet they were not failures, these people whose
hesitations have been described. They all achieved great things
afterwards, each in his own sphere. They honoured her ever-

lastingly in their lives. But it seemed she had to die before they could awaken fully. She, who liked completion, saw now the perfect completion of her own defeat. What she loved best in the world had failed her. She once gave the advice : " End all pains in pain." Now in her daily walks from her house to St. Peter's and back, she found all the physical infirmities that had pursued her for years intensified one hundred fold, so that she suffered in every fibre of her body. She knew well it could not last and that it must be a presage of the end. But her bodily affliction was consumed and almost forgotten in her lonely mental suffering. This, indeed, was the pain in which all pains end.

CHAPTER III

THE HOUR OF VIGIL

MEANWHILE Rome had all the atmosphere of a battlefield. The crashing bombardment of Castello Sant' Angelo daily filled the air. The Romans were roused to a savage pitch of fury against the French defenders, reducing them to desperate straits and cruelly mutilating all of them who fell into their hands. Urban had hired for his service the Company of St. George, made up of Italian mercenaries recruited by Alberigo da Barbiano, Count of Cunio, who was winning fame as a condottiere. This army was the nearest approach to a national army any Italian commune could yet boast of. All Urban's success in the field depended upon it. We therefore of course find Catherine writing to the captain of this poor ghost of the Roman legions, as confidently as she had once approached the redoubtable John Hawkwood. She mothers the whole Papal army, calling Alberigo her " dearest brother " and trying to exalt his service to the height of the greatest Christian chivalry.

"Now is the time of the new martyrs. You are the first to shed blood. Do you want to be very strong so that each one of you shall be worth many ? Then you must hold up before you the Blood of Christ, the humble Lamb."

She tells them to enter the fight with a right intention, to go to confession as often as possible. She explains to Alberigo her ideal of a Christian army. She had in mind a company of Galahads :

"Have wise and mature counsellors by your side, faithful and loyal. And choose for leaders virile and honourable men, of the best conscience you can find ; because good members

are found under good heads.   Watch attentively always that
there is no treason within or without.   And offer yourselves
first thing morning and night to that sweet mother Mary,
praying her to be your advocate and protectress.   Take heart,
take heart in Christ sweet Jesus, keeping before you that Blood
shed with such great fire of love.   Keep on the battlefield
with the standard of the most holy Cross ; think that the blood
of our glorious martyrs is always crying out in the sight of
God, invoking His help upon you.   Think that this soil here
is the garden of the blessed Christ and the beginning of our
Faith.''

In the Spring of 1379, the Urbanist cause seemed to be
springing steadily upwards to victory.   During April, the
soldiers beleaguered in Castello Saint' Angelo (despairing of help
reaching them from outside) were compelled to treat with the
city government.   They capitulated on the 27th.   At the end
of that month too, the Company of St. George was solemnly
blessed by Urban and marched out of Rome to encounter the
Clementine troops.   Both forces met at Marino on the morning
of April 30th and fought a notable battle there, Alberigo da
Barbiano coming off victorious.   It was a great achievement
because Italian soldiers defeated double their own number of
foreign mercenaries.   (To this Company, safeguarded so mater-
nally by Catherine's prayers and counsel, is traced the beginning
of an Italian national army.)   One-third of the Clementine troops
were killed or made prisoners, the latter including three famous
captains.   On that same day, Castello Sant' Angelo was razed
to the ground.   Urban had wished to take it and guard it but
the Romans would not give it up to him.   Although supporting
him as true Pontiff, they did not intend him to be supreme
temporal ruler within the city.

Meanwhile Clement VII had been moving around southern
Italy.   In his character of Pope, with astounding liberality, he
made over the greater part of the States of the Church to Louis
d'Anjou, to reward that prince for his support (a most unponti-
fical gesture, significant enough).   After the surrender of Cas-

tello Sant' Angelo and the defeat at Marino, he withdrew in some alarm to the gay court of the Queen of Naples. Joanna received him gladly, but her subjects viewed him with cold hostility. Almost the whole populace were in favour of the Neapolitan Pope, Urban. They would have no part in their Queen's policy. A few days after Clement's arrival in Naples, this disapproval was expressed by an ugly revolt in which the Queen's life was threatened. Clement had to flee again. He began to make preparations to leave Italy for Avignon. Joanna helped him secretly. Two days before his departure, she formally declared her allegiance to Urban (probably in order to pacify her kingdom). Clement then proceeded to Avignon. Urban's cause seemed secure in southern Italy.

Catherine was steadfastly in the background of all these scenes of battle, siege and revolution. She was in constant communication with the chief actors in the drama, beseeching in vibrant words right action from the most unlikely ; using every effort to smooth away the friction provoked by jarring wills even in her own camp. She persuaded Urban to commemorate his double triumph in a manner worthy of the great Popes of old. Before taking up his residence again in the Vatican (from which he had to retire during the bombardment of Castello Sant' Angelo), he walked barefoot in a solemn procession of thanksgiving from Santa Maria in Trastevere to St. Peter's. It was six hundred years or more since Rome had witnessed such a sight.

Then, when the wounded were pouring into the city after the Battle of Marino, she wrote to the Roman Governors to see that they were well cared for, in gratitude to the Company. She points out the example of Urban's act of humility, " a thing which has not been done for a very long time." There must have been dissension between the government and the soldiers, for she adds : " Be charitable and peaceable with them, so that you may retain their help and remove their cause for complaint. You must do this, dearest brothers, both from duty and from necessity." She reminds them, too, to be grateful to Giovanni Cenci, who had negotiated for them the surrender of Castello Sant' Angelo.

" He worked with great zeal and faithfulness and a pure purpose, solely to please God and serve us (this I know to be the truth), putting all else aside to deliver you from the scourge that Castello Sant' Angelo had become to you and settling the affair with great prudence. Now not only do you show no sign of gratitude, not even thanking him, but the vice of envy and ingratitude is poisoning you to slander and murmur against him. I do not like him to be treated thus." And still she pursued the Queen of Naples : " I have written to you several times out of compassion, explaining to you that what was offered you as truth is a lie. It is a human thing to sin, but to persevere in it is devilish. Alas, do not wait for time that you are not sure of having : do not ask my eyes to shed rivers of tears over your miserable little soul, which seems to be dead, because it is separated from the body of the Church. It is not Pope Urban VI you are persecuting, but the truth and our faith." She tells the Queen that, even concerning her temporal goods, she seems to have lost her reason. (Naples was a fief of the Holy See.) She warns Joanna that excommunication is hanging over her, and therefore deposition.

She wrote that letter on May 6th and on May 18th Joanna declared her allegiance to Urban again. Was it partly the effect of Catherine's letter ? Very likely. The latter had predicted revolution in Naples if the Queen declared for Clement and it had come to pass. Feign as she might to be deaf, Joanna must have had a confused horror of that voice ringing in her ears so persistently. She wrote to Catherine personally, confessing her belief that Urban was true Pope and promising to obey him.

At any rate, it was Urban's hour of triumph. The Italian communes held for him and, beyond Italy, the horizon seemed to be clearing : England was supporting him warmly ; also the new Emperor and King Louis of Hungary and Poland, who gave hope of armed assistance. At Whitsuntide, the Pope took up his residence in the Vatican and Catherine wrote to rejoice with him that " the most sweet Mother Mary and sweet Peter,

Prince of the Apostles, have restored you to your own place."
She invoked the fire of the Holy Spirit to work in his heart and
soul, to give him light, wisdom and strong patience. " Be
comforted, my holiest and sweetest Father, for God will refresh
you. Great consolation follows a great trial." During June,
all the rebellious castles around Rome submitted, making his
position more secure. From the Vatican, he sent a joyful brief
to the Christian world : " giving thanks to the Most High with
ineffable joy of mind."

Catherine seemed convinced that it was the tide of victory.
She rallied all her forces in a supreme endeavour to make the
truth prevail during this moment of success and bring the
schism to an end. Desperately she multiplied the efforts of her
exhausted body and mind. Time, streaming past her, seemed
to jeer at her flagging strength. It was apocalyptic : the
struggle waged by this solitary woman while her life was ebbing
away in mysterious maladies. She sent out her flaming letters
to the four corners of the world, imploring help for the Church.
She told the Italian cardinals that they could wash from head
to foot in the tears and sweat that were poured out for them.
The letters she wrote on behalf of Pope Urban VI form one of
the world's epics.

To the delicate King Charles V of France, surnamed the Wise,
who lived among his books, she said : " Do not go on in such
ignorance. I am amazed that a Catholic man, who wills to
fear God and be manly, should allow himself to be led like a
child." She tells him (what Father Delle Vigne should have told
him) the whole story of the election of Urban VI.

She warns the Government of Siena to pay their debts to the
Church (Urban badly needed money), and to treat the Pope as
the Vicar of Christ on earth and their dear Father, doing all in
their power for him. She wrote to her own Republic a second
time, telling them not to

" waver and limp in their minds through any illusion of the
devil. No matter what people say, do not think : Perhaps
he is, perhaps he is not ! Not so, for the love of God, but

affirm it cordially holding that our father is Pope Urban VI, whatever may be said to the contrary.

" You must obey him and help him and, if necessary, die for this truth."

She wrote to a religious confraternity (the Disciplinati) and to Maconi, bidding them bring pressure on the Sienese government to assist Urban with the money they owed the Holy See. She said to Maconi : " If you are what you ought to be, you will set all Italy on fire." The Florentines were also very slow in paying up their indemnities. She wrote to them too, reproaching them for their ingratitude and urging them to consider the Pope's need.

" I therefore implore you for the love of Christ crucified and for your own advantage to keep your heart firm and stable and do not waver, but strongly affirm this truth, that Pope Urban VI is truly the Supreme Pontiff."

She sent Neri on a personal embassy with a letter of hers to the Government of Perugia, admonishing them to help the Pope. She tells these worthy magistrates that they are like idiots, " not understanding the evil they have done nor the graces received up to now, giving no help except in words." She wrote to the King of Hungary (whose wife had once written her as *Amica Specialissima*), telling him to make peace with Venice and obey Urban, who is calling him to help.

" Postpone everything else. Can you endure that Anti-Christ, member of the devil, and a miserable woman should bring all our Faith to ruin, darkness and confusion ? Take hold of the little bark of Holy Church and help to lead her to a port of peace and quiet."

She wrote to this King's cousin, Charles of Durazzo, who was married to a niece of Queen Joanna, telling him to first purify his own life and then hasten to Urban's aid. " Do not wait for time ; it is dangerous. Come and hide in the ark of Holy Church under the wings of your father, Pope Urban VI, who holds the keys of the Blood of Christ." She wrote to the Cardinal of Padua : " Do not sleep any longer ; it is the hour of vigil,"

and in similar terms to the Senator of Siena, and to Bishop
Angelo Correr (who in after life was Pope Gregory XII). During
her struggle with Queen Joanna, she wrote to innumerable
women in Naples asking the help of their prayers and influence.
She wrote to hosts of private persons and religious everywhere,
mobilising them for prayer.

And these are *only the letters that have been preserved.* It is known,
for instance, that she wrote also to the King of England, but this
letter is lost, together with many others. She flung in against
the balance of evil all her power of prayer, every ounce of her
physical energy, all the fasting and vigil and penance of which
any human being was ever yet capable, all her eloquence, all
her organizing ability, all the force of her magnetic personality,
all the love she had ever won from men and women. She
exploited every gift of hers to the uttermost.

And yet they did not win on that flood-tide of victory. When
it began to recede, she knew with dismay that the ground was
slipping again from under their feet. Urban's triumph was
illusory. Too soon the reverses came. Joanna's change of
mind lasted little over a month. Then she again began to wage
a fierce persecution against the Urbanists in her kingdom.
Catherine, in a final effort, sent Neri and a certain Abbot on an
embassy to her, bearing the last letter she ever addressed to this
Queen. There was something very pathetic in those embassies
which the grave and sensitive young poet undertook so willingly
for Catherine, although he detested life apart from her : Avignon,
Perugia, Naples. He would be sure to loathe the Neapolitan
court. This mission proved the saddest one he ever embarked
upon. There was civil war in the Kingdom of Naples, the
Urbanists wearing a red rose for emblem and the Clementines
a white rose. To the Queen who had provoked this strife,
Catherine said :

"Alas, how does your heart not burst with grief to see your
people divided because of you ; one side wearing the white
rose and the other the red, one maintaining the truth and the
other a lie ! Can you not see that they were all created by

that most pure rose of the eternal will of God and recreated to grace in that most ardent crimson rose of the Blood of Christ."

She tells the beautiful and vain Queen what she least wanted to be reminded of : that her youth was over and death pursuing her. (The Queen was now nearer sixty than fifty, but still entrancing.) Joanna's husband had defeated the rebels. She felt secure and probably threw the letter aside as the message of a fanatic. She had bitter cause to remember it less than a year later. Neri remained on in Naples, trying to work for good there. He had learned from Catherine in Florence not to abandon an enterprise too soon.

Meanwhile, little aid was forthcoming for Urban from any side, except in words. Both claimaints to the tiara had summoned foreign princes into Italy to help decide the question and the peninsula was in troubled expectation of this clash of arms : Louis d'Anjou for Clement and the King of Hungary, helped by his cousin, Charles of Durazzo, for Urban. The three Italian cardinals continued neutral and appealed to a General Council to end the schism, until August 1379, when one of them, Jacopo Orsini, died. The other two went over to Clement afterwards. The King of France continued to support Clement, now comfortably installed in Avignon.

The worst feature of the case, from the point of view of the Roman claimant, was that he had trouble at his very door. Since the surrender of Castello Sant' Angelo relations between him and the Roman Government had been strained. Also some of the Roman feudal nobles opposed him, particularly Francesco di Vico, the tyrannical Lord of Viterbo and titular prefect of Rome. This man had long been in opposition to the Holy See. Urban had included him in the excommunications of last November. All this close of the year 1379 was clouded with apprehension of a revolution against Urban outside or even inside the city of Rome.

Probably what afflicted Catherine most was that the new cardinals he had created were not by any means exemplary in their lives. From that point of view, they were no improvement whatever on the schismatic group. Urban did not attack them as he had attacked the others. He seemed indifferent. Probably too harassed by exterior troubles, he was every day less zealous about reform.

Thus one of the Urbanists' best arguments was beginning to lose point : that the Pope's desire for reform had provoked all the trouble. There was not that shining light of holiness in their camp which would have helped Christendom to discern them. Catherine wrote urgently about this to Urban, telling him he was not as zealous as he should be.

" Do not let us wait until we are humiliated. But work virilely and do those things secretly and prudently (because if they are done imprudently, more is destroyed than rebuilt). Do it benevolently and with a tranquil heart."

And at last she speaks out to him about his explosive temper : " For the love of Christ crucified, restrain a little those hasty movements of your nature." She warns him also that there are spies in his household carrying out news to the Clementines. She adds : " I would have come, instead of writing, but I did not want to weary you by coming so often."

Then a Roman embassy went to parley with the fierce Francesco di Vico and were repulsed with insults. Catherine was desperately afraid that Urban would hopelessly aggravate the situation by a breach with the Roman Government, thus making enemies within and without the walls. He was no diplomat whatever. She tries once more to soften his bitterness, to bridle his outbursts :

" I have heard, most holy Father, of the reply that the impious prefect made you, truly impious in anger and irreverence to the Roman ambassadors : and it seems they must call a general meeting about that reply ; after which the leaders of the Rioni and certain other good men will come to you. I beg of you, most holy Father, that as you have begun, so do you continue to confer often with them ; and prudently bind them with the bond of love. And so I beseech you now, whatever they say to you, after they have held the council, receive them as sweetly as you possibly can, explaining what is necessary to them according as Your Holiness thinks.   Forgive me if love makes me say what perhaps should not be said. I know that you must know the nature of your Roman children, that they are led and bound more by gentleness than by other force or by harsh words ; and you realize also how necessary it is for you and Holy Church to conserve this people obedient and reverent towards you ; because here is the head and the beginning of our Faith.   I beseech you humbly, too, to aim prudently always at promising only what you can fully perform, so that there follow no harm, shame, cr confusion.   And forgive me, sweetest and holiest Father, for saying this to you."

She wrote frequently to Neri, whom she knew to be miserable in Naples.   Already she and her company were thinking of the chances of going back to Siena.   In her letter to Neri of December 4th, she discusses whether he ought to go back, but she does not definitely release him.   She tells him the news : " We have good news of Father Delle Vigne : that he is well and is working very hard for holy Church : He is Vicar of the Province of Genoa and shall soon be made Master in Theology.   I have had news from Siena of permission to alter Belcaro, and therefore see if you can get any assistance for the work down there.   We have taken a house near San Biagio, between Campo de' Fiori and Sant' Eustachio and we hope to go back before Easter by the grace of God."   She wrote to Maconi, telling him somewhat tersely he shall have no more indulgences from Rome, unless he comes for them himself.   She marvels why Pietro di Venture, Stefano's boon companion at this time, has not written her. She says :

" I have much to say to you, which I do not want to write. Neri is at Naples, where I sent him with Abbot Lisolo.   I believe they are very unhappy down there, especially suffering mentally in seeing God so much offended."

By Christmas (1379) the tide in Urban's favour had turned

even in Rome. It seemed an awful New Year. Catherine was tortured by persistent rumours and at last definite information of plots to kill the Pope. In her fevered prayers to prevent this horror, she seemed to be struggling physically with the powers of evil. Her letters became rarer. On the evening of January 30th, she told Barduccio she wanted to write to the Pope and to the cardinals. She dictated that last letter to Urban quoted above, between gasps, like one in great pain. Before she could go on to the second letter, she fell on the floor unconscious.

Chapter IV

THE MARTYR BY DESIRE

NOTHING could better illustrate the enormous gulf which always separated Catherine from the Fellowship than the letters they exchanged among themselves during that dark and terrible year of 1379. Those letters indeed form the light relief of the picture. One wonders if they at all grasped the situation. Anyhow, they were not extraordinarily helpful. Ser Cristofano writes Neri and hopefully quotes : " *Tu es Petrus et super hanc petram,*" as though that were all that need be said. The letters are all about Catherine, of course. " Tell Mamma that we are very scattered here and to give us some rules that we could obey out of reverence for her and which would induce us to meet together occasionally in her memory ; and tell her to write to us sometimes, showing she does not forget her little lost sheep, etc." When one thinks of the letters she was writing !

Vaguely impressed (but quite unable yet to rise to what the terrible crisis in the Church demanded of him), Maconi had doffed his chevalier's attire and wore the plain white of the nursing brothers of the Misericordia. We see him sitting at his table, in the room he had taken in that hospital with Matteo Cenni, writing long letters to Neri, which still breathe all a soldier's naïveté. " I tell you," he unnecessarily assures his friend, " that I firmly believe and so confess, that our most benignant Mamma *is* Mamma ; and I have firm hope that every day with clearer light, I will believe and confess with greater efficacy that she is Mamma. I do not believe my pain will ever be fully assuaged until I find myself again at the feet of my

dilettissima Mamma." He calls Clement (somewhat confusedly)
" that antidemon of Fondi."

He tells Neri that, at a rumour of a Clementine ambassador
coming to Siena, the people were making ready to stone him.
He and Pietro had gone with alacrity to the Town Hall to offer
to be the first to lay hands on the said ambassador, who,however,
had not been allowed inside the city gates (almost to Maconi's
disappointment, one feels). Again he says to Neri : " *Fratel
mio dolce*, prove to me by two signs that you do not forget me :
remember me to that venerable, sweet and joyful Mamma of
ours. Begin now before you put this letter out of your hands,
so that you do not forget. The second is, that you write to me
often," and so forth.

They heard afterwards in Rome that a Clementine envoy *had*
been received in Siena after all and Neri wrote Stefano rather
crossly not to tell any more lies, but to give them a correct report
of what was happening there. More in touch with reality,
Neri did not laugh so readily and he thought that if Maconi
would not come to Rome to help, he could at least keep them
accurately informed of events in Siena. Meekly Maconi
apologizes and says perhaps his desire that things should be as
he had described made him believe too readily that they were so.
In his subsequent letters, one can see him trying to be more
careful. He adds many assurances to his statements. (But
compare all this with Catherine's terrific correspondence.)

The great event for the group left in Siena was the arrival of
messages and couriers from Rome. Maconi relates about some
unsatisfactory Tommaso who came back from Rome with no
news :

" He had no news of you, nor of Barduccio, nor of anyone
else : only that Mamma is well. But we knew that much.
If time permitted, I would make you laugh a lot about it ;
because not only the others, but Misser Matteo, too, thought
he would die laughing."

A great number of the letters are concerned with indulgences.
Special ones were granted by Urban of course for special work at

this time. One can understand that all the friends of members of the circle wanted favours from the Papal court. But it was not always easy to get the irascible Urban to grant them, as Father Bartolomeo explains in a letter to Neri, while the latter was in Naples :

" When I spoke to Misser Tommaso about it, a few days after you left, he told me that our lord the Pope does not want to issue any more such bulls, if he has not proof first of the good lives of those persons. Then he fell ill, but is now better, although still weak. So recently the Master wanted those bulls for you and Pietro signed, as the minutes were drawn up a long while ago. Misser Tommaso read it to Christ on earth, Mamma and the Master being present : and Christ on earth answered that he should draw up the petition all over again and then he would sign it. Master Giovanni therefore does not know what to do and Misser Tommaso is so weary of it, he says he will not do anything more in the matter."

Father Simone had very characteristically promised some lady to obtain an indulgence for her and he wrote Neri a long string of Latin quotations, and then whisked in a reminder about this at the end.

Catherine did not seem the same since that stroke on January 30th. She rose up after some hours' unconsciousness and spent the ensuing days in a mysterious physical and mental agony, as though the evil around her were *palpable*. Rome was full of agitation and dread : of threats and murmurings against the Pope. On February 2nd, an armed mob assailed the Vatican and broke in through the gates. This time Urban seemed inspired to do the right thing. He received the insurgents, sitting on his throne in Pontifical vestments (very much as Boniface had received the French soldiers). He succeeded in calming them and the danger was averted for the moment. Rome began to breathe again.

In her house in the Via Chiara, Catherine had felt she was wrestling with demons. On February 15th, she wrote a description of this mystical experience to Delle Vigne. She would have been glad to tell him this personally. She could not readily talk about such things to anyone else.

" Father, Father and dearest son, God has worked admirable mysteries in me from the Feast of the Circumcision until now, such as no tongue could relate. But passing over that period, let us come to Sexagesima Sunday, on which Sunday took place those mysteries of which I am writing you briefly, and the like of which never happened to me before. For the pain in my heart was so great that in the spasm I tore my habit, as much of it as I could clutch, going round the chapel in an agony. If anyone had tried to restrain me, it would surely have cost me my life. When Monday evening came, I felt constrained to write to the Pope and to three cardinals : wherefore I had myself assisted into the study. And when I had written to Christ on earth, I could do no more, such were the pains that increased in my body. And after a little while, the terror of the demons began in such a way that they utterly stupefied me ; mad with rage against me that I, a worm, had been the means of wresting from their hands what they had long time possessed in holy Church. So great was my terror and bodily pain, that I wanted to fly from the study and go into the chapel ; as though the study had caused the pain. I rose up, therefore, and being unable to walk, I leaned upon my son, Barduccio. But I was immediately flung down : and lying there, it seemed to me that my soul had left my body ; but not in the way that once happened to me, when I had tasted the bliss of the immortals, enjoying supreme good together with them. This was quite different. I seemed no longer in the body, but I saw my body as though it belonged to another. And my soul, seeing the grief of him who was with me, tried to use my body to say to him : Do not fear, my son, but I saw that I could not move my tongue or any other member, no more than in a dead body. I therefore left the body as it was ; and my intellect remained fixed in the abyss of the Trinity. My memory was full of the needs of holy

Church and of all Christian people. I cried out in God's sight and confidently demanded divine aid, offering Him my desires and constraining Him by the Blood of the Lamb and by all sufferings borne : and I implored so insistently that it seemed certain He would not deny that petition. Then I prayed for all you others that His will and my desires should be accomplised in you. After which I prayed to be saved from eternal condemnation. And I remained thus for a very long while, so long that the family wept over me as one dead, during which time all the terror of the demons passed away. Then the Presence of the humble Lamb came before my soul, saying : Fear not ; for I will fulfil thy desires and those of My other servants. See, I am a good potter, marring and making again as I please. I know how to destroy and remake those vessels of mine : and therefore I take the vessel of thy body and I refashion it in the garden of Holy Church in a different wise from before. And as this sweet Truth held me close with ways and words most winning, which I pass over, the body began to breathe a little and show that the soul had returned to its vessel. I was full of wonder. And such great anguish remained in my heart that I still have it there. All joy and all refreshment and all food were then taken away from me. When they carried me upstairs, the room seemed full of demons, who began to wage another battle against me, the most terrible that I ever endured, striving to make me believe and see that I was not she who was in the body, but rather an impure spirit. I then called on the divine aid with sweet tenderness, not refusing labour, but saying : Incline unto my aid, O God ! O Lord, make haste to help me ! Thou hast permitted me to be alone in this struggle, without the help of my father, of whom I am deprived through my own ingratitude.

" Two nights and two days passed in these tempests. It is true that mind and desire received no injury, but always remained fixed on their object ; but the body seemed to be failing. Afterwards, on the Feast of the Purification of Mary,

I wished to hear Mass. Then all the mysteries were renewed and God showed what great need had existed, as was seen later ; because Rome had been then on the point of revolting, traducing miserably and with great irreverence. Only that God had poured balm on their hearts and now I believe it will end well. Then God imposed this obedience on me, that during all this holy season of Lent I should offer up the desires of all my family and have Mass celebrated solely with this intention, for Holy Church ; and that I should myself hear Mass every morning at dawn. You know that this is impossible for me, but in obedience to Him everything has been possible. So much has this desire become part of me that memory retains nought else ; the understanding sees nought else, the will desires nought else. And not only do I reject the things of earth for this ; but in conversing with the Just, the soul neither can nor will rejoice in their joy, but only in the hunger they still have, and used to have while they were pilgrims and wayfarers in this life.

" By this and other means, which I cannot relate, my life is consumed and distilled in this sweet Spouse, I doing this way what the glorious martyrs did with their blood. I pray the Divine Goodness soon to let me behold the redemption of His people. When it is the hour of Tierce, I rise from Mass and you would see a dead woman going to Saint Peter's. I enter anew to labour in the little bark of Holy Church. I remain there praying until nearly the hour of vespers ; and I would fain not leave that place, neither day nor night, until I see this people pacified and reconciled with their Father. My body remains without food, even without a drop of water ; with such sweet physical torments as I have never before endured : so that my life is hanging by a thread."

There was a final ring about this letter which must have troubled Delle Vigne. She says at the end :

" I beg of you and of Father Bartolomeo, Father Tommaso and the Master, to get all writings of mine into your hands, and the book in which I found some recreation ; and, together with Misser Tommaso, do with them what you think most to the honour of God. I pray you further, as much as shall be possible to you, to be the shepherd and ruler of this family, even as a father, and keep them in the joy of charity and in perfect union, that they be not scattered like sheep without a shepherd. I believe I shall do more for them and for you after my death than in life. I shall pray the Eternal Truth to pour out on you all that plenitude of graces and gifts he gave my soul, so that you may be like lamps placed on high.

" Pray fervently for me and have prayers said for me for the love of Christ crucified. Forgive me for having written you bitter words : and do not be afflicted because we are separated from each other. Although you would have been a great consolation to me, I have greater consolation and gladness to see the fruit you are producing in Holy Church."

During ten days after writing this letter, Catherine continued the way of life she had described in it. In the chapel of her house, she heard Mass at dawn (this being a privilege from the Pope). When she received Holy Communion, she had to be carried back to her couch. There she remained until Tierce, when she rose and walked with the others to St. Peter's, the distance of one mile. She remained in the basilica until Vespers and would then just succeed in dragging herself home, completely exhausted. During this time, her Family watched her with growing apprehension because, to use her own phrase, she was like " a dead woman."

A lifetime before this, Giotto and Cavallini in collaboration had adorned the vestibule of St. Peter's with a famous mosaic of the " Navicella." It represented in glowing colours that great scene out of St. Matthew's Gospel, to which Urban VI had so sorrowfully referred when imploring the spiritual help of the Church. During the night, the little ship containing the Apostles was buffeted by storm. In the fourth watch, they saw Christ walking towards them on the water and cried out in fear. He called to them reassuringly and Peter, at that voice, flung himself out of the boat to go to Him. But when the disciple

felt the strong wind around him, he gasped that he was sinking ;
whereupon Christ caught and steadied him, rebuking him for
doubting. When they both reached the ship, the storm was
stilled.

One can understand how profoundly the symbolism of this
great picture affected Catherine. Her sorrowful eyes always
rested on it when she entered the basilica. It consoled her.
The bark of the Church was indeed lost now in a stormy night,
and her daily life was a cry to God to walk over the waters to
them. Only such a miracle could save that frail vessel. On
the third Sunday in this Lent of 1380, she was praying before
the picture and, at the same time, she seemed to be struggling
with demons, who with noise and confusion were continually
trying to sweep her to the edge of despair.

She had hardly been able to contain herself for joy when
the Pope had restored the Holy See to Rome and now that
rich fruit of her endeavour had turned to dust. There
was a Pope again in Avignon, reigning securely, protected by
the French King, supported by the University of Paris and
acknowledged by one-half of Christendom.

She had worked all her life for peace, striving doggedly against
the indifference and discouragement of her contemporaries,
who thought hope for peace an Utopian dream. Now, even she
was defeated ; it was a bitter jest to talk of peace. The whole
peninsula was under arms again. Two foreign princes with
their armies were marching upon Italy to contend for it and add
to the misery of the communes, already exhausted by their
internecine struggles and by the depredations of the freelance
companies. It was an appalling prospect of bloodshed and ruin.

Catherine had failed to arrest this evil schism in its first
beginning. Desperately then she had tried to heal it, but the
monstrous breach had widened irrevocably. It was beyond her
strength. By now the fissure in Christendom stretched right
across Europe, even adding—can it be credited ?—to the divisions which sundered Scotland and England. All the weapons
she had used in that heroic defence of unity had been struck,

one by one, out of her hands. She had told the King of Hungary that the holy and just in the Church were on Urban's side. This was no longer true. Saints were beginning to speak from the Clementine camp. What she knew to be the truth was not manifest to the world ; the keenest and most sincere minds could not discern it. She had said it was Urban's zeal for reform that had alienated the schismatics ; but the new cardinals he had created were certainly no improvement and he was not attempting to reform *them*. It could no longer be claimed that the Urbanists looked for righteousness.

In those agonized interior debates on the situation (always beating in her mind), the demons had one weapon against her which she feared : her sense of responsibility. She knew that the cause of the cataclysm in which they were foundering, was commonly assigned to the inopportune return of the Papacy from Avignon. *She alone had provoked that.* She still knew she had done well. But what swarms of doubts did not the demons unloose upon her for her torment. She knew she was pointed out as a false prophet ; one who had helped to cause all the confusion and dismay.

Catherine fixed her burning eyes on the picture above her. Suddenly it seemed to her that the bark of the Church was lifted bodily out of that gorgeous mosaic and placed on her shoulders by invisible hands. Physically, she shrank to feel the cruel, intolerable weight of the dire thing. She was crushed beneath it and once more her friends saw her fall on the pavement unconscious. They lifted her up and carried her home. Later, they found she was paralyzed from the waist down. She never walked to St. Peter's again.

Unable to move, she insisted on lying only on bare boards as she had always done. They transformed her room into an oratory and every morning at dawn, Mass was celebrated before her eyes and she received Holy Communion. She could not swallow anything else, not even water. Besides the paralysis, she was racked with pains and consumed with fever. Her throat burned and her breath felt scorching.

The bad news spread and the Protonotary Apostolic, Misser Tommaso Petra, hastened to visit her. He had known her at Avignon and was deeply attached to her. He considered her condition very grave and suggested that she should say to her Family whatever messages of farewell she had in mind. She tranquilly agreed. That fantastic group of her " sons and daughters " were rallied from all around the city. This was the first intimation many of them had. In great grief and excitement, they crowded into her room and she talked with them for a long time, though her speech was difficult and painful. She knew them all, called each one lovingly by name and had a personal message for each. She spoke to them in general about mental purity. But by this she did not mean mere freedom from grossness. (Her very language is a reproach.) She meant utter abstention from mental judgment of others.

By this time Father Bartolomeo was back in Siena, having been made Prior of St. Dominic's there. During March, he was fortunate enough to be sent to Rome on business for his Provincial. Arriving on Holy Saturday, March 24th, he went first to find Catherine. Not having heard of her illness, he was utterly shocked when they brought him into her. The planks upon which she was lying were boarded up on each side, so that her couch looked disturbingly like a coffin. The suggestiveness overcame the priest. He found her terribly altered. She appeared to have shrunken in size : all her bones protruded so that they could be counted. Her skin had turned brown, as though bronzed by sun, and it adhered closely to her cheekbones like parchment. Indeed she resembled a mummified skeleton. Only her eyes were the same : she smiled through them as she always did. When Bartolomeo met that look, full of humorous and tranquil understanding, he seemed to find her again. He stammered enquiries, but had to bend his ear to her lips to hear her reply : " Very well indeed, by the grace of God." The following day was Easter Sunday and it also happened to be her thirty-third birthday. Father Bartolomeo celebrated the Mass in her room. While he was preparing to give Communion to the Family, they were all overwhelmed with amazement to see Catherine slip off her couch and walk over to join them. It was a pathetic little birthday and Easter celebration, though brief, because she became motionless immediately afterwards. But her speech was freer and she was able to talk for a few days. When his business in Rome was concluded, Father Bartolomeo could not make up his mind to go back. He lingered beside her, until she noticed it and insisted he should return to his duties. They argued it for some days and in the end she prevailed on him to go. He felt quite reassured the day he said good-bye. She was sitting up and was gay, almost her old self. Touched by his devotion, she held out her arms and embraced him. But a few moments after his departure, she was immobile again. " I was deceived by the Lord," said this faithful friend afterwards.

In Siena, Maconi had heard of her illness and was unspeakably wretched. He spent his days wandering between the churches, praying. He knew that always she was subject to mysterious prostrations and miraculous recoveries. But this sounded very grave. He did not know what to think. One night, as he knelt in the chapel in the vaults under the Scala hospital, he was overwhelmed by an intuition that she was dying. Running out in a kind of frenzy, he hastily dispatched his affairs and, taking horse, galloped out of Siena on the long road to Rome. He rode like a man riding for life. In that anguished journey southward, he grew up.

No one has ever described their meeting. When he arrived, she was clearly dying and her sufferings were very distressing to witness. She could still speak. She whispered to him to write to Father Bartolomeo in Siena and get prayers said in St. Dominic's there.

On Sunday, April 29th, about an hour before dawn, the watchers in her room noticed a change and hastily summoned the others. Unable to endure those boards, Alessa knelt down by the couch and lifted the dying woman into her arms. Catherine's breathing was very laboured and she could not

speak. Father Tantucci pronounced over her the plenary
indulgence which the Pope had granted her for the hour of death.
As soon as day lighted the room, the Abbot of Sant' Antimo
anointed her. She did not seem conscious of what was taking
place. The moment the Sacrament was administered, her face
which had been serene, clouded darkly and she began to struggle.
She raised her arm as though to shield herself and turned her
head from side to side with anguish in her eyes. They prayed
desperately around her, but the struggle lasted for nearly an
hour, during which time she never spoke. Then she began to
gasp some words ; *Peccavi Domine, miserere mei.* She repeated
this at least seventy times, her arm still working. Then she said :
" O God, have mercy on me. Do not take Thy memory from
me." Once she said in a louder voice as though answering
an opponent : " Never vainglory ; but true glory in Christ
crucified," and the words gave the bystanders some clue to the
thoughts that tortured her. At last she was still and her face
brightened again into serenity ; her eyes which had been so
pained and dim, became clear and joyful. The gladness passed
round all their faces. The change in her was so complete,
they half-believed she was miraculously cured. She made
efforts to rise and then Alessa sat on the edge of the couch and
raised her into a sitting posture, still holding her. They held
up before her a little table of relics which some cardinal had
given her. She fixed her eyes on the Crucifix in the centre of it
and began to pray. She made a general confession aloud and
asked for absolution. It was granted. She asked that the
plenary indulgence at the hour of death should be repeated,
saying with a hint of her old spirit, that two Popes had given it
to her. Father Tantucci pronounced it again. She asked for
her mother's blessing and poor old Monna Lapa bent over
her, choking with grief. Then Catherine blessed all her friends
and spoke of those who were absent. Neri being still loyally in
Naples, she sent him a special message. She told Stefano to
join the Carthusian order. Her voice began to sink inaudibly,
while she prayed for them all. They bent down in turn to listen,

each collecting a few phrases, which afterwards they put together and treasured. But besides the faintness of her voice, they were so shaken with emotion, they heard very little. She sank into silence ; then said fervently : " Blood, Blood, Blood ! " Her head fell forward. Alessa laid her down gently. It was nine in the morning.

Outside, Rome pursued its way unconscious of all this. Then the Fellowship did a curious, but most comprehensible thing. They closed the doors and windows and put out no sign of mourning, so that people would believe they were all out, as had often happened. Having jealously excluded the outer world, they gave themselves up to the grief that had stricken them. Their only glimmer of consolation was to be alone together with her. Knocks on their door went unheeded. (They were very much reproached for this afterwards.) They kept her death a profound secret until all arrangements were complete for removing her to the Dominican Chapel of Santa Maria sopra Minerva. Maconi claimed the supreme honour of carrying the sacred remains. They placed the bier behind an iron grille in order to safeguard the body from the people's devotion. Stefano and Barduccio remained on guard beside it, as long as it was left exposed.

The news then flew around Rome and the people immediately flocked to the church, pouring in " like tumultuous waves." The devotion of the Romans broke out impetuously around the still figure in the white dress and black cloak. They thronged before the grille for days, bringing their sick in an unending procession. Many miraculous cures strengthened the devotion and increased the excitement. The day after the body had been placed in the church, Father Tantucci went up into the pulpit to preach a panegyric of Catherine Benincasa, but he could not make his voice audible above that vast multitude acclaiming and praying. He said, " She speaks better for herself," and came down again.

On the Tuesday evening, the body looked just the same as immediately after death : fresh and fragrant, the face peaceful, the limbs still pliable. The Pope ordered all the details of a magnificent requiem, which was carried out with impressive solemnity. Giovanni Cenci, who was then Senator of Rome, had a second requiem offered in the name of the Roman people. Thus, around her bier, the Church and the State united to mourn her. The body was placed in a coffin of cypress, enclosed in a low marble sarcophagus, raised off the ground. This was afterwards deposited at the right hand side of the High Altar in the Minerva.

CHAPTER V

THE END

AT the moment of Catherine's death, Father Delle Vigne was
in Pisa, just setting out for the Chapter-General at Bologna.
He was there elected Master-General of the Urbanist half of
the Dominican Order (that is, in opposition to Father Elias, who
had declared for Clement). It was three years before he
could get to Rome. When he did so, he spent long hours by
that tomb in Santa Maria sopra Minerva. He obtained the
Pope's permission to have the coffin opened and the head
removed from the body, which was reverently replaced and the
sepulchre closed up again. Father Della Fonte and another
Dominican then secretly carried the sacred head back to Siena.

In the April of 1384, that is as soon as Delle Vigne was able
to come to Siena, the citizens of the Republic were informed of
what had been done. The head was carried through the streets,
borne by the Bishop in a silver casket, under a baldacchino, in
one of the most gorgeous and impressive processions ever seen
in Siena. The whole city was richly decorated ; there was a
public holiday, and all the bells rang out to honour Catherine
Benincasa. Maconi and Neri were in the cortege, side by side.
Among the tertiaries was the curved figure of old Monna Lapa.
(She lived to a great age and used to say, with a wry smile, that
God had put her soul athwart in her body so that she was not
able to die.) The head was finally carried to St. Dominic's and
solemnly deposited there. It is to-day that Church's greatest
treasure.

Father Delle Vigne spent the rest of his life labouring to bring
the schism to an end and to reform his Order. He accepted

many missions from Urban as Apostolic Legate. Shortly after Catherine's death, he began to write her life (the quarry from which all subsequent hagiographers have drawn). In this work, his view was polemic, because detractors were still busy with her name. Burdened with illness and his heavy work, he did not complete it until 1395. He was one of the greatest mediaeval reformers. He died in Nuremberg in 1399, while working for Dominican reform in Germany.

Alessa Saracini was the first of the Fellowship to die. She survived Catherine only a few months and passed away in Rome, having never seen Siena again.

Barduccio was the second. He returned from Rome to Siena and died there on December 9th, 1382, having developed consumption. At the moment of his death, he was seen to look upwards with a joyous laugh and that laugh remained carved on the boy's face in death. They said he must have seen her whom he had loved so much.

Ser Cristofano had six children, all of whom died in infancy. His wife also died. He then gave up his notary work and devoted his goods and person to the Scala Hospital, as one of the nursing brothers. He became its director later on. He wrote his " Memoirs," in which he gave Catherine the place of honour. In his old age, his wife, his children, his political work, seemed to fade out of his mind as unimportant, and he looked back on his acquaintance with Catherine as the supreme event of his life. He died while actually talking about her to Maconi.

Even Francesco Malavolti did her credit. His wife and children died too, whereupon he became an Olivetan monk. He got hammered into shape then. He kept up a correspondence with Neri, and we can mark his progress through the letters. Once the Prior went away and left him in charge of fourteen brethren. He writes the news to Neri in a frantic state : how he has to please everyone and finds himself between the hammer and the anvil. There is a comic element in Malavolti's experience of religious life. As Catherine had prophesied, she yoked him to her at last in such wise that he never escaped again.

Maconi had no intention of becoming a monk when he went riding down to Rome. The moment Catherine was dead, he could think of nothing else. He made arrangements immediately to enter the Carthusian order. He was clothed at Pontignano less than a year afterwards, on March 19th, 1381. His progress in the order was extraordinary ; his work for it admirable. He was Prior of Pontignano a year after being clothed ; thence he was transferrred to Milan, where he was concerned in the founding of the great Carthusian monastery of Pavia. In 1398, he was elected General of the whole Carthusian order in Urban's obedience. In this office, he strove honourably to bring the whole order together under one head and finally resigned the generalship to accomplish this. He survived Catherine forty-four years and outlived the schism. Throughout his long life, he could never hear her name spoken, without being overwhelmed by a rush of emotion. He headed all his letters " in her holy memory " ; he died pronouncing her name.

Neri had been very faithful and was curiously denied the sad privilege of being with Catherine at the end. He had less luck than the more graceless Maconi. He heard the news at Naples and went straight to a hermitage outside Florence, as though to hide his broken life. While the Family comforted each other, they could not comfort him. He flung himself into such austerities that, after ten years of it, he had a very bad nervous breakdown, which lasted nearly two years. At the end of this period, he had an accumulation of letters from the Fellowship, reproaching him for his silence. He moved later to a hermitage near Siena, where he had a devoted band of disciples. There exists a letter from one of these, describing his death in terms of poignant grief, and the distribution of his poor belongings among his friends. This letter is Neri's great Christian monument. From the pathetic list of his effects, the poor hermit's figure rises before us. These were the possessions of the patrician poet, who had been a society favourite : three chest-protectors ; an old cloak ; an old grey felt hat ; an old torn shirt ; a broken bed ; two worn-out feather pillows ;

a pair of torn sheets ; an old torn bed-cover ; a pair of spectacles ; an old chair ; a bag ; an old torn towel ; seventy soldi.

While Neri lived, he and Maconi were bound together in an exceptional friendship. Despite Don Stefano's increasing responsibilities, he always found time for long letters to Neri. He became in some sort Neri's protector, constantly asking him to his monastery to rest. When the latter fell ill, he sent a message to Maconi by a beggar, asking for some wine. Stefano promptly sent the wine with an affectionate letter, and wrote at once to his brother in Siena to visit Neri and provide him with all his needs. Then we find Neri sending him some of his poems, which the Carthusian has illuminated and gives away. These two consoled each other with memories. Catherine lived all the time in their correspondence, only now she is the " *santa Mamma*," " *beatissima Mamma nostra*." Once a mutual friend of theirs was in trouble and Maconi, writing to Neri, pauses to think of a consoling message to send. It was then twelve years after Catherine's death, when Stefano framed this passage, unconsciously memorable : " Say that our holy Mamma is waiting for us and calling us, so that we must walk quickly." Thenceforward, the Fellowship looked on life like children facing a long road home in the evening, who hasten their tired feet at the thought of their mother's welcome at the door.

Chapter VI

THE CULT OF SAINT CATHERINE OF SIENA

As we have seen, Catherine Benincasa was practically worshipped as a saint by a large circle during her lifetime. Immediately after her death, she passed into the language of her friends as the "beatissima," or the "santa." One of the first writings that appeared about her was a letter from Barduccio to a nun, describing her passage from this world. The letter is a long, detailed narrative of Catherine's last hours, most poignant in its unaffected simplicity. It has been described as "*presqu'un long sanglot.*" Already from this letter, it is clear that Catherine's disciples believed she would help them henceforth from "the splendour of Living Light Eternal."

But the most ardent promoter of her cult was not one of her very close friends. Father Tommaso di Nacci Caffarini knew Catherine, corresponded with her, but did not play any conspicuous part in her life, perhaps mainly because his religious duties kept him at a distance from Siena during her lifetime. But, shortly after her death, Caffarini sprang into prominence as the most active promoter of her cause. He really seemed to make it the dominant motive of his life. He laboured more than twenty years for her triumph. He wrote of her, spoke of her, preached about her incessantly. He collected every document relating to her, copying, correcting and diffusing them with amazing industry and perseverance. Posterity would never have been so well informed about Catherine, were it not for this priest's single-hearted devotion.

First of all, he pestered the Master General of his Order

(Delle Vigne) to finish the " Life " of Catherine he was writing. Four years after Catherine's death, Delle Vigne had taken up this task with great reluctance. Not that his devotion was not as ardent as Caffarini's, but he was overwhelmed with the burdens of office, ill-health, and the trials consequent upon the schism. It was 1395 before he completed the work, that is, fifteen years after Catherine's death. During all this time, Caffarini pursued him relentlessly. When they happened to meet, Caffarini would talk of nothing else. He wrote parts of it at Delle Vigne's dictation, in order to hurry the thing up. He wrote to members of the Fellowship to write the Master-General, urging him to complete it. At last, mainly thanks to Caffarini, the " Life " was completed. It was written in Latin and Caffarini immediately turned it over to Maconi to have it put into Italian. The Master-General now had a rest and it was Maconi's turn to be pestered. We find him not answering Caffarini's repeated letters for " that vernacular version ! " But at last that, too, was finished. And meanwhile the indefatigable Caffarini had been keeping Neri and others busy copying and collecting Catherine's letters.

It is worthy of note that the cult of Catherine advanced always with reform of the Order. Both were invariably found together. The three most active promoters of her cause, Caffarini, Delle Vigne and Bartolomeo da Ferrara were the three greatest reformers of the day.

When Caffarini had well digested Delle Vigne's " Life " (or " Legend " as it is usually called), he wrote a compendium of it for more general use, " The Minor Legend." Believing, too, that Delle Vigne's work was not exhaustive, he also wrote a Supplement to it, containing additional matter.

Thirty-one years after her death, Caffarini and Bartolomeo da Ferrara preached on Catherine Benincasa in Venice to such effect that a number of citizens there made representations to the Bishop about it. The Bishop cited the two Dominicans to appear before him and answer the charge of preaching the cult of a person not officially recognized as a saint by the Church.

The defence was easy (since the Bishop was himself a devotee of Catherine). But the incident gave rise to the collection of documents known as the " Processus." This collection is not a real Process of Canonization, since it was not compiled specifically for that purpose. Neither does it savour of a Legal process, since plaintiffs, accused and judge are all in agreement before the end. After a certain number of testimonies are collected, the plaintiffs reappear on the scene, declaring themselves fully satisfied and offering to defray the expense of collecting further evidence. Once started on this track, Caffarini never stopped until he had exhausted every available source of evidence. In all, he collected the testimonies of twenty-six persons (including most of the *Famiglia* still living). It needed time and patience ; in fact the work was spread out from 1411 to 1416. Each document included in the collection was signed by witnesses and sealed by a notary with all possible formality. Caffarini left no loophole. He checked and scrutinized each word to see that no undesirable matter was included, nor anything too much at variance with Delle Vigne's " Legend," so that nothing should injure the great cause.

He did not live to see the realization of his dream. The confusion of the Schism and other troubles in the Church prevented Catherine's cause being fully considered until the pontificate of Pius II. This Pope, who happened to be a Sienese too (Aeneas Sylvius Piccolomini), issued the Bull of Canonization in 1461. In the interval of eighty-one years since her death, an enormous number of petitions for Catherine's canonization had piled up in the Vatican from all over the world.

When Augusta Drane wrote her " Life of Saint Catherine," she estimated that there were sixty lives of her in circulation. The number is now nearer one hundred in all languages, many of them notable. A vast literature has grown around the name of the woman whom Pastor describes as " one of the most marvellous figures in the history of the world." Beside the " Lives," there is a great body of incidental writing. Artists, similarly, have clustered round her. The representations of St.

Catherine are legion. In order to unify and, in a sense, dominate this vast output, a group of Sienese "Catherine" students determined in 1920 to form an international society for the prosecution of such studies : the *Società Internazionale di Studi Cateriniani*, and to publish a quarterly bulletin devoted to the latest literature and art concerning the Saint. The first number of this Bulletin was issued in September, 1923 ; it has been issued regularly since and maintains a high standard of scholarship and interest. The Società has done notable work in the eight years of its existence. It has been instrumental in forming a group of "Caterinati" in Rome, Florence, Pisa, Bergamo, Turin, Bologna and elsewhere. Through its efforts also, a Chair of Catherine Studies has been inaugurated in the University of Siena. This great idea was first mooted in 1925 and became effective on January 31st, 1926. There is now a regular course of studies, with the usual diplomas, etc., and the titular professor is the Marchese Piero Misciattelli. The formal inauguration of the Chair was followed by the opening of a Catherine Hall (Sala Cateriniana) in the University, devoted exclusively to the lectures, and furnished out of the offerings of the women of Siena. The University of Siena has thus happily become the natural centre of all further study of Saint Catherine. It is hoped in time to form a complete library in the Sala Cateriniana.

The first statute of the Società lays down that, although it has a purely cultural character, it proposes to adhere perfectly to the Catholic Faith, obedient to the supreme authority of the Church, and therefore to include in its Council an ecclesiastic, nominated by the Archbishop of Siena, to revise all the publications of the Società. It numbers already fifty-seven founders and a most encouraging list of ordinary members.

To understand how exhaustive Catherine studies are, it is sufficient to read some of the conference titles in the academical course : " The Historical Value of the Legend," " The Supplement by Caffarini," " St. Catherine and the English," " Saint Catherine in Art," " The Sky of Saint Catherine " (by a pro-

fessor of astronomy !), " Saint Catherine and the Civic Ideal of
Siena," and so on.

Here, at those conferences in the Sala Cateriniana of the
University of Siena, the modern pilgrim can find the " Famiglia "
again. For this audience, not only St. Catherine lives but
every member of her circle. No allusion escapes them.
They discuss those men and women of the fourteenth century,
their idiosyncrasies, their outlook, as keenly as though they were
living persons. One feels that at any moment Stefano Maconi
and Neri may walk through the door, or Ser Cristofano mount the
rostrum to harangue them ponderously ; or, turning round,
one may see Alessa Saracini reproaching Malavolti in the corner.
It might only have been yesterday William Flete refused to stir
from his wood. (And let the Englishman beware of giving
umbrage to this discriminating audience, or they immediately
remark, thus and thus must Guglielmo have acted, he probably
pronounced *bosco*, *bōsco*, and said little else but " *molto bello* "
in the uninspiring manner of the tourist !). On the alert and
smiling faces of this group of *Caterinati* shines still the bland light
of that glorious Fellowship.

The religious world in Siena keeps pace magnificently with
all this. As Saint Catherine's feast-day approaches (April 30th),
there is a tremendous ferment of activity in the city. To make
the Novena in good style, that is attend *all* the religious functions,
means a hard day's work for nine days ; even then, it is not
possible to see all that goes on, because so many of the functions
overlap. During the preceding week, a Retreat is preached in
her house, and there are two Masses, three discourses, and
Benediction daily. Every evening, in the chapel consecrated
to her in the Basilica of San Domenico, part of her life is read out
on the altar before Benediction. In this way her whole life is
read during the Novena. The walls of the chapel in which it is
read were decorated by Bazzi with frescoes representing scenes
from her life ; the figures are life-size and they glow palely
from the walls in the Spring dusk. The most moving of all the
ceremonies in this great week is the distribution of bread to the

poor in Catherine's house the day before her feast-day. No commemoration could be more divinely appropriate. The ragged, the blind, the deformed, the diseased, the verminous, in short, all the offscouring of the city make their way to her house on that afternoon of golden charity. They climb her stairs in an endless, shuffling procession and carry away armfuls of bread. One sees, for instance, a blind man led up : a shrunken old creature, wearing cast-off patent leather boots, so over large for him that the toes turn up ludicrously. All the way upstairs, he apologizes in a high, cracked voice for his blindness, as though it were a social misdemeanour : " *Scusino, Signori, ma non ci vedo. Scusino, eh !* " One feels that at this pitiful feast, Catherine is truly at home. These are the guests she would welcome with such burning, compassionate *interest*. Her house re-echoes again with those dead voices : her brothers complaining loudly to her father because she has given away all the wine, the angry hubbub as her friends retrieve her cloak from a beggar.

By a privilege, her feast is celebrated on April 29th, in her house (the day of her death), but the liturgical date is the 30th. Therefore, on the 29th, her house is thrown open and throngs visit it freely all day, peering behind the altar in one of the chapels to see what remains of Monna Lapa's hearthstone, and pressing into Catherine's cell to look at the relics hanging there : the handle of the stick she used to walk with ; the lantern she carried with her when going out at night ; the scent-bottle she took to the sick during the plague. In the principal chapel upstairs is exposed for veneration the picture of the Crucifix, before which she received the Stigmata at Pisa ; it is a most unusual representation of the Crucified : a strangely unmoved figure, inspiring fear. In the evening, the Saint's head is exposed in St. Dominic's, shining faintly behind the silver bars of the reliquary. On the morrow, the crowds are drawn up from her house to the Basilica. Candle-vendors throng the steps and allow no-one in (if they can help it) without a candle a yard long to burn before her shrine. Masses are celebrated at all the principal altars from dawn to noon. There is a blaze of candles and flowers around the sacred relic. All the banners of the city wards are hung in the nave. In the evening, the pages of the wards appear in their gorgeous mediaeval costumes to take part in the procession. This takes place after the panegyric is preached, before Benediction. The relic is carried solemnly around the Basilica and the great multitude take up St. Catherine's hymn and send it soaring through that vast nave. It does not end then. There is nothing half-hearted about the Sienese festas. The celebrations are prolonged during all the subsequent week and culminate on the Sunday after her feast. Then all Fontebranda is decorated with flags and bunting, and there is a gorgeous procession outdoors, in which the pages of the wards duly appear again in their splendid dress and the " alfieri " toss their banners, making the streets through which they pass a whirling riot of colour. So thoroughly is the city permeated with the presence of Saint Catherine in this great commemoration every Spring, that the children sing her hymn to themselves for weeks afterwards on their way to school, and their Latin is perfectly clear and confident. Climbing down the steep hillside to Fontebranda, one can hear boys of eight shrilling it to the high heavens :

> Virgo decora et fulgida,
>   Ornata Regis purpura :
>   Electa, puro in corpore
>   Christi referre imaginem.

> Nobis novum cor impetra,
>   Transfige dulce, et concrema ;
>   Tecumque ad Agni nuptias
>   Sorde expiatos advoca.

APPENDIX I

BIBLIOGRAPHY

This is by no means a complete Catherine Bibliography, but a selected one upon which the present work is mainly based.

I. FIRST BIOGRAPHICAL SOURCES

There were two contemporary records of Saint Catherine :

1.—THE MIRACLES. " *Miracoli di Santa Caterina da Siena*," a narrative of miracles worked through her intervention up to October, 1374, written by an anonymous Florentine, between June and October, 1374. Two mauscripts of this work are preserved in Florence. It was published for the first time by F. Grottanelli in *Alcuni Miracoli di S. Caterina secondo che sono narrati da un anonimo suo contemporaneo*, Siena, presso Onorato Porri, 1862. This book is out of print and most rare. But the " Miracoli " have been reprinted by Dr. Robert Fawtier in the first Appendix to his work : *Sainte Catherine de Sienne —Essai de Critique des Sources*, Paris, E. de Boccard, Editeur, 1921 ; and by P. Misciattelli in " *Epistolario*," Siena, 1922, Vol. VI.

2. SINGULARIA ET MIRA SANCTAE CATHARINAE SENENSIS, dictated during the Saint's lifetime by Fra Tommaso della Fonte, her first confessor, to Fra Bartolomeo Dominici. This record seems to have disappeared shortly after the Saint's death. But upon these notes of Fra Tommaso della Fonte was largely based :

3.—THE LEGEND. " *S. Catharinae Senensis Vita*." Auctore Fr. Raimundo Capuano. Acta Sanctorum, Aprilis, Tom. III. New Edition, Paris, 1866. *La Vita della Serafica Sposa di Gesu Cristo S. Caterina da Siena*. Translated from the Latin Legend of Fra Raimondo into Italian by Bernardino Pecci, in *L'Opere della Serafica Santa Caterina da Siena*, Girolamo Gigli, Siena, 1707, and reprinted in Rome, 1866, Vol. I.

4.—THE SUPPLEMENT. " Libellus de Supplemento legendae prolixae Virginis Beatae Catharinae de Senis." Biblioteca Comunale di Siena, MS. T. 1. 2 ; Biblioteca Casanatense (Rome), MS. 2360. This text has never been published, but a very loose Italian translation, or rather summary of it, has been published as follows :

Supplemento alla vulgata leggenda di S. Caterina da Siena. Translated from the Latin of Fra Tommaso by P. Ambrogio Ansano Tantucci, Vol. V. *Opere*, Girolamo Gigli.

Note.—This Supplement of Caffarini is also based largely on Della Fonte's lost notebooks. Part of the Latin text omitted by Tantucci in his translation has been published by M. Joergensen in Appendix II to his " *Life of St. Catherine of Siena*," Italian version, p. 565.

5.—THE PROCESS. " Processus quorundam dictorum et attestationum super celebritate memoriae ac virtutibus, vita et doctrina Beatae Catherinae de Senis." Part of this collection of evidence has been published by Martène et Durand in *Veterum Scriptorum et Monumentorum*, etc., Amplissima Collectio. Tom. VI. Paris, 1729. Three of the testimonies omitted from this work have been published by Eugenio Lazzareschi as follows : that of Francesco Malavolti in *Santa Catherina da Siena in Val d'Orcia*, Florence, 1915 ; and those of Fra Agostino da Pisa and Fra Baronto da Pisa, in the Appendix to *S. Caterina da Siena ed i Pisani*, Florence, 1917.

6.—THE MINOR LEGEND. " *Epitome Vitae beatae Catarinae de Senis*," by Fra Tommaso da Siena. In the Sanctuarium of Boninus Mombritius, Milan, 1479, Vol. I. For Italian translation, see : *Leggenda minore di S. Caterina da Siena e lettere dei suoi discepoli*. F. Grottanelli, Bologna, 1868.

7. LETTERA DI SER BARDUCCIO DI PIERO CANIGIANI nella quale si contiene il transito della serafica vergine S. Caterina da Siena. A suor Caterina Petriboni nel monasterio di S. Piero a Monticelli presso Fiorenza. Vol. I. *Opere*. Girolamo Gigli. (This letter is translated into English at the end of Thorold's translation of the Dialogue. See II below.)

8.—For an analysis and discussion of all the above sources, see : *Sainte Catherine de Sienne—Essai de Critique des Sources*. Sources Hagiographiques. Robert Fawtier. Paris. Ed. De Boccard, 1921. Compare with Appendix III.

II.   SAINT CATHERINE'S WRITINGS

1.—THE LETTERS. " *L'Epistole della Serafica Vergine S. Caterina da Siena*." Vols. II and III. *Opere*. Girolamo Gigli.

Le Lettere di S. Caterina da Siena a cura di Piero Misciattelli. Siena, Libreria Editrice Giuntini Bentivoglio & C. 1922. Six Volumes.

Saint Catherine of Siena as seen in her letters. A selection of the letters, translated and edited by Vida D. Scudder. London, Dent, 1905.

2.—THE DIALOGUE. " *Il Dialogo della Serafica Santa Caterina, etc.*" Vol. IV. *Opere*. Girolamo Gigli.

Libro della Divina Dottrina, volgarmente detto Dialogo della Divina Provvidenza, Nuova Edizione secondo un inedito Codice Senese a cura di Matilda Fiorilli. Bari, Laterza, 1912. (This is the best Italian edition, Gigli's being incomplete.)

The Dialogue of the Seraphic Virgin, Catherine of Siena, together with an account of her death by an eye-witness. Translated from the Original Italian and preceded by an Introductory Essay on the Life and Times of the Saint, by Algar Thorold. (London, Burns Oates, 1925.) (This translation is from Gigli's edition.)

III.   HISTORY

Belloc, H. *History of England*. London, Methuen, 1925-28. 3 Vols.

Buonsignori. *Storia della Repubblica di Siena in Compendio*. Siena, Landi, 1856. Vol. I.

Capecelatro, Alfonso. *Storia di S. Caterina da Siena e del Papato del suo tempo*. Naples, Lauriel, 1856. Two volumes.

Capponi, Gino (the elder). *Il Tumulto de' Ciompi*. Parma, Fiaccadori, 1856.

Capponi, Gino. *Storia della Repubblica di Firenze.* Florence, 1888. Vols. I and II.

Carpellini. *Gli Assempri di Fra Filippo da Siena.* Siena, 1864.

Cronica Sanese by Agnolo di Tura and Neri di Donato.

Drane, Augusta Theodosia. *The History of St. Catherine of Siena and of Her Companions.* London, Longmans Green, 1899. Two volumes.

Gardner, E. G. *Saint Catherine of Siena.* A Study in the Religion, Literature and History of the Fourteenth Century in Italy. London, J. M. Dent, 1907.

Gardner, E. G. *The Story of Siena and San Gimignano.* London, J. M. Dent, 1904.

Gasquet, Francis Aidan Cardinal. *The Black Death of 1348 and 1349.* London, George Bell, 1908.

Gayet, Louis. *Le Grand Schisme d'Occident* d'après les documents contemporains. Florence, 1889. Two volumes.

Gherardi, A. *La Guerra dei Fiorentini con Papa Gregorio XI.* In Archivio Storico Italiano, Seria III, Vol. V, VI, VII, VIII.

Guidini, Cristofano. *Memorie di Ser Cristofano di Galgano Guidini da Siena,* scritte da lui medesimo nel secolo XIV. Ed. C. Milanesi. (Arch, Stor. It. Seria I, Vol. IV.) Florence, 1843.

Heywood, William. *The Ensamples of Fra Filippo.* A Study of Mediaeval Siena. Siena, Torrini, 1901.

Heywood, William. *Palio and Ponte.* Siena, Libreria Editrice Senese, 1928.

Langton, Douglas R. *A History of Siena.* London, 1902.

Landucci, Ambrogio. *Sacra Leccetana Selva.* Rome, 1657.

Magnan, I. B. *Histoire d'Urbain V et de son siècle.* Paris, 1862.

Malavolti, Orlando. *Historia dei fatti e guerre de' Senesi.* Venice, 1599.

Michaud. *Histoire des Croisades.* Paris, Furne, 1841. Four volumes.

Misciattelli Piero. *Mistici Senesi,* Siena. Tip. S. Bernardino, 1911.

Pastor, Dr. L. *History of the Popes.* Edited by Frederick Ignatius Antrobus of the Oratory. London, Kegan Paul, 1923. Vol. I.

Professione, A. *Siena e le Compagnie di venture.* Siena, 1898.

Sismondi. *Histoire des Républiques Italiennes du Moyen Age.* Paris, Furne, 1840. Vols. IV, V and VI.

Temple-Leader and Marcotti. *Giovanni Acuto (Sir John Hawkwood).* Florence, Barbèra, 1889.

Valois, N. *La France et le Grand Schisme.* Paris, 1896. Four volumes.

Villehardouin & Joinville. *Memoirs of the Crusades.* (Marzials.) London, J. M. Dent, 1908.

Zdekauer, L. *Il Constituto del Comune di Siena dell'anno,* 1262. Milan, Hoepli, 1897.

Zdekauer, L. *Il Mercante Senese nel Ducento.* Siena, 1900.

Zdekauer, L. *Lo Studio di Siena nel Rinascimento.* Milan, 1894.

IV. GENERAL

Antony, C. M. *Saint Catherine of Siena*. London, Burns & Oates, 1915.

Bartoli. *Lettere del B. Giovanni Colombini*. Lucca, 1856.

Bernardy, Amy A. *Santa Caterina da Siena*. Florence, Le Monnier, 1926.

Bianco. *Laudi spirituali del Bianco da Siena*. Bini, Lucca, 1851.

Flavigny, Comtesse de. *Sainte Catherine de Sienne*. Paris, 1895.

Gigli, Girolamo. *Vocabolario Cateriniano*. Lucca, 1760.

Hurtaud. *French translation of the Dialogue*. Paris, 1913.

Huysmans, J. K. *Sainte Lydwine de Schiedam*. Librarie Plon, Paris.

Joërgensen, Giovanni. *Santa Caterina da Siena*. Rome, Ferrari, 1919.

Malan, Emile Chavin de. *Vie de Sainte Catherine de Sienne*. Tournai, Casterman, 1848.

Misciattelli, Piero. *Lo Spirito, Il Cuore, La Parola di Caterina da Siena*. Tommaseo. Siena, Guintini, 1922.

Olmi, Gaspero. *I Senesi d'una Volta*. Siena, S. Bernardino, 1889.

Regolamenti di Disciplina della Ven. Confraternità della Misericordia di Siena. Tip. Bindi, 1844.

Revelations of St. Bridget of Sweden. London, Richardson, 1874.

Rossetti, D. G. *The Early Italian Poets*. London, Dent, 1908.

Scudder, Vida D. *The Disciple of a Saint.*—Being the Imaginary Biography of Raniero di Landoccio dei Pagliaresi. London, Dent, 1907.

Sorio, Bartolommeo. *Lettere del B. Don Giovanni dalle Celle*. Rome, 1845.

Statuti Volgari de lo Spedale di S. Maria Vergine di Siena. Siena, Banchi, 1864.

Steele, F. M. *St. Bridget of Sweden*. London, Washbourne, 1909.

Studi Cateriniani. Bullettino della Società Internazionale di Studi Cateriniani. Siena. From September, 1923, onwards.

Tozzi, F. *Antichi Scrittori Senesi*. Siena, 1913.

APPENDIX II

HAGIOGRAPHICAL SOURCES AND DR. ROBERT FAWTIER

(a) DR. FAWTIER'S METHOD.

(b) COUNTER-CRITICISM BY REV. FATHER I. TAURISANO, O.P.

(c) FURTHER COUNTER-CRITICISM BY THE SAME.

(a) DR. FAWTIER'S METHOD

In 1921, an eminent French scholar, Dr. Robert Fawtier, published the thesis presented to the Sorbonne University for his doctor's degree, being a critical essay on the hagiographical sources of St. Catherine : *Sainte Catherine de Sienne—Essai de Critique des Sources*. Sources Hagiographiques. (E. De Boccard, rue de Mèdicis, 1, Paris.)

This book caused great consternation among students of the Saint's life, because it seriously questioned the long-established chronology and impugned the historical value of most of the original sources. Indeed, only two documents emerge with any honour from this crucible of criticism : the " Miracoli," by an anonymous Florentine, and Barduccio's famous letter relating the Saint's death. Dr. Fawtier's findings were considered of the very utmost importance, because he had made a prolonged and meticulous study of the documents. Every statement of his is backed by a formidable array of references. His book is closely and admirably documented throughout and is apparently exhaustive. Although weighty, it is far from being dull. A wide circle of readers found it of fascinating interest, because the style is forceful and brilliant in its succinctness.

But the student who examines this essay, with a view to reconstructing the Saint's life from it, finds much matter for bewilderment. The work is marred throughout and its value rendered almost negligible by one capital defect : an arbitrary use of the Letters, amounting in some cases to *misuse*. Dr. Fawtier begins by placing the Letters in a category apart, promising to deal with them separately in a second volume. He cannot concede to them the title of " historical " documents because (as has been frequently remarked) out of the odd four hundred which Catherine dictated, we possess only six original copies. Further, in the collected transcriptions, many passages have been suppressed and there are obscurities in the text. But, in deprecating the historical value of the Letters, the critic raises one new point : he discusses whether any register of them was kept during the Saint's lifetime and decides in the negative, thus of course reducing still further the value of the transcriptions we possess. For the refutation of this assertion, the reader is referred to Father Taurisano's article republished herewith. However, Dr. Fawtier then explains that he intends to examine the hagiographical sources without reference to the Letters : "*Nous examinerons les premiers comme si les seconds n'existaient pas.*" (p. XIII.) This is a piquant promise and the fulfilment of it would have been a notable achievement. Either set of documents can usually be understood only in the light of the other ; they are inter-dependent. Unfortunately, he, too, finds he cannot develop his theme without reference to the Letters. We are undeceived about that piquant promise in a footnote to the preliminary chapter, in which he explains that he must refer to the Letters occasionally and he gives the numbering adopted. And at first the Letters are kept strictly to the footnotes as befitting " unhistorical " documents in a category apart. But presently they make little incursions into the text ; then they invade it openly ; presently they dominate it. On page 195, we find Dr. Fawtier hemmed in on every side by the Letters, only escaping by a most resolute effort. It is very amusing.

But what *did* he mean, when he said : "*Nous examinerons les premiers comme si les seconds n'existaient pas.*" In practice, what veto does he observe in using the Letters ? Regrettably, one is forced to conclude it is this : such letters are cited as *seem* to support his arguments ; those that contradict it are ignored.

Here are five examples of this amazing method :

1. THE TESTIMONIES OF WILLIAM FLETE.—In examining this body of evidence, Dr. Fawtier takes Catherine's letters into account, p. 54. He shows the agreement between the Saint's letters, a papal bull and an ambassador's report, p. 56. But on p. 73, he apparently decides to consider the letters as non-existent. Speculating as to the audience to which Flete could have delivered the sermon attributed to him, the critic says he cannot understand why the Sienese should be reproached on Catherine's account. He has, therefore, never heard that the Saint was constantly being slandered by her fellow-citizens ; she even protested to the Government about it, using the very same terms attributed to Flete : " Ma non si lascerà però per la *ingratitudine e per le ignoranzie* de' miei cittadini . . . " Lett. No. 121, Vol. II, Misciattelli, p. 244. " Increscemi dell' affanno e della fatica che i miei cittadini hanno nel pensare e menare la lingua verso di me ; che non pare ch'egli abbiano a fare altro che tagliarmi le legne in capo, a me ed alla compagnia che ho con meco." Lett. 123, Vol. II. M. p. 262. It is strange to find Dr. Fawtier quoting this same Letter, No. 123, in the text of page 195. If he uses it for one purpose, why not use it here to illuminate why a Sienese audience could be reproached about their consistent attitude to Catherine Benincasa ? And all those other letters, in which she tells her agitated friends how to meet this continual campaign of slander : Nos. 93, 119, 120, 121, 122, 123, Vol. II, M. and No. 250, Vol. IV ? The critic adds that Flete was too diplomatic with his compatriots (sic) to be capable of such an outburst. But what profile of Flete emerges from Catherine's letters to him ? No one who has read the Saint's exhortations to the English recluse (Letters Nos. 64, 66, Vol. I, No. 77, Vol II, and especially No. 328, Vol. V) could imagine Flete in the guise of a suave diplomat.

2.—CATHERINE'S MISSION IN AVIGNON. In examining the documents bearing on this part of Catherine's life, Dr. Fawtier discusses in detail Catherine's letter to the Eight of War (p. 177). He finds no confirmation in it that the Saint had an embassy, unofficial or otherwise, from the Florentines. But why omit all reference to Letter No. 234 (Vol. IV, p. 12), written by Catherine from Avignon to Buonaccorso di Lapo, in which she complains of the Florentines' conduct and repeats the very terms on which she agreed to negotiate for them? Further, Dr. Fawtier doubts whether Catherine really played such an important part in restoring the Papacy to Rome. The greater part of the proof for this resting on ten letters from the Saint to Gregory XI (Nos. 185, 196, 206, 218, 229, 231, Vol. III, M., and Nos. 233, 238, 239, 252, Vol. IV, M.), the critic dismisses them (pp. 181, 182) to his promised second volume and concentrates on the remaining evidence, which he finds insufficient, of course. Yet on p. 184, he falls back on those luckless Letters to quote a phrase from one of them which happens to be useful for his purpose (Letter No. 211, Vol. III). Is not this method of criticism more calculated to exasperate than to instruct?

3.—CATHERINE'S SOJOURN AT ROCCA D'ORCIA. On p. 195, Dr. Fawtier uses no less than seven of the Saint's letters to support his argument : that her business in the Val d'Orcia was not to make peace between the rival Salimbeni. He makes a fairly plausible case, but completely ignores two letters of capital importance in the discussion. The first is Letter No. 117, Vol. II, M., in which Catherine explains her absence to her mother ; the second is Letter No. 121, Vol. II, M., written from the same territory, in which Catherine says : " *Diravvi Pietro a bocca la principale cagione per la quale io venni e sio qua.*" Cf. Letter No. 218, Vol. III for the same procedure for greater secrecy.

4.—CATHERINE'S MEETING WITH RAIMONDO IN ROME. Dr. Fawtier thinks Delle Vigne invented this meeting to give himself a little importance ! He says it cannot be proved and skims through the evidence : Catherine's letter to the Prior of Gorgona only mentions that Raimondo has left for France : Catherine does not say explicitly that she saw him, etc., p. 209. But if Letter No. 323 is quoted, why not also Letter No. 329, Vol. V, M, p. 105, in which Catherine says to Stefano : " *Conforta misser Matteo : di' che ci mandi prima informazione di quello che vuole, perche a me si e scordato ; e frate Raimondo si partì si tosto che non la potemmo avere da lui.*" She does not say she did not see Raimondo in Rome ; she says he left there so quickly (after their arrival) that she could not get this information from him. (Probably it was about some request for indulgences and they had other things to talk about in those few days !)

5.—WHO WAS GIVEN CHARGE OF THE FAMIGLIA, AFTER CATHERINE'S DEATH ? Raimondo says it was entrusted to him (Leg. Mag. P. III, Ch. IV, 4, 8) and that Alessa was given the care of the women disciples (Leg. Mag. P. III, Ch. I, 8). But Nigi di Doccio, in his letter to Neri about the Saint's death, says she gave the Family into the care of the Bachelor (probably William Flete) and Matteo Cenni. (Lettere dei Discepoli, No. 17.) Dr. Fawtier, therefore, concludes that Nigi di Doccio, of whom we know almost nothing, was right ; and that Delle Vigne, of whom we know so much that is admirable, lied. So the critic leaps ahead to one of those conclusions which can only be qualified as detestable ; p. 212 :

" Jusqu'aux derniers moments de la sainte, Raymond de Capoue n'a pu résister au désir de se donner un rôle même aux dépens de la vérité, qui pourtant, selon la prescription de saint Dominique, eût dû lui être chère par dessus toute chose."

Once again, Dr. Fawtier ignores a letter of capital importance : Catherine's last one to Raimondo, in which she confides to him, in poignant words, the care of her fantastic Family : Letter No. 373, Vol. V. It is useless for the critic to say he is excluding the Letters from this volume. In this same chapter, he introduces into the text Catherine's Letters, Nos. 292, 319 and 323 (p. 205 and p. 209), to support his statements.   Also, Lettere dei Discepoli, No. 17, is quoted, but not letter No. 41, in which Raimondo, writing to Neri and Gabriele after Catherine's death, gives them certain directions and speaks to them as one who takes the lead in the affairs of the Famiglia.

No, this method is indefensible.   Either the Letters should be dealt with in a separate volume, as promised ; or, if introduced into the text of Volume I, they should be considered in their entirety.   No doubt the reasons for this curious arbitrary selection will be made clear by Dr. Fawtier's second volume, though the charge of great confusion of method still remains.   But here again one has ground for complaint.   In his provocative first volume, the author stated that the material for the second was already collected.   It was to complete the argument.   The public have been impatiently waiting for this second volume for *seven years !*   One cannot sufficiently regret this lapse of time.   As this book goes to press, we hear that there is no hope of its appearance in 1929.

The most painful breach of Dr. Fawtier's promise to reserve the Letters for adequate treatment in a separate volume occurs on p. 169, where he attempts to destroy (in his stride, as it were) the authenticity of the famous letter about the execution of Niccolò di Toldo, perhaps the most treasured document and certainly the best-known, of the whole Epistolario.   In the article hereto appended, Father Taurisano defends the authenticity of this letter on the critic's ground, but asks in amazement if there is no longer such a thing as the literary criticism of a document.   One is indeed almost led to believe that Dr. Fawtier represents a new school of criticism unconcerned with internal evidence.   It is not so, however.   On pp. 71 to 75, one finds with relief that the style of a document, its form (p. 79), its tone (p. 81) have all their value for Dr. Fawtier.   Then what of the style, form and tone of this letter he rejects as a forgery of Caffarini ?   It is sufficient to compare it with the letter we possess from Caffarini to Catherine (Lettere dei Discepoli, No. 1) to be over-whelmed with the wild improbability of the suggestion.   The friar's style, scholarly, colourless, but coldly coherent, is the very antithesis of the Saint's. As Signora Rosmini remarked (when describing his contributions to the *Processus*), Caffarini is the scholastic who ennumerates and catalogues every-thing in species like a botanist, even down to crosses and the different qualities of glory !   He never wrote Catherine's letters for her and, therefore, never used the faintest echo of her phraseology, as her secretaries did, Barduccio especially, cf. Caffarini's letters to Neri in Lettere dei Discepoli, Nos. 29, 30 and 31.   This rejected letter is the most " Catherine " of the whole collection ; every word in it speaks of her.   It is full of her images : " *Voglio dunque che vi serriate nel costato aperto del Figliuolo di Dio, il quale e una bottiga aperta* " (cf. Dialogo, Cap. XXVII).   She almost invariably breaks off to apostrophize the images she evokes : " *Oh botte spillata, la quale dài bere ed inebri ogni inna-morato desiderio . . .* "   And that invariable description of a dominant thought : " *. . . altro non puo ritenere, nè altro intendere, nè altro amare . . .* " Cf. Dialogo, Cap. LXXIX and Lett. No. 373.   What reader of the Letters does not know that when anything pleased her, she must go the whole round of this sentence : " *Mi fu di tanta dolcezza che'l cuore nol puo pensare, ne lingua parlare, nè l'occhio vedere, nè l'orecchio udire ?* "   Then the confusion of that final vision !   Caffarini would have been ashamed to perpetrate such a descrip-tion.   He liked the clear precision of a graph.   But Catherine shows us the clarity of the sun, blood and the fire of divine charity and swings us upward, in her wild profusion of words, to that image of the open side of the Son of

God which seemed to obsess her. Could it ever be conceded that Caffarini achieved this? And even admitting the improbability : that he collected her images and phrases and concocted a document with such miraculous precision of style and form, could he ever have informed the forgery with its unmistakably feminine tone? Who but Catherine would have put in that eloquent little detail : " *la mattina innanzi la campana andai a lui.*" (It was forbidden by law in Siena to go out before the bell.) Who but she could have described that scene in the dungeon with the condemned man, so vibrant with reality? Who else would have " felt his fear " and offered to stand by him on the scaffold? Who but Catherine would have been so overwhelmed with joy at the description of the scaffold as *holy*? She breaks off to exult about it.
. . . " *Vedete che era giunto a tanto lume, che chiamava il luogo della giustizia santo !* " Here is the literary ear vibrating at a word, seeing whole realms of light in one single word. And who but Catherine would have *thought* of saying at the supreme moment : " *Giuso ! alle nozze, fratello mio dolce !* "

One last comment. When Dr. Fawtier tries to prove that Catherine went through her " *crise de mondanité* " *after* her entry into the Third Order, Father Taurisano asks whether the critic can really be serious? The same suspicion of levity must occur to every reader. There are passages in the book which make one wonder whether it is not after all a gigantic and elaborate joke, a tremendous leg-pulling ! Take for instance this excerpt from p. 128 :

" Les récits faits à Raymond par tous les personnages qu'il cite n'ont pas davantage été donnés par écrit, il nous le dirait ; il les rapporte de mémoire et la sienne déclinait, il l'avoue. D'ailleurs que valaient ces récits ? Quand on voit monna Lapa, la mère de la sainte, raconter le plus sérieuse- ment du monde que Catherine étant petite fille portait la charge d'un âne ou d'un cheval, sur ses épaules jusqu'au dernier étage de la maison, et quand on constate que la Légende Majeure enrégistre gravement ce racontar, j'allais écrire cette, ' galéjade,' on est en droit de se demander quel fond on peut faire sur un tel texte."

The passage which aroused the critic's wrath is then quoted :

" Narravit enim quandoque mater ejus quae adhuc superest quod ante- quam filia tantis poenitentiis se incepisset affligere, tanti vigoris et forti- tudinis erat in corpore, quod onus jumenti seu asini dorso delatum ad ostium domus suae ipsa sine difficultate super se levans, agiliter per duas scalas longas multorum graduum usque ad superiora domus propriis humeris deferebat."

Still fuming, Dr. Fawtier adds : " Ceux qui ont vu sur les routes toscanes les petits bourricots et leurs charges apprécieront l'imagination de Lapa ! " In the Spring of 1928, the present writer fell to counting (while pondering the ways of historical critics) some fifteen of those " petits bourricots " on the road from Siena to San Gimignano. Their burdens varied from what a child could easily carry to what a docker might grumble at ! It seems necessary to establish what loads they carried to the Benincasas' door ! But what puerilities to introduce into a text claiming to be serious.

The most notable replies that have appeared to Dr. Fawtier are as follows, and the student who wishes to make a fair estimate of the critic's work would do well to consult them. Professor Jordan's article shows clearly that Dr. Fawtier missed the ludicrous contradictions in which he involved himself. No one who has really entered into the matter will fail to endorse Father Mandonnet's conclusion ; "*L'autorité de la documentation historique de cette vie reste après les nouvelles recherches ce qu'elle était auparavant.*" Of these replies, the best—that of Father Taurisano, is reprinted here in full with the Author's kind permission, together with a copy of a Conference given by him on the same subject :

I. r. p. I. Taurisano, o.p., in " Letture Cateriniane Nella R. Università di Siena." Libreria Editrice Senese, Siena.　8th August, 1928. "*Le fonte agiografiche Cateriniane e la critica di R. Fawtier.*"

II. Prof. Jordan, in "Analecta Bollandiana," Tomus XL.　Fasc. III et IV.　15 Novembre, 1922.　Société des Bollandistes, 24, Boulevard Saint-Michel, Bruxelles.　"*La Date de Naissance de Sainte Catherine de Sienne.*"

III. Fr. P. Mandonnet, O.P., in " L'Année Dominicaine," Janvier-Fevrier, 1923.　Faubourg Saint-Honore, 222, Paris. "*Sainte Catherine de Sienne et la Critique Historique.*"

IV. Prof. G. Pardi, in " Studi Cateriniani," An. II, N. 2.　Bulletino della Societa Internazionale di Studi Cateriniani, Siena. "*Elenchi di Mantellate Senesi.*"

See also r. p. Taurisano, o.p., in " Studi Cateriniani," An. I, Nos. 1 and 2 ; and Eugenio Lazzereschi, *S. Caterina da Siena e i Salimbeni.* Roma, Rassegna Nazionale, 1927.

It would be a mistake, however, to suppose that Dr. Fawtier seeks to detract in any way from the essential glory of Saint Catherine.　Exasperating though his method is, he has sincerely tried to find out the truth about the great Dominican saint.　He is really an ardent " *caterinato,*" and this debate to which the reader is introduced is strictly a discussion " *entre famille.*"　Of course, expressions of devotion and admiration have no place in a critical essay, and Dr. Fawtier concentrates austerely on his task.　Nevertheless, he betrays his sentiments.　It is to him we owe that fine description of Barduccio's letter, " qui n'est presque qu'un long sanglot."　Occasionally, he has to jerk back his pen from a lyrical flight : " Considérée comme la plus exquise fleur mystique éclose au jardin de saint Dominique . . . "　And when he reads the lamentations of John of the Cells over the dead Saint, Dr. Fawtier cannot forbear the comment : " Sa personalité dût cependant être singulièrement remarquable pour provoquer de tels regrets chez une âme d'élite, comme celle du grand solitaire de Vallombreuse."

(b) LE FONTI AGIOGRAFICHE
CATERINIANE E LA CRITICA DI R. FAWTIER

(Reprinted with the author's kind permission, from "Letture Cateriniane," Libreria Editrice Senese, Siena, August, 1928.)

Dal 29 aprile 1380, giorno in cui Caterina di Jacopo Benincasa, dopo un'agonia più dura di un martirio, rese al Creatore l'anima sua ardente come fuoco, da quel giorno sino a noi, intorno al suo nome, alla sua opera, ai suoi scritti, alla sua vita, si è formato un immenso coro, un concerto stupendo di lodi, che ne canta, magnifica, esalta e propaga come onda concentrica, l'opera meravigliosa, opera altamente cattolica, altamente romana.

Dinanzi a questa musica che scuote e fa vibrare nella nostra anima latina arcane voci, voci lontane di sangue, di fede, di dolori, di battaglie, voci di un passato che non si annulla, ma si accumula in noi come strati geologici, questo fondo ricchissimo che è in noi, alla voce di Caterina freme, perchè Caterina è nostra ; e allora vogliamo ansiosi prendere partre al concerto, vogliamo intonare il nostro inno, offrirle un piccolo, profumato fiore di omaggio, simbolo di una fraternità di sangue e di fede.

Il nostro omaggio, il nostro entusiasmo deve essere però, sereno, cosciente, dignitoso, illuminato. Non è il momento di ammirare Caterina nei suoi possenti amori verso i poveri, verso la Patria, la Chiesa e il Papato ; il nostro compito deve essere molto più severo ; dobbiamo porci e risolvere un problema di critica storica : le fonti cateriniane, le biografie, cioè, scritte dai discepoli della Santa, quale valore hanno di fronte alla critica ?

FRA TOMMASO DELLA FONTE. Il primo religioso che influì, si può dire, insensibilmente su l'anima di Caterina fu Fra Tommaso della Fonte. Era della contrada dell'Oca, anzi era stato allevato sotto il medesimo tetto della Santa, quel tetto che racchiudeva, tra figli, nuore e nipoti, un quaranta bocche. Fra Tommaso subì il fàscino dell'abito bianco e nero, sentì attrarsi ad entrare, in età già matura, verso il 1356, in San Domenico, tra quei religiosi dotti, pii, levantisi a mezzanotte per cantare le lodi di Dio e osservanti il magro perpetuo. Elevato alla dignità sacerdotale, il primo apostolato lo esercitò naturalmente nella casa che gli aveva dato il pane, e Caterina lo prese a suo confessore e direttore. Non era dotto, ma buono tanto ed aveva un'attrattiva speciale nel confessare le donne, dice un cronista. Oltre ad essere il primo confessore della Santa ne fu anche il primo biografo, scrivendo i " Miracula." (*)

---

* Di fra Tommaso della Fonte farò uno studio a parte. Cfr. p. 230.

— Un giorno — racconta il Caffarini — visitando Fra Tommaso della Fonte Caterina, ella gli disse : " Cosa facevate ieri sera verso le tre ore di notte ? " " Cosa facevo ? " E lei cominciò a ridere. E di nuovo Fra Tommaso : " Cosa facevo ? " Ella rispose : " Scrivevate." Stupefatto, il confessore disse che non scriveva. E Lei : " Un altro che era con voi scriveva." Di nuovo disse : " Cosa scrivevo ? " Non volendo dire altro, Fra Tommaso le comandò di parlare. Allora Caterina, costretta, disse : " Scrivevate le grazie che Iddio nella sua misericordia ha fatto a questa serva inutile ! " Così era infatti, poichè un confratello del confessore, la sera precedente fu con lui fino alla quarta ora di notte, e alcune cose riguardanti la vergine scrisse di sua mano.*

Quei *Miracula* dettati da Fra Tomaso furono la prima fonte agiografica, cioè il primo scritto in lode di Caterina, scritto che non ci è pervenuto nella sua completa redazione, ma sparso in frammenti nelle biografie successive.†

---

* *Supplementum legenda prolixe*, cod. T. I. 2 della Bibl. Comunale di Siena f. 31-32.

Di quest'opera di fra Tommaso Caffarini che integra la leggenda del Beato Raimondo si hanno due codici originali, uno a Siena sopra citato (in perg. di f. 112 + 4, m. 29-20, scritto su due colonne di 43 linee ciascuna, scritto nei primi del XV secolo) ; contiene in margine delicati e bellissimi disegni a penna illustranti i fatti principali della vita di S. Caterina.

L'altro codice, poco conosciuto, è stato studiato con molta competenza da Carlo Frati in *Bibliofilia*, a. 1923 fsc. lugio-settembre pp. 97-129, il quale attribuisce i desegni a Giovanni Bellini.

Una copia fu fatta a Venezia in S. Domenico nel 1460, e certo non fu la sola, ma non sappiamo dove oggi, sia ; cfr. *Dialogo di S. Caterina* a cura di P. Taurisano, Firenze, 1928 p. XLIX.

Altra copia del *Supplementum* si trova nella Casanatense di Roma n. 2360 ; e un'altra copia sconosciuta è nell'Archivio del Collegio Angelico in Roma, Lib. H. fatta nel 1705.

† Il B. Raimondo da Capua autore della *Legenda maior* edita di Bollandisti Aprile III. 29, p. 903 n. 164, tra l'altro dice : " *Veruntamen tam pro presenti quam pro futuro protestor, quod cunctaque scribo aut mihi confessa est, aut in scriptis fratris Thome reperi, primi confessoris sui, aut a fratribus Ordinis mei vel matronis fide dignis sociabus eius quas superior nominavi.*" E al n. 126 dice : " *Simile in scriptis primi confessoris reperi. . . .* " Pag. 883 n. 82 " *Unde, prout confessor eius, qui me in hoc precessit officio, et refert et in scriptis redegit.*"

P. 898 n. 142 " *Fratris Thome predicti et fratris Bartholomei Dominici de Senis, nunc sacre theologie magistri ac prioris provincialis Romane Provincie narratio et scriptura.*"

P. 902 n. 162 " *Simile in scriptis fratris Thome primi confessoris reperi.*"

P. 904 n. 167 " *Igitur sicut in secreto ipsa mihi confessa est et in scriptis reperi confessoris me precedentis.*"

P. 977 n. 181 " *. . . que aliquoties hoc experte retulerunt fratri Thome confessori eius, qui diligenti facta inquisitione postquam comperit ita esse, in scriptis redegit ad memoriam sempiternam.*"

P. 908 n. 186 " *Narrat autem post hec omnia frater Thomas primus confessor eius, in cuius scriptis reperi dictam visionem. . . . Et hoc dixit dictus frater Thomas factum fuisse anno Domini 1370 in festo Margarete virginis et martiris* " (20 lugio).

A p. 911 n. 199 con più forza il B. Raimondo scrive : *Enimvero plenos quaterniones per fratrem Thomam confessorem eius, sepe superius nominatim, scriptos invenio de excellentia visionum eius.*" E al n. 210 " *Aliam etiam eorumdem verborum expositionem inveni, legendo scripto fratris Thome primi confessoris eius, que fecit de verbis et gestis eius.*"

Così anche ai nn. 189, 202, 230, 244, 283.

Anche fr. Tommaso Caffarini nel *Supplementum legende prolixe* p. 4 enumerando le fonti scrive : " *plures quaterni per primum confessorem dicte Virginis de gestis eiusdem virginis transcripte* " E a pag. 53 più chiaramente ricorda : " *omnia supradicta ego habui ex certis quaternis scriptis per manus principaliter primi confessoris qui dictus est frater Thomas de Fonte et etiam per manus secundi confessoris ipsius virginis qui appellatus est frater Bartolomeus Dominici qui fuit postmodum sacre theologie professor. Et ambo fuerunt de Senis.*"

Il frate che scrisse sotto dettatura e che fu poi il secondo confessore di Caterina, si chiamava : *

FRA BARTOLOMEO DOMINICI. Se Fra Tommaso fra le virtù sacerdotali ebbe il dono della bontà, Fra Bartolomeo fu il religioso dotto, il vero tipo del domenicano, che ha per lo studio una grande ed immensa passione, non sterile passione, ma quale mezzo per imporsi alle intelligenze, illuminarle e farvi penetrare la luce, la verità.

L'influenza di questo dotto nella formazione intellettuale e spirituale di Caterina, non è stata da nessuno notata, e credo che proprio a lui si debba, dopo Dio, se l'intelligenza di Caterina acquistò quella profondità e limpidezza, quella *forma mentis*, direi quasi, machile, capace di avventurarsi negli abissi della Fede.

Fra Bartolomeo fu uno dei domenicani più illustri del suo tempo, prese la laurea dottorale in Bologna, fu priore, provinciale, vicario dell'Ordine e professore nelle scuole pontificie ; cooperò con Fra Raimondo da Capua alla rinascita della vita domenicana, lavorò con Fra Tommaso Caffarini ad eternare la memoria di Caterina, ed al processo di canonizzazione della Santa fece una deposizione della più importanti, storicamente. Morì in Rimini nel 1415 a 72 anni.†

IL CENACOLO CATERINIANO. Questi due Domenicani formarono il primo nucleo di quel cenacolo cateriniano che fece di Fontebranda la vera fonte, dove correvano a dissetarsi non solo le pie donne, le madri sventurate, i malati di corpo e di coscienza, ma in modo speciale e continuo le intelligenze, le quali, tra il turbinio di quella società che si disfaceva nell'odio delle fazioni comunali e nazionali, tra la corruzione morale e politica, cercavano nella Fede il lievito restauratore e rinnovatore.

Tra quei spiriti agitati troviamo Neri di Landoccio dei Pagliaresi, nobile, colto, poeta e studioso di Dante ; anima privilegiata, che avendo sentito parlare di Caterina, va, e, come tanti altri, resta preso e avvinto.‡ Conosciuto il dono ricevuto, non abbandonò più Caterina ; fu lo scrittore di moltissime lettere e di una parte del Dialogo, andò per ordine di Lei a Napoli presso la Regina Giovanna II, e dopo la morte della Santa fu l'anima della grande famiglia di Caterina, raccogliendo anche per sua gioia molte lettere di Lei e scrivendo poesie in suo onore.

---

* *Supplementum* ff. 31-32.

† Anche di fra Bartolomeo Dominici scriverò a parte.

‡ Del Pagliaresi parla il Caffarini nel *Supplementum*, f. 1740 e quel pezzo fu edito da Grottanelli in *Leggenda minore*, p. 382 nota 121, dove pubblica molte lettere scritte o ricevute dal Pagliaresi, p. 262-67, 273-93, 298-305, 308-314, 318-37. Una lettera di Benvenuto da Munistero a ser Iacomo racconta gli ultimi momenti del Pagliaresi e ci dà notizie sulla sua eredità. Morì il 12 marzo 1406 (1407).

Nessuno finora si è preoccupato di darci un profilo completo del Pagliaresi che fu un centro di apostolato cateriniano prima e dopo la morte della Santa.

Di lui parala il Guidini nelle sue memorie. Cfr. *Fioretti di S. Caterina* p. 115 ; il Mala volti nella deposizione al *Processo* e spesso il B. Raimondo nella *Legenda maior* parlano di Neri.

A lui diresse la Santa 12 lettere, la 8, 42, 46, 99, 106, 178, 186, 192, 212, 228, 269, 281 (ed. Tomm.).

Il Pagliaresi era poeta e naturalmente scrisse laudi in onore della sua Mamma, edite nelle antiche edizioni del *Dialogo*. Scrisse anche due legende in versi, quella di S. Eufrosina che è nel codicetto della Nazionale di Firenze, Strozziano cl. XXXVIII n. 130, autografo del Pagliaresi, e una leggenda di S. Giosafat nella biblioteca Bodleiana di Oxford, cod. 53 ; cfr. Mortara, *Catalogo dei codici italiani detti Canoniciani italici*, 1864, *v.* 31.

Di mano del Pagliaresi sono i due codicetti Strozziani, cl. XXXV n. 599 e cl. XXXIX n. 90 contenente lettere dealla Santa. Vedi p. 336.

Il Pagliaresi condusse giù a Fontebranda molti amici, tra i quali Francesco Malavolti*, figura bizzarra di nobile gaudente, che fu poi monaco di Monteolliveto e al processo mandò una testimonianza, ancora inedita, dove confessa senza reticenze, la vita sua tormentata. Di un altro nobile senese, Gabriele di Davino Piccolomini, trovo citato, che scrisse un libro di ricordi su Santa Caterina, ma in nessun archivio Piccolomini mi è riuscito finora di trovarlo.†

Condusse il Pagliaresi alla Santa, Ser Cristofano di Gano Guidini, notaio letterato e uomo politico, che ebbe anche uffici importanti nel reggimento della republica senese. Fu segretario della Santa ed il primo a raccogliere il materiale cateriniano, specialmente quello custodito dal Pagliaresi ; anzi la prima collezione delle lettere fu opera sua ; tradusse in latino il *Dialogo* e lo divulgò. Scrisse infine le sue memorie, che sono veramente deliziose.‡

Nelle sue memorie Ser Cristofano non si contenta di parlare solo delle cose sue, ma preso dall'onda dei ricordi nel parlar di Caterina, ci dà notizie preziose sugli altri discepoli, fermandosi in modo speciale sull'eremita agostiniano Fra Guglielmo Flete, inglese, personaggio molto in vista nei suoi tempi, per dottrina e santità. Era chiamato per antonomasia *el Baccelliere*. Fra Guglielmo scrisse in lode di Caterina delle lettere e dei trattati molto importanti.§

IN S. MARIA NOVELLA. Ma il nome di Caterina ormai non poteva più essere nascosto tra la cerchia angusta delle mura cittadine ; la missione ricevuta dall'alto la portò irresistibilmente a guardare più in là, molto in là, nonostante che la malignità, l'invidia ed il verme terribile della gelosia la circondasse di ostilità, di calunnie e dicerie d'ogni genere, specialmente nell'ambiente chiesastico e anche fra le consorelle, le mantellate, e tra is suoi confratelli, i domenicani. Il rumore fu grande, così da giungere alle orecchie del generale dell'Ordine domenicano ; tanto più che quella monaca voleva immischiarsi anche un po' nella politica della sua città, della Toscana, e, ciò che era peggio, guardare più in alto, e scriveva parole amare ai Cardinali Legati ed ai Principi.

---

* Del Malavolti resosi olivetano dopo la morte di Caterina nel 1388 parla il P. Lugano O. M. O. in *Rivista storica benedettina*, a. VII, pag. 162-73 ; il Grottanelli nella *Leggenda minore, passim*. Morì dopo il 1413. Scrisse una lunga deposizione per il processo rimasta inedita.

Fu pubblicata in parte con ampie notizie sul Malavolti dal Lazzareschi in *S. Caterina in Val d'Orcia*, Firenze 1915, appendice.

Al Malavolti scrisse la Santa la lettera 45 (ed. Tomm.).

† Di Gabriello parla il Grottanelli c. p. 335, 336, 355, 338, riportando ciò che di lui scrisse il Caffarini nel *Supplementum*. Morì il 12 nov. 1399.

‡ Del Guidini vedi le notizie pubblicate nei *Fioretti di S. Caterina* pp. 113-34. Di lui parla il francescano fra Angelo Salvetti nel *processo*, cfr. Martene et Durand, *Collectio Monumentorum* vol. VI, col. 1367 n. 115, e *Dialogo di S. Caterina*, edizione del P. Taurisano, Firenze, Libr. Editr. Fiorentina, 1928, p. XL.

§ Di fra Guglielmo parla con grande ricchezza di documentazione il Fawtier, *Ste. Catherine de Sienne, essai de critique des sources, sources hagiographiques*, Paris, De Boccard, 1921, p. 53-81 ; il Caffarini o. c. f. 1710 ; il Guidini, cfr. *Fioretti ;* il Baluzio, *Miscell. I.*, pag. 1085 ; Grottanelli o. c. p. 270.

Una notizia inedita su fra Guglielmo è nell'archivio generale degli Agostiniani, regesto I. 118, (1359) "*fr. Guglielmus di Anglia sacre pagine professor positus est pro regente in conventu Pragensi cum socio.*"

A fr. Guglielmo sono dirette 6 lettere, la 64, 66, 77, 227, 292, 326 (ed. Tomm.).

Così fu che, radunandosi il congresso internazionale dei domenicani in Firenze nel 1374, Caterina per ordine dei superiori fu chiamata a presentarsi nel meraviglioso cappellone degli Spagnoli per dar ragione di sè.*

I biografi antiche e moderni, fino a qualche anno fa, trascurarono del tutto questo fatto importantissimo nella vita di Caterina, che conosciamo soltanto da un prezioso scritto redatto in volgare da un discepolo fiorentino, forse Giannozzo Sacchetti, e intitolato *Miracoli*, che publicai nei *Fioretti*.†

Quei *Miracoli* sono la prima fonte agiografica giunta integralmente a noi, scritta vivente la Santa, dal maggio all'ottobre 1374 ; di un valore quindi molto grande.

FRA RAIMONDO DA CAPUA. Conseguenza di quel, direi quasi, processo, fu che l'Ordine domenicano, avendo conosciuto quale spirito animasse l'umile mantellata senese, a salvaguardia contro l'ambiente ostile formatosi in Siena, le pose a lato un frate di un'autorità indiscussa, dotto, prudente e pratico nell'arte difficilissima di dirigere le anime, fra Raimondo da Capua, discendente di quel Pier delle Vigne, *che tenne—del cor di Federico ambo le chiavi.*‡

Dal 1374 al 1380 fra Raimondo fu per Caterina lo scudo, la luce, il Padre e anche il discepolo. La missione completamente nuova di una donna-apostolo, di una donna, vorrei poter dire, missionaria, che non potendo predicare perchè donna, usa la penna come la spada più possente, per tagliare, ferire, e tagliando sanare, quella missionaria doveva procedere per la via maestra dell'ortodossia, e fra Raimondo fu l'uomo provvidenziale. Egli non era un meridionale, intelligente sì, ma immaginoso e impulsivo. Nobile per sangue e discendente da una generazione di giuristi, ebbe un carattere freddo e realistico. Conoscitore profondo della teologia, della mistica e delle forze della natura, studiò a lungo la sua discepola, e si convinse solo dinanzi alla voce di Dio.§ Da allora diresse Caterina nel molteplice apostolato di pace tra i popoli, di purificazione della vita cattolica nella Chiesa, di vita religiosa negli ordini monastici e nel grandioso progetto della crociata contro gli infedeli. Egli fu così il capo, il padre di quella numerosa e scelta famiglia iniziata in Fontebranda da Fra Tommaso della Fonte, ed il Papa e l'Ordine domenicano ebbero in lui piena fiducia.

LA " LEGENDA MAIOR." Morta Caterina, i discepoli vollero, ostinata-mente vollero, che lui fosse il solo a scriverne la vita o *leggenda*, come allora si diceva, da *leggere*, della loro indimenticabile *Mamma*. Ma Fra Raimondo era stato appunto nella Pentecoste del 1380 eletto generale dei domenicani rimasti fedeli a Roma, e l'opera di restaurazione dell'antica disciplina e le missioni continue del Pontefice, in quell'agitatissimo periodo dello scisma di occidente,

---

* Cfr. il mio articolo *S. Caterina e Gregorio XI*, in *Rosario Memorie Domenicane.*

† Sono stati anche pubblicati dal Fawtier o. c. in appendice p. 217-23 e dal Misciatelli nel VI volume delle lettere, pp. 183-215.

Circa l'autore dei *Miracoli* inchino a credere che sia Giannozzo Sacchetti per delle ragioni che dirò in altro lavoro.

‡ Su fra Raimondo vedi le notizie date dal Fawtier o. c. pp. 118-27 dove si trova la biblio-grafia, ma incompleta ; cfr. il Caffarini o. c. f. 169-71 ; il regesto del medesimo B. Raimondo nell'archivio generale dell'Ordine Domenicano IV-1 ; il P. Denifle nel Charthularium Universitatis Parisiensis, I. IV., dove pubblica i documenti riguardanti il B. Raimondo come legato pontificio i Francia. Cfr. anche il Novati, *Epistolario di Coluccio Salutati,* dove in un carme dello Stella diretto al Salutati si parla bene di fr. Raimondo.

§ Il fatto avvenne a Montepulciano e fr. Raimondo lo racconta con grande sincerità nella *Legenda maior.*

gli impedivano un lavoro che richiedeva tranquillità, raccoglimento e serenità. Accettò finalmente, ma ci vollero *dieci anni* per poter leggere la *legenda* di Catorina. Venne alla luce solo nell'anno 1395.*

Il metodo di lavoro usato dal B. Raimondo può dirsi unico in tutta l'agiografia medioevale. Si possono benissimo sfogliare i numerosi *in folio* dei Bollandisti e credo si troveranno poche vite scritte con metodo direi così scientifico come quella di Raimondo. Nel prologo secondo dice : "Affermo dunque a chiunque leggerà questo libro, che, essendo testimonio essa Verità, la quale non inganna e non è ingannata, io non porrò in esso alcuna cosa finta e non vera, ne anco nella substanzia della cosa facta, quanto la mia fragilità à potuto investigare. E, acciocchè più fermamente fede si renda alle cose che si diranno, porrò in ogni capitolo onde e come io ebbi quello che narro." †

La leggenda del Beato Raimondo che fu detta *maggiore* per distinguerla dalle *minori* e meno importanti, è la fonte principale di tutto il materiale cateriniano, ma non è la sola.

FRA TOMMASO CAFFARINI. Accanto al B. Raimondo troviamo un frate senese, fra Tommaso di Naccio Caffarini, coetaneo della Santa, e che fu, dopo la morte di B. Raimondo, avvenuta nel 1399, la figura più importante. A lui dobbiamo eterna riconoscenza per aver raccolti e pubblicati tutti i documenti riguardanti la Santa, e per avere preparato il processo di canonizzazione, chiamato *Processo Castellano*, perchè fatto in Venezia nella curia di Castello.‡

Il Caffarini non ha l'ingegno ed il carattere di Fra Raimondo ; mite, osservante e buono, avvolge la sua vita religiosa in un'atmosfera di misticismo che propaga interno a sè con ansia di asceta e di santo. Ma il metodo che usa è quello stesso di Fra Raimondo ; e nell'archivio de' Frati in Venezia ho potuto toccar con mano la verità.

---

* Cfr. la lattera del B. Raimondo ai discepoli di Siena sulla compilazione della *Legenda* in P. Cormier, *B. Raymundi Capuani, Opuscula et litterae*, Romae, 1899, p. 73-74 e 164.

† "Protestor autem cuilibet qui leget hunc librum, quod teste ipsa veritate, quae nec fallit nec fallitur, nihil fictum, nihil adinventum inseritur in ea, nec, saltem in substantia rei gestae, quantum mea fragilitas investigare potuit, quomodolibet falsum. Ut autem fides adhibeatur his quae dicentur praestantior, in quolibet capitulo ponam unde et qualiter habui ea quae narro ; et videat quilibet unde traxi quae narro ; et videat quilibet unde habui pro animabus potandis in hoc libello propino." Acta SS., aprile III., p. 867, n. 21.

Così a pag. 875 n. 51 dopo il secondo capitolo si legge : " Haec autem sunt in hoc recitato capitulo, habui, a Lapa matre, a Lysa uxore eius germani, ab aliis qui tunc erant in domo sua, necnon quaedam quae alii scire non potuerunt, ut dictum est, ipsa sacra virgine didici revelante."

E nella terza parte preso sempre da *scrupoli storici* il B. Raimondo sente il bisogno di parlare più diffusamente delle sue fonti ; così parte III. cap. II. n. 338 dice : "Verum ne allegando testes in generali lectorem videam subornare, ipsos et ipsas nominaliter hic ponam, ut fides non mihi sed eis tanquam dignioribus adhibeatur ; novi enim quod ipsi et ipsae eam perfectius in sacris actibus sunt imitati, et ideo perfectius eius actus intellexerunt." Nomina prima le mantellate Alessia Saracini, Francesca di Clemente Gori, e Lisa Colombini. Tra i discepoli nomina fra Santi eremita, Barduccio Canigiani, Stefano Maconi e Neri di Landoccio.

‡ Le notizie sul Caffarini si trovano nel *Supplementum*, f. 180-83, nel regesto del B. Raimondo da Capua, IV-1 *passim*, nel Trattato sul Terz'Ordine, edito da Flaminio Corner, t. XI, nel necrologio di S. Domenico di Siena f. 25, nell'attestazione al processo di Canonizzazione in parte inedita, e negli Script. O. P., I. p. 785, II, 822 ; cfr. anche il mio articolo in *Studi Cateriniani*, a. I. p. 76-83 ; Carlo Frati, *Leggenda di S. Caterina con disegni attribuiti a Iacopo Bellini*, in *Bibliofilia*, a. XXV, luglio-settembre 1913 ; Pietro Rossi, *La "Laude" di fr. Tommaso Caffarini in onore di S. C.*, in *Studi Cateriniani*, a. IV, pp. 70-99.

Prima di chiudere l'enumerazione delle fonti, bisogna ricordare brevemente altre cinque figure di caterinati : due senesi : Stefano Maconi certosino e Angelo Salvetti francescano, ed i fiorentini Barduccio Canigiani, il B. Giovanni Dominici cardinale ed il famoso asceta Don Giovanni dalle Celle.

DON STEFANO MACONI. Stefano Maconi, gentiluomo, letterato e gaudente, conobbe Caterina nel 1376, in occasione di una pace tra la sua famiglia ed i Tolomei. Da quel giorno non l'abbandonò più. Ne fu il segretario preferito e Caterina ebbe per lui delle finezze materne, ricambiate con inestinguibile affetto filiale. L'accompagnò a Firenze, ad Avignone, a Roma, e fu testimonia dei fatti più importanti negli ultimi quattro anni della vita di Caterina.

Tradusse in latino *Il Dialogo*, raccolse, ancor vivendo Caterina, molte lettere, di cui poi fece una collezione a parte, testimoniò al processo di canonizzazione, tradusse la leggenda minore del Caffarini, fece tradurre la leggenda maggiore e postillò di sua mano molti manoscritti contenenti la vita della Santa, postille sfuggite ai biografi e che illuminano mirabilmente l'apostolato di Caterina a Firenze e ad Avignone.*

Morta la Santa, si fece certosino, fu a Passignano, a Milano, indi nella meravigliosa certosa di Pavia, poi in Austria, fu generale del suo Ordine, lavorò molto per la cessazione dello scisma e per diffondere gli scritti e lo spirito di Caterina. Morì nel 1424.†

Un uomo quindi superiore, di fama indiscussa come Fra Raimondo da Capua. La sua corrispondenza con Neri Pagliaresi, di cui per fortuna si conservano gli autografi nella biblioteca di Siena, forma un materiale dei più preziosi per la conoscenza dell'ambiente cateriniano.

FR. ANGELO SALVETTI. Tra i discepoli francescani di S. Caterina, quali fra Lazzarino da Pisa e fra Gabriele da Volterra, il Salvetti non occupa l'ultimo posto. Da giovanetto visse nell'ambiente Cateriniano e anche sotto l'abito del frate minore, pur occupando altissime cariche quale il provincialato e il generalto de suo Ordine non dimenticò la *Mamma :* fu sempre un forte assertore della sua santità e al processo di canonizzazione mandò deposizione che è tra le più importanti. Morì nel 1423.‡

I DISCEPOLI FIORENTINI. Non ancora è stata studiata ed illustrata la famiglia spirituale che Caterina si formò in Firenze. Basti ricordare Niccolò Soderini, Bonaccorso di Lapo, l' Arcivescovo Ricasoli, e poi il sarto Francesco di Pipino e Giannozzo Sacchetti che finì tragicamente e scrisse forse i *Miracoli*. Ma tre personaggi bisogna ricordare di più : un giovane fiorentino della famiglia dei Canigiani, Barduccio, che fu segretario della Santa, e fu presente in Roma alla morte di Lei, scrivendone una relazione che è fra i documenti più belli delle fonti caateriniane. Trascrisse di sua mano *Il Dialogo* e molte lettere, conservate in un manoscritto della Casanatense in Roma. Morì in Siena nel 1382 di mal sottile.§

* Molte di quelle postille le ha pubblicate il Fawtier o. c. pag. 115.

† Così per il Maconi vedi *Supplementum* f. 178-80 ; le sue lettere pubblicate dal Grottanelli in *leggenda minore ;* le lettere di S. Caterina a lui, e la vita di lui scritta da B. Bartolomeo Scala e dal De Vasseux.

‡ Del Salvetti scrissi nell'articolo : *S. Caterina e i Francescani* in *Antonianum*, a. 1927.

§ Il biografo più completo del Canigiani è stato il B. Raimondo, il quale nella *Legenda maior*, A. SS., p. 947 n. 341 traccia un profilo molto delicato di Barduccio. Fu l'ultima conquista di Caterina, fatta in Firenze durante quel torbido periodo di storia in cui la Santa ebbe parte sì importante.

Una figura più alta e complessa è quella del domenicano Fra Giovanni Dominici cardinale, e autore di quella graziosa laude che tutti conoscono :

Di Maria dolce con quanto desio . . .

Predicatore famoso, umanista, teologo, artista, riformatore di conventie monasteri, a Fiesole e Venezia, scrittore elegante, uomo politico dei più importanti, lavorò e riuscì a far cessare lo scisma : questo cardinale domenicano, che la Chiesa venera come Beato, ebbe per Caterina una venerazione filiale e scrisse di Lei delle parole riboccanti di affetto e di fede.*

Chiude la serie dei discepoli quel profondo asceta che riempì del suo nome lo scorcio del trecento, Don Giovanni dalle Celle. Fu così entusiasta di Caterina, che, benchè vecchio, scrive delle espressioni da far invidia ad un secentista.

" Io dico di Caterina mia, così angelica come divina, la quale come sole illumina el nostro emisferio "—" O Angela terrestre, o rosa di caritade, o giglio di verginitade e viola d'umilitade, chi t'ha rivelato questa celestiale dottrina ? "—" Caterina mia è piena di sapienza e scienza di Dio, secondo che manifestano l'altissime sue pistole."†

L'accenno del B. Giov. Dalle Celle alle lettere di Caterina ci spinge a chiudere la enumerazione delle fonti cateriniane dando un rapido sguardo all'epistolario della Santa.

Le lettere e il Dialogo. Queste lettere sono un monumento meraviglioso di fede, di pietà, di battaglie per il bene, dove vibra e freme l'anima di Caterina,

---

Barduccio era discepolo di Don Giovanni dalle Celle e, conosciuta Caterina, abbandonò la patria e la famiglia per seguirla. Divenne presto il beniamino di Caterina e dei Caterinati, fu segretario della Santa e la seguì a Roma, descrivendone con accenti commossi il transito, pubblicato in tutte le antiche edizioni del *Dialogo*, dal Gigli e nelle *Elevazioni e preghiere di S. Caterina*, Roma, Ferrari, 1920. A Roma si ammalò di petto e fu ordinato sacerdote ; il B. Raimondo lo rimandò a Siena ove morì nel 1382 e fu sepolto in S. Domenico insieme con i religiosi : " 1382 Presbiter Barduccius Pieri Chanigiani de Florentia sepultus est die nona decembris cum fratibus ad pedes figure sancti Iacobi ad altare B. Thome." Sepultuario di S. Domeninco, Bibl. Com. di Siena C. III. 2 f. 280. Di Barduccio e del *Transito* parla il Fawtier o. c. pag. 84-88 ; della copia del *Dialogo* con alcune lettere nel codice casanatense 292 parla il Prof. Bacchisio Motzo, *Alcune lettere di S. C. in parte inedite* in *Bullettino storico senese* a. XVIII (1911) f. II-III.

Di tutte le lettere di S. Caterina abbiamo solo 7 originali, e tutti questi originali sono di mano di Barduccio, secondo la dimostrazione che ne fa il signor Giovanni Ioergensen nella bella vita di S. Caterina pp. 553-55.

* Molte notizie del Domimici le raccolsi nel quarto centenario della morte sua, cfr. *Analecta O. P.*, Roma 1919, pp. 39-56. Del Dominici e della sua attività parla il Caffarini in *Tractatus super reformatione et approbatione III. ordinis* edito del Corner in *Monumenta Ecclesiae Venetae*, dec. XI p. I. passim ; per la vita cf., il Rosler e per le opere il Quetif-Echard, *Scriptores o. v.*, T. I. p. 768, e *Dictionnaire de Théologie catholique*, alla voce : Dominici.

† Il lavoro più completo su D. Giovanni dalle Celle è quello della signorina Pia Cividali edito tra le *Memorie della R. Acc. dei Lincei*, classe scienze morali, storiche e fiologiche CCCIV, ser. V. Vol. XII., fasc. I., 1907.

Di Don Giovanni dalle Celle parla anche il Caffarini, *Supplementum*, f. 173 dove inserisce anche notizie su Barduccio Canigiani.

Il Caffarini parlando delle lotte sostenute da D. Giovanni a Firenze contro i fraticelli, scrivendo anche un libretto, accenna a S. Caterina che combatte in Firenze contro i Fraticelli : " unde contra quosdam de ipsis et etiam hec Virgo quando fuit Florentie, ut percepi, personaliter disputavit, eosque convicit oraculo vive vocis." Est autem dictus libellus (*di D. Giovanni contro i Fraticelli*) ad presens hic in Venetüs apud sorores dicti Ordinis de Penitentia B. Dominici per manus cuiusdam Neri Landocci de Senis."

Sono forse le molte lettere che Don Giovanni scrisse contro i fraticelli, cfr. Pia Cividali *Il B. Giov. dalle Celle*. Roma, 6907, pp. 395 e sgg.

ora supplicante come madre, ora ardita, impulsiva, tagliente come spada ; sempre luminosa, saplente, ispirata, piena di umanità, di fascino, di civismo altissimo ; scritte nel delizioso suo volgare, ricco, immaginoso, che porta lontano, nelle corti dei principi e dei re, tra i cardinali, papi, baroni, religiosi, uomini d'arme, di lettere, tra gli astuti politici, porta la sua passione, la sua arditezza, il suo mònito, il rimprovero, l'accusa, la parola di pace ; porta in Italia e fuori il fremito di una domenicana che vedendo offesa la Verità, profanato il Tempio, calpestato il suolo della patria dai predoni, grida, implora, comanda, fino a che le rimane un alito di vita, un palpito del suo immenso cuore trafitto.

I discepoli, diciamolo francamente, si affannarono con ansia filiale a descrivere, a raccontare, a darci la fisonomia della figlia del tintore di Fontebranda ; raccolsero tutto ciò che era uscito dal suo labbro, tutto il bene operato, le grazie straordinarie ricevute, vollero innalzare alla loro madre un monumento costituito appunto da tutte le fonti sopra enumerate, ma il vero, il grande, l'emperituro monumento, Caterina se l'è costruito con le sue stesse mani, con l'epistolario, dove scrisse involontariamente la sua autobiografia, e col Dialogo, che fu il canto del cigno, dove vediamo quali inaccessibili altezze raggiunse quell'intelligenza anelante, sitibonda di Luce.

IL LAVORO CRITICO. Come, dopo una faticosa ascesa, l'occhio corre ansioso ad ammirare l'ampio orizzonte, il panorama stupendo, così dopo la pesante e diciamo anche con sincerità, la noiosa enumerazione delle fonti cateriniane, dando uno sguardo d'insieme a quel ricco materiale, notiamo con piacere che, intorno alla popolana senese, digiuna di ogni cultura umana si formò un cenacolo intellettuale che pochi uomini e pochi Santi ebbero intorno a sè. Caterina era una domenicana, discepola di quel Domenico

che in picciol tempo gran dottor si feo,

esercitò quindi un fàscino sulle intelligenze più forti del suo tempo, attrasse nella sua orbita uomini politici, letterati, uomini d'arme, ecclesiastici di ogni gerarchia, persone insomma di un valore morale, di una sincerità, di una fede profonda e indiscussa.

Le fonti quindi cateriniane risentono di quel periodo di battaglie, in cui ogni personaggio è al suo posto di combattimento. Intorno a Caterina vi sono delle volontà, delle intelligenze abituate a dire la verità, a difenderla, senza fiori e senza svenevolezze leggendarie.

Tutto il ricco materiale agiografico cateriniano, dai *Miracula* del suo primo confessore al *Processo di canonizzazione* (materiale di cui non abbiamo ancora un'edizione critica, e di cui, una parte è ancora inedita),* non era stato ancora toccato dalla critica storica letteraria ; il chirurgo nè il clinico si erano permessi di sottoporre ad un esame di gabinetto o di tavola anatomica sia la vita della Santa che l'attività dei discepoli in tramandare a noi le sue gesta. La critica spesso ha die pudori di fanciulla, fino a che la necessità, mi si passi l'espressione, non impone di operare.

---

* Il *Supplementum* di fr. Tommaso Caffarini, che è una specie di zibaldone, dove sono raccolte un pò alla rinfusa tutte le notizie sfuggite al B. Raimondo nella sua *Legenda* fu tradotto liberamente dal P. Tantucci ma è tutto inedito nel testo latino. Uno studio molto importante sul *Supplementum* è stato fatto dalla Signora De Sanctis, edito negli *Studi Cateriniani*, a, V, n. 4.

E' inedita una parte del Processo di canonizzazione, edito solo in parte dal Martène et Durand in *Amplissima collectio*, T. VI. coll. 1238-1386 ; così pure alcune leggende minori dei discepoli S. Caterina, cfr. Taurisano, *Catheriniana*, in *Studi Cateriniani*, a. I, pag. 2.

Al periodo delle fonti successe, con l'invenzione della stampa, che coincise con la canonizzazione di Caterina e col rinascimento, un periodo di intensa divulgazione del pensiero e delle gesta della Santa, non disgiunti da un senso critico specie per la ricerca delle lettere e dei còdici gelosamente custodili da privati e da conventi. L'edizione del *Dialogo* nel 1472 (Bologna), l'Aldina delle lettere (Venezia 1500) ne furono i frutti.

La rinascita cattolica, che aveva avuto in Caterina una precorritrice, attinse nelle dottrine sue energia e luce. Col seicento però troviamo in S. Domenico di Siena un centro di studi cateriniani con a capo il Carapelli, seguito da sapienti eruditi senesi, che ebbero in Girolamo Gigli un condottiero ardente e combattivo, coadiuvato dal gesuita Burlamacchi che annotò criticamente le lettere raccolte dal Gigli, formando così una edizione che rimane ancora l'edizione principe degna del secolo del Muratori e del Mabillon.

Seguì un periodo in cui si copiò e ricopiò il già fatto fino alla metà dell'ottocento, dove troviamo tre nomi : il Tommaseo, il card. Capecelatro e il Grottanelli senese.

Ai magistrali lavori dal cardinale Capecelatro sulla vita e del grande Niccolò Tommaseo sulle lettere, dove fissarono per sempre in una sintesi mirabile la figura e l'opera di Caterina, non tenne dietro un'analisi corrispondente ; e, solo dopo la biografia scritta dall'inglese Gardner* si incominciò il lavoro necessario di revisione. Il Prof. Motzo dell'Università di Cagliari scoprì e pubblicò nuove lettere, da un codice casanatense† ; il dottor Lazzareschi trattò la relazione tra Lucca e Caterina. Le relazioni molto più importanti fra Pisa e Caterina, ed infine le peregrinazioni della Santa in Val d'Orcia.‡. La baronessa Sekendorff studiava con senso critico le lettere politiche, § il Domenicano P. Hurtaud scriveva una magistrale prefazione al *Dialogo* ‖ e la Signora Matilde Fiorilli pubblicò nel 1912 un'edizione critica di quell'opera, e preparava una edizione delle lettere, quando immaturamente morì.

LA CRITICA DI R. FAWTIER.   Come si vede, la spinta era data e, finalmente, nel 1921 il francese Roberto Fawtier, dopo una larga ed intensa preparazione, dopo aver trovato e pubblicato cose nuove ed interessanti,** diede alle stampa la sua tesi di dottorato alla Sorbona, un saggio cioè di critica sulle fonti cateriniane, saggio, che, invece di suscitare tra i numerosi ammiratori della grande senese un grido di gioia, strappò accenti di dolore e di sdegno.

---

* S. Catherine of Siena, London, Dent 1907.

† Dei saggi critici sulle lettere e specialmente sul codice di Modena e di Torino avevano fatto sentire il bisogno di un'edizione critica.

‡ I.—Santa Caterina da Siena e i Lucchesi, Firenze, 1912.

II.—S. Caterina da Siena in Val D' Orcia, Firenze, 1915.

III. Zucchelli—Lazzareschi, S. Caterina da Siena ed i Pisani, Pisa 1917.

§ Die Kirchenpolitische, Tatigk eit der beilingen Katerina von Siena unter Papst Gregor XI (1371-78) Berlin 1919.

‖ Le Dialogue de S. Cat. de Sienne, Paris, Letiellieux 1913.

** I.—Sur le portrait di S. Cat. di Sienne in Mélanges d'archéologie et d'histoire, a. XXXI (1912) f. III.

II.—La legende mineure di S. C., ibidem, ff. IV-V.

III.—Catheriniana ibidem, a. XXXIV (1914) pp. 5-158.

Non è questo il momento della gioia e dello sdegno ; l'ambiente in cui siamo impone serenità e calma. Alla critica non si risponde con improperi, ma con documenti e con severa controcritica.

* * * * *

Il Fawtier divide il materiale che sopra abbiamo illustrato, in tre categorie :

1.—documenti *personali*, cioè le *Lettere* e il *Dialogo ;*

2.—documenti *agiografici*, cioè tutti gli scritti in lode della Santa o per promuoverne il culto ;

3.—documenti *storici* che prescindono dal culto.*

Inoltre i documenti agiografici e storici sono dal Fawtier divisi così :

I.—Le *leggende* minori (S. Antonino, fr. Antonio della Rocca, D. Girolamo da Praga, camaldolese, fr. Massimino da Salerno, fr. Giovanni d'Ivrea e fr. Tommaso Caffarini), pp. 17-25.

II.—Il *processus* di canonizzazione della Santa, pp. 26-44.

III.—Il *supplementum* alla leggenda maggiore di fr. Tommaso Caffarini, pp. 45-52.

IV.—Le testimonianze di fr. Guglielmo Flete agostiniano inglese, pp. 53-81.

V.—I racconti della morte di S. Caterina, pp. 82-91.

VI.—I *miracoli* di S. Caterina, di un anonimo fiorentino, pp. 92-98.

VII.—I *miracula* di fr. Tommaso della Fonte, pp. 99-108.

VIII.—L'*epitaphium* di Don Stefano Maconi, pp. 109-117.

IX.—La *legenda maior* di fr. Raimondo da Capua, pp. 118-130.

Dal suo studio scarta i documenti personali, cioè le lettere, perchè, egli dice, delle 400 lettere nemmeno una è di mano di Caterina, e furono scritte tutte da quei discepoli che le raccolsero per promuoverne la canonizzazione ; bisogna—egli dice—prima vedere come i discepoli hanno lavorato la leggenda nella parte agiografica e poi esaminare le lettere.†

E' possibile ammettere uno studio sulle fonti cateriniane, trascurando il documento principale, personale, l'epistolario, sol perchè S. Caterina ebbe dei segretari, i quali, nel raccogliere quelle lettere, ne tolsero alcuni punti riguardanti persone viventi ? Non si fa anche oggi, così ? Il Fawtier, è bene qui dirlo di passaggio, non ha fatto caso di una lettera di Stefano Maconi a Neri Pagliaresi del 22 giugno 1379, quando Caterina era ancora in vita, e a Roma :

" Non mi ricorda come io ti scrissi di non avere avuta da te se non quella lettera di Perugia, forse che per la fretta errai nello scrivere. Ma questa è la terza lettera, e la seconda fu di quelle lettere o novelle dello imperadore,

---

* *Introduction*, p. XI.

† *Nous possédons environ quatre cents lettres de sainte Catherine de Sienne, e de cette vaste correspondance nous ne possédons pas un mot de la main même de sainte Catherine.* . . . . *Or, de ces lettres écrites sous la dictée de la sainte, nous possédons seulement six originaux.* E dopo aver discusso sul modo come i discepoli hanno potuto formare le collezioni delle lettere, e osservando che dai devoti era facile avere delle copie non così dai grandi, soggiunge, sottolineando in corsivo come le parole precedenti ; *aucune des lettres de S. C. adresséesà des personnages étrangers à son groupe religieux ne nous a été conservée en original.*

nella quale mi promettesti di mandarmene la copia e mai non l'ebbi. Anco le scrissi io allora a Riccardo a Fiorenza secondo che mi dicesti, ma quest'altra lettera con quella copia di quella che andò al re d'Inghilterra, io non l'ho avuta. Dici che 10 la procacci, ma 10 non so da cui. Scrivimi per cui la mandasti. Secondo che io ho scritto costà a te, almeno in due lettere, che tu procacci da 36 lettere ch'io vi mandai quando el Maestro ne venne ed a cui, e nondimeno non m'hai risposto se l'avete avuto o no e maraviglianei un poco se l'avete avute, che non avete mandata mai alcuna risposta."*

Queste parole del Maconi ci mostrano chiaramente come vivente ancora la Santa, si conservavano le minute e le copie†, e come poi ne vennero le diverse collezioni personali, quella del Guidini, notaio, abituato alle imbreviature, quella del Maconi, l'altra del Pagliaresi, poi quella del Canigiani, infine quella del Caffarini, domenicano, che fu l"ultimo, e non fece altro che dare alle lettere raccolte dal Guidini un ordine, secondo le persone a cui furono dirette.‡

Questa ansia di raccogliere le lettere ancor vivente la Santa, sfuggita al Fawtier, ha avuto per conseguenza un grave errore di metodo nell'esame critico delle fonti cateriniane, che ha influito poi su tutto il lavoro.

* * * * *

1.—Incomincia quindi il Fawtier il suo studio con un esame delle leggende minori, più o meno derivate da quelle del B. Raimondo ; e bisogna, con sincerità, ammirarne la ricchezza della documentazione e le scoperte da lui fatte di molti nuovi manoscritti e la serenità nel giudizio (pag. 17-25).

2. Non così nell'esame del processo di canonizzazione della Santa (pagg. 26-44). Ha portato nell'esaminare le 26 testimonianze il metodo che si usa oggi nei processi giudiziari. In uno storico e in un critico l'ignoranza di ciò che è un processo di canonizzazione è grave. Si spiegano quindi e si compatiscono le conclusioni completamente arbitrarie tratte da quel processo :

---

* Grottanelli, *Leggenda minore*, p. 280. L'accenno alla lettera mandata al re di Inghilterra non è stato notato dai biografi, e quella lettera non è nell'epistolario di Caterina, segno dunque che non scrivevano a mente i discepoli ma conservavano le lettere in minute o in copie. Anche una lettera al B. Raimondo è perduta.

† Il passo sopra citato del Maconi, che fu appunto uno dei raccoglitori della lettere, fa cadere tutte le sottili argomentazioni del Fawtier, il quale a p. XI dice : "*il semble établi qu' elle dictait ses lettres à des secrétaires pris souvent au hasard parmi ses disciples. Rien n'indique une organisation méthodique de cette chancellerie improvisée, aucune trace n'est restée d'une enrégistrement des minutes, quelques indices même tendraient à faire croire qu' il n'avait pas lieu.*" A queste ultime frasi ha risposto esaurientemente il Maconi, non solo per la sua raccolta che faceva delle lettere vivente la Santa, ma anche il Pagliaresi che faceva la sua e di cui sono rimasti due codici autografi nella Nazionale Fiorentina, Magliab. XXXVIII, 130 e XXX, 199. E va notato che tanto il Maconi che il Pagliaresi e così il Canigiani erano stati i segretari della Santa ed avevano scritto essi medesimi quelle lettere, di cui certo conservarono copia o minuta, e se le scambiavano per formarne raccolte per propria gioia ed edificazione. Nè v'è dimenticato che il primo a collezionare le lettere dopo la morte di Caterina, in modo completo, fu ser Cristofano di Gano Guidini, notaio di professione e discepolo della Santa. Il quale da buon notaio, uso alle imbreviature, non avrà dimenticato, vivente Caterina, di raccogliere tutto ciò che gli fu possibile.

Sulla genesi delle raccolte vedi il breve ma prezioso studio della signora Florilli, pubblicato dal suo degno marito, il Comm. Carlo, in *Miscellanea Dominicana*, Roma, Ferrari, 1923 pp. 196-205

‡ Il Caffarini parla nel *Processus* col. 1274-7 delle varie raccolte di lettere ; anzi alla col. 1290 n4. 2 parla degli *scriba* veneziani i quali trascrissero le opere in onore della Santa.

Alcuni pezzi inediti di quella deposizione del Caffarini riguardanti le opere della Santa furono pubblicati dal Lazzareschi *S. Cat. e i Lucchesi*, pp. 36-42. Della raccolta di Guidini parla anche il francescano fra. Angelo Salvetti nel *Processus*, col. 1367.

" Ce document nous apparaît comme extrêmement tendancieux." Eppure questo processo, come avrò occasione di dimostrare più a lungo, non è soltanto un documento agiografico ma essenzialmente storico, poichè la maggior parte dei testi parlano di cose vedute, di fatti personali, completano la biografia del B. Raimondo e mettono Caterina nell'ambiente vero di famiglia, così come si era venuto formando nella piccola casa di Fontebranda.

3.—Nel capitolo riguardante il *Supplementum* del Caffarini, dove questo instancabile discepolo raccoglie, ciò che era sfuggito al B. Raimondo, il Fawtier aggiunge nuovi elementi contro il Caffarini, che già nel processo ha tentato di mettere in una falsa luce (pagg. 45-52), concludendo che " le *Supplementum* nous apparaît comme une œuvre dont l'histoire même de la Sainte ne peut à peu près rien tirer."

4.—Lo studio sulle testimonianze del grande agostiniano inglese, fr. Guglielmo Flete,* venerato e rispettato dai contemporanei e dai discepoli della Santa per la profonda dottrina e la santità, il quale ebbe per Caterina una venerazione immensa, se è ricco per nuovi documenti e per intuizioni giuste, è sempre arbitrario nelle conclusioni, poichè toglie ogni valore a quelle testimonianze, aggiungendo nuovi elementi di colpabilità contro il Caffarini, che il Fawtier accusa di aver per lo meno alterati gli scritti del Flete (pagg. 53-81).

5.—Gli unici documenti che si salvano dalla critica, sono la lettera scritta da Barduccio Canigiani in morte della Santa (pagg. 92-98) e quel delizioso documento intitolato : *I miracoli della Beata Caterina* (pagg. 92-98). Per il Fawtier questi due sono gli unici documenti storici su cui possiamo fondarci.†

6.—Se i *Miracoli* dell'anonimo fiorentino hanno trovato benignità, non così i *Miracula* dettati a Fra Bartolomeo Dominici da Fra Tommaso della Fonte (pagg. 99-108). Que sti *Miracula* non sono giunti fino a noi, ma solo degli estratti nel Caffarini e nel B. Raimondo. La sparizione di questa fonte il Fawtier la crede *dolosa*, e ne incolpa il Caffarini con questa violenta invettiva : " Mi sembra bene che si possa affermare con quasi certezza che i *Miracula*

---

* " *Les témoignages de William Flete, pour nombreux qu'ils soient, ne nous seront pas d'un grand secours ; ou bien leur attribution est douteuse ou bien ils ne présentent pas les caractères d'authenticité nécessaires. Caffarini ne les a peut-être pas forgés entièrement, ce que nous savons de lui jusqu'à présent ne nous autorise, peut-être pas à le charger aussi lourdement mais il les aurait remaniés au point de les rendre méconnaissables qu' il ne s'en faudrait pas étonner. Dans tous les cas l'histoire de sainte Catherine n'en pourra rien tirer* " (pag. 81.)

† " *Les* MIRACOLI *seront donc pour nous un texte important au premier chef ; certes il faudra l'utiliser avec précaution, mais il semble que bien l'on pourra l'utiliser. Si nous jetons un regard en arrière sur les divers documents que nous avons examinés. de combien peut-on en dire autant ? Seuls avec la lettre de Barduccio Canigiani, tous deux écrits en langue vulgaire, ils apparaissent comme susceptibles d'une véritable utilisation historique* " (pag. 98). A pag. 96 il Fawtier scrive " *il semble donc bien que Miracoli e légende majeure se sont mutuellement ignorés.*" Eppure se si esaminano attentamente i miracoli appare evidente che l'ispiratore o per meglio dire il corrispondente da Siena con l'anonimo fiorentino sia appunto fr. Raimondo.

Finora nessuno ha pensato ad individuare quell'anonimo fiorentino ; quasi tutti hanno pensato a Niccolò Soderini, senza riflettere che il Soderini non poteva lasciare a mezzo un libro di ricordi di colei che fu per lui una vera madre. Credo che si debba pensare a Giannozzo Sacchetti che fu decapitato nel 1377 e lasciò in sospeso quel libretto di ricordi per tutte le vicende politiche in cui fu immischiato e di cui parlerò altrove.

Il Fawtier esagera enormemente l'importanza di quei miracoli, fino a scrivere, (pag. 96). " *C'est là vraiment le texte fondamental pour l'étude de la légende cathérinienne et l'on est en droit de s'étonner a priori de l'abandon dans lequel ce document capital a été laissé.*"

Nella seconda edizione dei *Fioretti di S. Caterina* ho cercato di studiare un po' più criticamente quel documento, facendone rilevare le inesattezze e contradizioni proprie dei documenti contemporanei scritti per sentita dire.

di Tommaso della Fonte e di Bartolomeo Dominici, *documenti unici in agiografia,* sono stati scientemente soppressi, senza dubbio dopo la morte di Raimondo da Capua, e l'autore di questa soppressione è Tommaso Caffarini."* Quest'accusa è grave, ma per fortuna manca di base.   Il documento fatto sparire prima del 1411, era stato scritto da fra Bartolomeo Dominici, di cui sopra abbiamo parlato, morto nel 1415, quando tutte le fonte cateriniane erano state scritte e divulgate.   Il Fawtier non ha pensato che quei *Miracula* che il Dominici mise a disposizione di fra Raimondo e di fra Tommaso e da essi largamente sfruttato, erano sua proprietà ; egli ne usufruì certamente per la sua deposizione bellissima al Processo e, dopo la sua morte, andarono dispersi, insieme ad altri materiali, come i quaderni di fra Raimondo, la leggenda minore in latino del Caffarini e una leggenda scritta dal Piccolomini.†

7.—Un personaggio che attira l'attenzione del Fawtier è Don Stefano Maconi, il generale dei certosini, di cui fortunatamente non mette in dubbio la veridicità e l'onestà.   Anzi si lamenta (pagina 114) che questo santo monaco, invece di scrivere una vita della Santa, si sia limitato a postillare quelle del B. Raimondo e del Caffarini.‡

8.—Indi, attacca direttamente la leggenda maggiore di Raimondo e la demolisce completamente (pagg. 118-130).   Sia come uomo politico che quale storico e scrittore, il B. Raimondo da Capua non è degno della fama che finora, egli afferma, ha usurpato.   E la dimostrazione la dà nei cinque capitoli seguenti, dove, passando in rassegna i principali fatti della vita di Caterina, dalla nascita alla morte, arriva alle seguenti conclusioni, (cito le più importanti) :

* Il Fawtier con un metodo critico insolito e assolutamente personale vuol fare apparire i *Miracula* di fra Tommaso della Fonte come contrari alla *Legenda maior,* e di qui la necessità del Caffarini di far sparire quei *miracula.*   Eppure abbiamo sopra visto quante volte il B. Raimondo nella sua *Legenda* cita con grande fedeltà quei quaderni del primo confessore, anzi nel *Supplementum* del Caffarini f. 168 leggiamo : " *dictus confessor* (fra Tommaso della Fonte) *presentavit ipsi fratri Raimundo cuncta que de virgine usque tunc contingerant ac etiam quaternos in quibus facta et dicta prout melius noverat in scriptis redigerat.*"   Un fatto veramente strano è questo : che il Fawtier con una minuziosità ammirevole cita anche tutti i passi del *Suppementum* dove il Caffarini ricorda i *quaderni* di fra Tommaso (pag. 105-6). In 86 punti il Caffarini ricorda fra Tommaso esplicitamente ; e dopo questa constatazione come è possibile pensare ad una voluta soppressione di quei quaderni ?   Le testimonianze dei *nemici* non si fanno così.   Riesce dunque inesplicabile la seguente asserzione del Fawtier (p. 104).   " *Il me semble bien que l'on peut avancer avec une quasi certitude que le miracula de Tommaso della Fonte et de Bartolomeo Dominici, document unique en hagiographie, ont été sciemment supprimés sans doute après la mort de Raymond de Capoue et que l'auteur de cette suppression est Tommaso Caffarini.*"

† Nella biblioteca nazionale di Brera in Milano il cod. AD.-IX. 11, proveniente dalla certosa di Pavia, contiene la *leggenda minore* del Caffarini con note autografe del Maconi. In quel manoscritto il Maconi ricorda una visione avuta di S. Caterina a Varazze e dice : " *Item inveni scriptum propria manu R. P. Magistri Raymundi sub tali forma.*"   Da queste parole il Fawtier deduce giustamente che fra Raimondo mentre era ancora in vita la Santa prendeva degli appunti e ricordi che sono poi andati perduti.

Per la leggenda minore del Caffarini cfr. lo studio molto interessante e decisivo del Fawtier, in *Mélanges,* a. XXXII (1912) p. 399.

Per la leggenda del Piccolomini la notizia è tratta dal P. Ugurgeri, *Pompe senesi.*

‡ Il Fawtier fu molto fortunato nello scoprire nei manoscritti della Brera di Milano alcuni codici maconiani provenienti da Pavia, AD. IX-38 ; AD. IX. 11 ; AD. IX. 35 ; ai quali ne va aggiunto un altro della Bibl. Vaticana : il Vatic. Lat. (10151), contenenti tutti la leggenda maggiore, la minore del Caffarini è il *Processus.*   Tutti questi quattro codici hanno delle note marginali, delle quali è autore il Maconi.   Però il Fawtier dubita che siano autografe, dal fatto che incontra spesso alla fine di quelle note un *etcetera,* segno dice di una trascrizione da un primo codice.   Osservazione sbagliata del tutto, non solo da un esame calligrafico con gli autografi conservati a Siena del Maconi, ma anche dal fatto de quell'*etcetera* è solo un segno convenzionale per indicare la fine del discorso precedente, come ho potuto constatare in altre note autografe marginali del Caffarini nel codice 3002 del Collegio Angelico in Roma.

" La Santa non è nata nel 1347, come finora si era creduto, ma almeno 10 anni prima ; entrò tra le mantellate non nel 1363*, ma nel 1352 (pag. 145); la lettera dove Caterina racconta la decapitazione di Toldo, è un falso del Caffarini† (pagg. 165-169) ; il suo uffiico di ambasciatrice dei Fiorentini presso Gregorio XI (pagine 172-180) non provato ; il ritorno del Papa a Roma per opera di Caterina (pagg. 180-188) è inverosimile ; l'azione della Santa per mettere pace tra la repubblica di Siena ed i Salimbeni, non si può provare (pagine 193-196) ; così il secondo viaggio della Santa a Firenze (pagg. 196-203). Il progetto di mandare Caterina alla regina Giovanna di Napoli, una faba (pagg. 206-8) ; la morte infine di Lei passa inosservata, non solo presso tutte le città italiane, ma anche in Siena ; solo un cronista fiorentino ed i suoi discepoli la piangono amaramente (pagg. 210-213)."

La chiusa è veramente glaciale.

Ma la conclusione di tutto il volume è quanto mai radicale.

Dopo aver detto che vi è stato un lavoro di *deformazione*, per lo più *cosciente*, per dei fini speciali, e di *cristallizzazione* in un periodo successivo, si domanda : " Che cosa può cavare lo storico da tutta la letteratura cateriniana ? " "Anche ammettendo—egli dice—che non si può esigere da un agiografo la stessa precisione di un cronista, poichè il suo fine è di edificare i suoi lettori più che informarli, bisogna riconoscere che l'esame fattone gli è singolarmente sfavorevole. Scartiamo anche il rimprovero che abbiamo fatto ad alcuni di tacere dei fatti importanti ; non consideriamo che le notizie dateci su fatti precisi, naturali, verificabili ; ebbene, non vi è quasi un caso dove non si debba constatare un lavoro di *deformazione ;* vi sono anche degli errori, e ciò che è più grave, degli errori volontari. *Il processo di Venezia* non è che una manifestazione organizzata per ottenere la canonizzazione, *una parodia* di *processo*. Il *supplemento* (del Caffarini) un *corpus* di documenti selezionati, appropriati e forse inventati. Ciò che abbiamo sotto il nome di Guglielmo Flete non è che una collezione di testi sospetti. La leggenda maggiore di Fra Raimondo, infine, è talmente piena di invenzioni, di errori e deformazioni, che bisognerebbe esitare a invocarne la testimonianza, anche nei punti dove ci dice la verità, tanto sono pochi. Solo due testi in lingua volgare, i *Miracoli* e la lettera di Barduccio Canigiani sembrano di un'utilizzazione meno azzardata. Ma cosa ci dicono ? Alcune notizie sui primi anni della Santa e un racconto dettagliato della sua morte."

" Su ciò che fa Caterina un personaggio importante nella storia, sul suo influsso nei grandi avvenimenti del secolo XIV, su la sua azione storica in uno parola, sembra che yi sia molto poco da tirare da l'agiografia cateriniana ; in

---

* Le ricerche dell'autore sulla famiglia sono molto interessanti (pp. 131-36).

† Un altro falso del Caffarini l'autore (p. 156) lo vede nella lettera 272 (ed. Tomm.) diretta a fr. Raimondo, dove la Santa nel 1377 racconta il modo miracoloso come imparò a scrivere. E come argomento cita la testimonianza dei *Miracoli* dell'anonimo fiorentino, scritti nel 1374, dove si dice che Caterina leggeva molto. Il Fawtier ha dimenticato che saper leggere non è sinonimo di saper scrivere, ed il modo come leggeva Caterina non era ordinario, poichè sapeva leggere ma non *sillabizzare*, come dice il B. Raimondo. Altro argomento forte sarebbe quello dei confessori. Tutti dicono che fr. Tommaso della Fonte fu il primo confessore, mentre il Fawtier riporta una cronaca di S. Maria Novella del sec. XVIII, dove si dice che nel 1352 fra Angiolo Adimari essendo *lettore* a Siena fu il *primo* confessore di Caterina bambina. L'Adimari fu a Siena nel 1352 ma non come lettore, bensì nel 1360 genn. 20, e allora potè essere confessore di Caterina. Il cronista fiorentino del 700 dovè confondere le date e da quella confusione il Fawtier ne à tratto un argomento per accusare di falso fr. Raimondo e il Caffarini. Tommaso della Fonte fu il vero direttore e confessore di Caterina, ma ciò non esclude che l'Adimari possa qualche volta aver confessato la bambina.

ogni modo è talmente tendenziosa, da non accettarne la minima asserzione, a meno che non sia confermata da testi completamente indipendenti da Raimondo da Capua e dai discepoli della Santa."*

Dopo una critica così radicale, dove di tutto il magnifico materiale cateriniano tramandatoci dai discepoli, non rimangono in piedi che due ruderi, dove quasi tutti i cateriniani appariscono come falsari, e la figura di Caterina Benincasa, gloria di Siena, dell'Italia, della Cristianità, viene ridotta a proporzioni miserabili, prego tutti di ascoltare le parole che il Fawtier scrisse sulla copia del volume che volle gentilmente offrirmi ; è una indiscrezione, ma necessaria :

"Al R. Padre Innocenzo Taurisano questo libro scritto con grande amore e rispetto della Santa e del suo Ordine Santo."

L'ANNO DI NASCITA. Esaminiamo con calma i due problemi fondamentali sui quali il critico francese basa tutto il suo lavoro : *la data di nascita e l'entrata di Caterina fra le Mantellate :* 1347 e 1363, secondo la testimonianza del B. Raimondo da Capua e degli altri discepoli.

Il Fawtier nega recisamente che Caterina sia nata nel 1347 e la fa nascere verso il 1337 ; poi accusa Raimondo di avere falsata la verità, e, ciò che è più grave, coscientemente.

Raimondo scrisse che Caterina morì in Roma nel 1380 nell'età di 33 anni. " Ora,—scrive il Fawtier a pag. 138—la Leggenda Maggiore ha contro di essa il fatto che l'età di 33 anni in cui il suo autore fa morire la Santa, è sospetto : è l'età del Cristo. Vi sarà forse una coincidenza, ma però è curioso. Ed è ugualmente curioso constatare come Raimondo da Capua non ci dice in verità quando Caterina è nata, dice solamente che è morta a 33 anni nel 1380. Come sapeva egli l'età della Santa ? Da lei stessa ? Ma si può accordare credito a questa ipotesi che non ha per appoggio nemmeno una parola di Raimondo ? Bisognerà credere che Monna Lapa, la madre di Caterina, ha informato il nostro autore ? Ma noi abbiamo visto quale credito dare a questa buona persona. Nè bisogna dimenticare che abbiamo a

---

* " Quel parti peut tirer l'historien de toute cette littérature ? Même en ne perdant pas de vue que l'on ne saurait exiger d'un hagiographe la même précision que d'un chroniqueur, que son but est d'édifier ses lecteurs plutôt que de les renseigner, il faut reconnaître que l'examen que nous venons de faire leur est singulièrement défavorable. Ecartons même le reproche que nous avons pu faire à certain d'entre eux, de passer sous silence des faits importants, ne considérons que les renseignements qu'ils nous donnent sur des faits précis, naturels, vérifiables ; il n'y a presque pas de cas où l'on ne puisse constater un travail de déformation, il y a même un certain nombre d'erreurs, et, ce qui est plus grave, d'erreurs volontaires.

Des légendes mineures, serviles reproductions de l'œuvre de Raymond de Capoue, il n'y a rien à tirer. Le Procès di Venise n'est qu' une manifestation organisée pour amener la canonisation, une parodie de procès. Le *Supplementum,* un *corpus* de documents triés, appropriés, ou peut-être fabriqués. Ce que l'on nous donne sous le nom de William Flete n'est qu'une collection de textes suspects. La légende Majeure enfin est tellement encombrée d'inventions, d'erreurs et de déformations, que l'on devrait hésiter à invoquer son témoignage, même sur les points où son auteur nous dit la vérité, si peu nombreux soient-ils. Seuls, deux textes, en langue vulgaire, les *Miracoli* et la lettre de Barduccio Canigiani, semblent d'une utilisation moins hasardeuse. Mais que nous donnent-ils ? Quelques renseignements sur les premières années de la sainte, un récit détaillé de sa mort.

Sur ce qui fait de Catherine un personnage important dans l'histoire, sur son rôle dans les grands évènements du XIV siècle, sur son action historique en un mot, il semble qu'il y ait vraiment bien peu à tirer de l'hagiographie cathérinienne et, dans tous les cas, celle-ci est tellement tendancieuse qu'on ne saurait en accepter la moindre assertion, à moins qu'elle ne soit confirmée par des textes complètement indépendants de Raymond de Capoue et des disciples de la sainte " (pp. 215-16).

are con gente del popolo, con dei Toscani, per i quali il tempo non ha che un valore relativo e la cronologia non ha nessun interesse."

Questo significa far della critica scientificamente !

A queste domande del Fawtier risponde lo stesso B. Raimondo, il quale nella chiusa del primo capitolo, dove parla della nascita di Caterina e dei primi anni, scrive :*

" Queste cose le quali io ho dette in questo capitolo, parte sono note quasi a tutta la città o vero grande parte di essa, e parte ne ebbi da essa sacra Vergine e da la predecta Lapa madre sua e parte da più religiosi e più secolari e quali tucti furono vicini e noti o vero parenti di Jacopo (padre di Caterina)." E come nel primo caso, alla fine di ogni capitolo mette fr. Raimondo le fonti viventi o personali da cui à attinte le sue informazioni.

Secondo il Fawtier, dunque, Raimondo ha fatto morire Caterina a 33 anni per trarne una conformità con Cristo e opporla a S. Francesco, di cui appunto in quegli anni uscì il famoso libro delle conformità con Gesù. Ora bisogna sapere che Raimondo cerca, sì, un paragone dei 33 anni di Caterina, non però con quelli di Gesù, ma con gli anni della penitenza di S. Maria Maddalena ; anzi dice espressamente che è *una bestemmia paragonare il Cristo con i Santi.†* Chi ha dunque alterata e deformata la verità ?

Il Fawtier cerca un documento ed una nuova prova alla sua tesi in quel prezioso scritto dei *Miracoli della Beata Caterina*, che principia così :

" Venne a Firenze del mese di maggio anno 1374, quando fu il Capitolo de' Frati Predicatori, per comandamento del Maestro dell'Ordine, una vestita delle pinzochere di Santo Domenico ch'ha nome Caterina di Jacopo da Siena, la quale è d'etade di *venzette anni*, quale si reputa che sia santa serva di Dio, e con lei tre altre donne pinzochere del suo abito, le quali stanno a sua guardia, ecc."

Se nel 1374 aveva Caterina ventisette anni, ne segue che nacque nel 1347.

Questa testimonianza chiara, lampante, indipendente dal B. Raimondo e da Lapa, vien dichiarata dubbia dal critico francese, per aver trovato, nel corso della narrazione, un errore, spiegabile d'altronde, dell'autore dei *Miracoli*, circa la morte del padre di Caterina. Allora, costruisce due crono- logie : A e B : la prima desunta dalla data sopra riferita e l'altra dall'errore commesso dal cronista fiorentino ; e accetta la seconda per cogliere in fallo Raimondo (p. 137). Anzi, a confortare la sua tesi, giunge sino a supporre un'alterazione nel manoscritto dei *Miracoli*, e, ciò che è peggio, a battezzare il codice Laurenziano‡, che contiene quel testo, per un codice scritto dopo la canonizzazione della Santa, verso il 1480, sol perchè . . . un copista aggiunse al volume, in due pagine rimaste bianche, i distici composti da Pio II in onore della Santa. Chi giudica di lontano gli argomenti del Fawtier può rimanere

---

* Vedi sopra p. 328.

† " Verum nolo putes, amantissime lector, me per omnia supra dicta, hanc virginem in sanctitate omnibus suprasceptis sanctis praeponere voluisse, aut etiam inter sanctos odiosas comparationes fecisse. Non ita desipio lector bone, nominari inter ceteros Salvatorem, cui aliquem sanctum comparare scio blasfemiam esse. . . . " A SS. n. 65.

‡ É lo Strozziano XXXI che contiene una copia del *Dialogo*, i *Miracoli*, il *Transito*, tutti di una mano della fine del XIV secolo. In fondo al codice, in due fogli bianchi, uno scrittore umanista trascrisse i versi di Pio II in lode di Caterina. Cfr. Fiorilli, *Libro della Divina Dottrina*, Laterza, Bari, 1912, p. 427.

sorpreso, ma ho esaminato diverse volte quel codice fiorentino insieme ad insigni paleografi e tutti sono d'accordo che il manoscritto è di poco posteriore alla morte di Caterina, cioè verso ll 1395 ; cade dunque tutta la cronologia A e B, architettata dal Sig. Fawtier.

Qui bisogna aggiungere qualche cosa di più grave. Abituato a controllare sempre, volli andare a Milano per vedere i codici annotati da D. Stefano Maconi, scoperti dal Fawtier. Il manoscritto della *Legenda Major* porta 10 postille marginali, tutte con precisione descritte dal Fawtier (p. 115). Esaminando però il codice prezioso*, m'accorsi di un fatto : il critico aveva saltato il foglio 2, dove, accanto al racconto della nascita di Caterina, il Maconi aggiunge in margine : *videlicet anno Domini MCCCXLVII ;* cioè : *nell'anno del Signore* 1347.

Ebbi uno scatto. Perchè il Fawtier ha taciuta la testimonianza di quel Maconi, di cui non mette in dubbio la veridicità, anzi lamenta che non scrisse una vita della Santa ? Gli sfuggì forse ?

L'ENTRATA NELL'ORDINE. Ma lo sforzo principale, il cavallo di battaglia del critico francese, per battere in breccia l'opera del B. Raimondo è sulla data dell'entrata della Santa tra le Mantellate, data che il Fawtier crede di avere scoperta in un piccolo quadernetto in pergamena che si conserva nella biblioteca comunale di Siena, inchiodato alla coperta di un altro codice cateriniano†. Contiene tre elenchi di Mantellate, il primo del 1321 con 65 nomi, il secondo del 1352 con 99 nomi, scritto da sedici mani differenti, il terzo del 1378 con 94 nomi tutti di una medesima mano, a cui furono aggiunti altri 26 nomi da altre mani.

La seconda lista del 1352, è stata, diciamo così, il raggio di luce rivelatore per il Fawtier, il quale ne à fatto il perno di tutto il suo volume ; tanto è vero, che ad una mia lettera di alta meraviglia per la distruzione operata, mi rispondeva : " bisogna demolire la lista del 52 se si vuol riabilitare la Leggenda Maggiore " ; e sottolineò *demolire.*

Nel 1352 delle voci calunniose si sparsero in Siena contro le Mantellate, ed i superiori, per tagliar corto a quelle dicerie, l'11 agosto riunirono tutte le mantellate senesi alla presenza del priore del convento, fra Matteo Maconi, fra Bartolomeo Mini, priore di S. Gemignano e del loro direttore fra Corrado di Pistoia, professore in convento, perchè giurassero solennemente di portar sempre fino alla morte l'abito di mantellata. 27 nomi, tutti di una mano, seguono l'intestazione e poi seguono altri nomi a piccoli gruppi di 4, di 6, di 10. Al 58.o posto troviamo *Katerina Jacobi Benencasa,* e all'82 *Domina Lapa Jacobi,* la madre.

Di fonte a questa lista così varia nelle scritture, viene naturale il pensare che il primo gruppo, di 27, fu quello che giurò nel 1352 di portar sempre l'abito, mentre gli altri piccoli gruppi sono le nuove ascritte degli anni successivi ; gruppi che aumentano dopo l'entrata di Caterina, e la ragione è intuitiva.

---

*AD. IX. 38. Le postille del Maconi sono ai ff. 4, 93, 110, 142, 150 v., 155 v., 167, 170, 170 v., 171.

† Fu pubblicato per la prima volta dal Grottanelli, *Regole del terzo ordine di S. Domecio, volgarizzata nel buon secolo della lingua da fra Tommaso Caffarini,* Torino, 1864, pp. 35-40 ; ultimamente negli *Studi Cateriniani,* a III. ff. I.-II. pp. 35-65 dal Marchese Piero Misciatelli.

E che le Mantellate sieno state 27 in quell'anno 1352, e non più, è facile arguirlo dal fatto che nel 1347 e 48 la valanga della peste in Siena e nel contado fece perire 80 mila persone, e le vecchie mantellate non furorno certo risparmiate.

Ma per il Fawtier non è così : tutta la lista per lui è del 1352 ; ed allora egli argomenta : se Caterina nel 1352 era già terziaria, non potè essere nata nel 1347, come afferma Raimondo, altrimenti si verrebbe ad ammettere questo assurdo : che la Santa fu Mantellata a 6 anni ; dunque, conclude trionfalmente, Raimondo da Capua ha detto il falso, e volontariamente, per far rassomigliare Caterina a Gesù con i 33 anni.

Ed in che modo cerca di spiegare la differenza delle scritture ? Se ne sbriga dicendo, che, essendo molte le Mantellate e sparse in tutta la città, non vennero tutte nel '52, ma un po' per volta nelle successive adunanze. Sicchè, secondo il Fawtier, alla solennissima riunione, tenuta nell'agosto del 1352, nella quale le Mantellate dovevano giurare di portar l'abito fino alla morte, su 96 ascritte se ne presentarono appena 27, e persino S. Caterina, che abitava presso la Chiesa, la madre, la cognata e il gruppo delle più fervorose furono assenti e si presentarono dopo, in altre adunanze. . . . Ogni commento guasta !

Qui bisognerebbe addentrarsi nell'esame interno del documento, ma non è questo il luogo nè il momento.* Del resto è stato già fatto dal Prof. Jordan della Sorbona, dal P. Mandonnet e in modo speciale dal Prof. Pardi. Aggiungo solo alcune considerazioni.

Se Raimondo e il Caffarini vengono accusati dal Fawtier, come sopra è stato accennato, d'aver fatto sparire i *Miracula* di fra Tommaso della Fonte, come mai quei due falsari non fecero sparire quella lista di mantellate che è il principale atto di accusa, e che è rimasta nel convento di S. Domenico di Siena fino al 1780 ? Quella lista il Caffarini la conosceva benissimo, anzi la cita in un suo lavoro pubblicato da Flaminio Corner, in quell'opera stupenda sulle chiese venete.†

E se queste argomentazioni non fossero sufficienti, vorrei ricordare che ammettendo l'entrata di Caterina fra le Mantellate nel 1352, si verrebbe ad una constatazione molto piccante. Sia i *Miracoli* dell'anonimo fiorentino che fra Raimondo e fra Bartolomeo Dominici, sono concordi nel dire che la morte di Bonaventura, sorella della Santa, avvenuta nel 1362, trasse Caterina dalla piccola, passeggera crisi di mondanità, subìta più che voluta, spingendola totalmente a Dio. Ora, durante quella crisi, sappiamo che Caterina si fece i capelli biondi, per piacere ! Se quindi, secondo il Fawtier, Caterina nel 1352 era già mantellata, ne segue che dieci anni dopo, pure essendo vestita da Mantellata si ossigenò i capelli per piacere. . . .

A questo proposito bisogna osservare che uno dei lati più caratteristici della critica del Fawtier è questo : dopo aver provato e riprovato una tesi, si fa da se stesso le difficoltà, e naturalmente se le scioglie ad uso e consumo suo.

---

* A tutti gli argomenti del Fawtier per sostenere essere quella lista tutta del 52 hanno esaurientemente risposto il prof. Jordan della Sorbona, *La date de naissance de S. Ch. de Sienne* in *Analecta Bollandiana* a. 1922 ; P.P. Mandonnet O.P., *S. Cath. de Sienne et la critique historique*, in *Année dominicaine*, Janvier 1923 pp. 6-17 e Fevrier 1923 pp. 43-52. La lista è stata poi oggetto di un acuto esame da parte del Prof. Pardi, in *Studi Cateriniani*, a. II (1925) n. 2.

† *Ecclesiae venetae antiquis documentis*, Venetiis 1749, Dec. XI pars prior, pag. 19-20.

Così a p. 149 si pone la difficoltà della morte di Bonaventura nel 1362 e della crisi di mondanità subita da Caterina prima di quella sventura. E come la scioglie ? Dice che si può benissimo affermare che la Santa si fece mantellata nel 1352, poi subì la crisi mondana spinta dalla sorella (durante la quale si fece i capelli biondi), e poi dopo la morte di Bonaventura, ritornata in sè, si tagliò i capelli. . . . E' così illogico e anormale questo ragionamento e questa alchimia per salvare una tesi da farci dubitare seriamente sulla serietà del signor Fawtier.

NICCOLÒ DI TOLDO. Ciò che ha dato però un senso di rivolta è stato l'aver negato l'autenticità della mirabile lettera di Caterina, dove la Santa racconta con accenti meravigliosi la decapitazione del perugino Niccolò di Toldo che aveva sparlato della repubblica.* Il Fawtier ebbe la fortuna di trovare due lettere del cardinale legato di Perugia ai reggitori di Siena per intercedere e avere grazia ; lettere che avrebbero dovuto confermarlo e dargli una prova di autenticità ; invece no, sol perchè non ha trovato nell'-archivio senese una risposta, nè l'accenno della decapitazione in qualche cronista, chiama apografa la lettera (pp. 169 e 171). E' una leggerezza imperdonabile per un critico.

Con sincerità di storico, il Fawtier doveva dirci che dal 1374 al 1380 nell'archivio di Stato di Siena vi è un solo libretto di minute di risposte date dalla Repubblica alle lettere ricevute ; quel libretto è del 1376, gli altri sono perduti. Perchè ha taciuto questo ? Ed aggiungo : non è solo in quella mirabile lettera che Caterina parla di Toldo, ma anche in un'altra†, e poi anche nel *Dialogo*, segno che l'affare era molto grave, e ne parla in modo misterioso, quasi paurosa di rivelare il segreto, ciò che ci fa supporre il silenzio voluto dalla repubblica su quel fatto e la fretta avuta nella decapitazione.

Come è poi possibile giudicare un documento apografo con i soli criteri esterni ? Non esiste più la critica letteraria di un documento ?

---

* Fedele al suo metodo il Fawtier esaminando la vita di S. Caterina sotto un titolo generale : *histoire et legende* dal 1352 al 1380, tocca soltanto i punti dove crede di poter cogliere in fallo fra Raimondo. Così nella questione dello scrivere (p. 155-57) ; il supplizio dei due banditi sulle forche (p. 157) ; la conversione della famigli Tolomei (p. 157-58) ; l'altra di Andrea Naddini (p. 158-59). Uno studio speciale dedica l'autore al silenzio conservato dai biografi di Caterina sulla venuta a Firenze per essere esaminata dal capitolo generale.

Le sue osservazioni sono in parte giuste ; e certo appare inesplicabile quel silenzio, se non conoscessimo i metodi tutto speciali usati dai cronisti medioevali, i quali mentre si fermano su dei fatti trascurabili passano sopra con una disinvoltura che disorienta su fatti gravissimi che interessavano tutti.

Si può anche supporre, in questo caso, che gli agiografi domenicani e secolari, sia per rispetto ai superiori dell'Ordine sia per non rivelare cose intime di famiglia abbiano voluto sorvolare su quella pagina dolorosa, che conosciamo solo dall'*anonimo* fiorentino autore dei *Miracoli*.

† Nella lettera 90 (ed. Gigli) e 272 (ed. Tomm.) scritta di sua mano dalla Rocca di Tentennano nel 1377, la Santa nelle 4 petizioni fatte a Dio (come poi nel Dialogo) ricorda appunto la quarta : " dimandando l'aiutorio e la provvidenza di Dio, di provvedere in alcuno caso che era divenuto d'alcuna creatura, il quale per iscritto non vi posso contare, ma con la parola viva vel dirò se già Dio non mi facesse tanto di grazia o di misericordia che l'anima mia si partisse da questo miserabile corpo prima che io vi vedessi." E più oltre, riportando la risposta del Padre celeste, dice : ". . . E mirando con ansietato desiderio dimostrava (Iddio) la dannazione di colui per cui era divenuto il caso e di cui era pregato, dicendo : Io voglio che tu sappi che per camparlo dall'eterna dannazione nella quale tu vedi ch'egli era, io gli permisi questo caso acciocchè col sangue suo nel sangue mio avesse vita, perocchè non aveva dimenticato la riverenza e amore che aveva alla dolcissima madre Maria. Sicchè per misericordia gli ò fatto questo che gl'ignoranti tengono in crudeltà."

Di questo episodio di sangue che lasciò traccie sì profonde nella vita di S. Caterina vedi anche ciò che ho scritto nel *Dialogo*, prefazione.

Avignone. Man mano che l'opera di Caterina grandeggia e da angelo di pace entra animosa nel campo sociale e religioso, l'opera del critico francese si intensifica così, da volerne ad ogni costo sminuire l'importanza, facendoci di continuo vedere in Raimondo da Capua un deformatore e spesso un mentitore.

Il viaggio ad Avignone per intercedere pace per i Fiorentini, missione di cui negli archivi fiorentini non si trova, è vero, traccie, ma che viene attestata da Raimondo, da Stefano Maconi e da Bartolomeo Dominici, e specialmente dalle lettere di aspro rimprovero di Caterina verso gli astuti mercanti che la ingannarono, trova nel Fawtier un tremendo giudice (pp. 72-80).*

Più terribile è la requisitoria contro Raimondo e compagni quando il Fawtier esamina l'opera di Caterina per il ritorno del Papa in Italia (pp. 180-188). Vi è un accanimento che sconcerta, e non si comprende bene il perchè di tanto livore, da giungere sino a dire, che Caterina andò in Avignone per la Crociata soltanto e che vide una sola volta il Papa in Avignone ; e con quale lusso di documenti !

Per il Fawtier tutto è tendenzioso.† Egli appartiene ad una moderna scuola storica francese che cerca di esaltare i papi di Avignone ; egli vuol farci apparire Gregorio XI come pontefice dalla ferma volontà, mentre nella medesima pagina,‡ disinvoltamente contraddicendosi, lo dice in balìa dei varî umori della corte pontificia. *Gregorio XI*, egli dice, *non è una marionetta nelle mani di una piccola religiosa italiana.* Caterina, conclude, non à avuto nessuna parte nel ritorno del papato a Roma. E toglie così dalla corona d'oro che cinge il capo della nostra Santa la perla più fulgida.§

Ma è stato, per fortuna, un semplice tentativo di furto. Il Fawtier ha detto il falso, come ho provato e documentato in una conferenza tenuta all'Università di Torino e in quella di Siena, la prima il 16 maggio e la seconda il 12 giugno 1928.

Più acre e violenta è la requisitoria del critico contro il frate nel discutere l'opera di Caterina in Roma presso Urbano VI e presso la voluttuosa regina Giovanna di Napoli, durante lo scisma (p. 204-7). Egli cerca di impicciolire, sminuire, svalutare i documenti, l'attività mirabile di quella donna che vedeva naufragare con lo scisma il suo sogno ; il Papa in Roma, la pace in Italia e

---

* Sulle relazioni tra S. Caterina e Firenze ho trattato in una conferenza tenuta a Siena nell'-Università nel maggio 1927. La conclusione del Fawtier è questa : " Nous croyons donc pouvoir conclure que Sainte Catherine de Sienne n'a nullement été chargée d'une ambassade officielle—secrète ou non—par les Huit, et que le moins que l'on puisse dire du rôle que lui fait jouer Raymond de Capoue est qu'il a été exagéré au point d'en devenir méconnaissable " (pag. 180).

† Spinto dalla smania di tutto negare nega anche le notizie date dal Maconi e dal Domnici i soli discepoli che lui crede degni di fede. Ma per il ritorno del Papa in Roma è implacabile. A pag. 184 dice : " Il semble donc sage de ne pas parler du rôle de S. Cath. dans le retour de la papauté à Rome, rôle que les circonstances rendent invraisemblables, et que le silence de tous les documents contemporains n'est pas fait pour faire accepter sans preuve." . . .

‡ " Ce n'est pas le cas de Grégoire XI, dont tout le monde s'accorde à reconnaître la ferme volonté, dont la cour et la famille étaient nettement hostiles au retour en Italie. . . . E più sotto nella medesima pag. 182 dice : "Adversaires et partisans de l'idée du retourà Rome surveillaient soigneusement le Pape, leurs ambassadeurs rendaient compte de ses fluctuations à leurs gouvernements." . . . Dove è quindi la ferma volontà con quelle *fluctuations ?*

§ Invece il Fawtier vuol provare che la Santa andò ad Avignone solo per la Crociata e vuole assolutamente escludere la sua missione pacificatrice per Firenze e il ritorno del papato in Roma.

nella Chiesa e la Crociata. Bisogna distruggere tutte le fonti agiografiche per togliere a Caterina l'onore di essere stato il baluardo del papato.*

CONCLUSIONE. Ammainando le vele, ecco la sintesi di questo studio :

A Raimondo da Capua, Tommaso Caffarini ed a tutti i discepoli, venne da Caterina affidata una delle più nobili ed insieme più gravose eredità che madre potesse lasciare ai figli ; essi dovevano proseguire l'opera appena sbozzata, appena iniziata da Lei, dovevano purificare la Chiesa dai cattivi pastori, ricondurre la pace nell'ovile insanguinato e disperso di Cristo, dovevano spingere l'Ordine domenicano e gli altri Ordini religiosi verso le loro origini. E, raggiungere questo altissimo ideale in nome di Cristo e in nome di Caterina. Responsabilità tremenda che solo l'amore poteva rendere leggera ; ed i discepoli, benchè di tanto inferiori alla loro Madre, consacrarono tutta la vita a questo nobilissimo ideale. Parlare dunque, scrivere, far conoscere la Santa, divulgarne gli scritti, ottenerne la canonizzazione, far sentire nella società convulsa dei loro tempi la parola possente di Lei, portare Cristo nella società nel nome di Caterina, ecco l'opera magnifica dei *Caterinati*. E per adempiere a questo mandato vi era forse bisogno di *deformare* e, ciò che è peggio, *cristallizzare* la vita della Santa?

Questo non ha pensato nè poteva immaginarlo il Fawtier. Non sono stati i discepoli a creare, come vuol far leggere fra le righe, ad immortalare Caterina ; Dante non è Dante per i suoi commentatori, anzi, ma è la vita, le opere e gli scritti, la scintilla divina che alita in ogni vero genio, che hanno immortalato Caterina !

Conosco le esigenze della critica e dei suoi metodi ; ma è bene ricordarlo, la critica è come il ferro in mano del chirurgo : se la mano non è ferma, se non è guidata dall'occhio clinico e dalla lunga esperienza, il ferro sarà mortale.

L'errore fondamentale del Fawtier, è stato di cominciare il suo studio delle fonti cateriniane con la sicurezza matematica di trovarvi un materiale avariato, alterato, una *deformazione ;* necessaria quindi una operazione radicale di sfrondamento e di distruzione. Errore questo proprio della scuola ipercritica del secolo scorso e che tante rovine ha accumulate. Il restauro di uno storico ed artistico edificio non si compie distruggendolo dalle fondamenta.

Il secondo errore, e questo di metodo, è di aver studiate le fonti agiografiche prescindendo dalle lettere di Caterina ; studio che doveva precedere, non seguire.

Terzo errore : di aver trascurato di darci la figura morale dei discepoli, studiandone la vita ed inquadrandola nell'ambiente storico.

Quarto errore : di considerare tutto un testo sospetto e falso sol perchè vi è stato riscontrato qualche errore di dettaglio o non vi è conferma in altri

---

* Le lettere autografe dei discepoli pubblicate dal Grottanelli o. c. sono la conferma più viva di ciò che Caterina fece in Roma a prò della Chiesa e per ricondurre sulla retta via la regina Giovanna di Napoli ; cfr. la lettera XVI (Grottanelli, p. 288) di fr. Bartolomeo Dominici al Pagliaresi che era a Napoli mandatovi da Caterina appunto per la regina Giovanna. Tra l'altro dice : " La mamma à creduto più volte venire e non pare che Dio l'abbia ordenato, nè el Vicario suo non à consentito, bene che avesse detto che gli piaceva." . . . Queste parole scritte privatamente confermano pienamente la testimonianza del B. Raimondo che il Fawtier vorrebbe intaccare. A queste lettere fanno riscontro le lettere dell'ambasciadore senese presso la corte Romana, il quale in due lettere, tra quelle rimaste, parla del grande favore che godeva Caterina presso il Papa, Questi documenti come al solito, hanno poco valore per il Fawtier. Una lettera del 30 nov. 1378 è stata pubblicata dal Grottanelli, o. c. pag, 274 ; cfr. anche il Fawtier, p. 205-8 che riporta il passo del Dominici e trova *strana* la coincidenza col racconto di fra Raimondo. . . .

documenti. Con un metodo simile non sarebbe più possibile scrivere la storia. Inoltre non è sana critica accanirsi, qual cane con uno straccio, con fra Raimondo da Capua che la Chiesa annovera fra i Beati,* buttare il ridicolo su persone venerabili ; far dello spirito con delle freddure ; trovare tutto curioso ; spargere su tutti il sospetto, accusare gratuitamente di mala fede : scrivere insomma senza quella serenità che è la dote essenziale dello storico e del critico, che deve sollevarsi e dominare uomini e cose. La mancanza di serenità ha avuto questa fatale conseguenza nel suo studio : una contraddizione continua, aggravata da un latente fine politico.

Eppure, nonostante questi difetti gravissimi, nonostante le conclusioni arbitrarie e illogiche, questo saggio di critica letteraria sulle fonti cateriniane si impone per la ricchezza della documentazione, per la risoluzione di molti problemi, e per averci fatto conoscere dei materiali nuovi.

Se non fosse mancato al Fawtier l'equilibrio e la serenità, avremmo sicuramente avuto un capolavoro di ricostruzione storica.

I. TAURISANO, O.P.

---

* Dispiace dover constatare e dire come sia sfuggito agli scrittori di cose cateriniane il fine speciale che spinse il Beato Raimondo da Capua a scrivere la vita della sua santa penitente. Le contradizioni accanite e insistenti a cui fu esposta la santità di S. Caterina non finirono con la morte di Lei, ma seguitarono ancor più violente, e la *legenda maior* del B. Raimondo ha un fine prevalentemente polemico, per far tacere i contradittori, i quali ostacolavano così la canonizzazione di Caterina voluta dai buoni. Quel fine polemico se tolse alla *legenda maior* l'incanto delle antiche vite di santi, la semplicità ed il candore, ci diede però una vita scritta direi con criteri scientifici, tutta a base di controlli e di citazioni di persone viventi, unico esempio questo nell'agiografia medievale. Alla fine di ogni capitolo, come è stato sopra dimostrato, l'autore cita con cura le fonti da cui attinse le notizie, precorrendo così le moderne fonti bibliografiche. La *legenda maior* fu pubblicata nel 1553 a Colonia dal certosino Teodoro Loher a Stratis, ma quell'edizione è rarissima ; poi dai Bollandisti in *Acta Sanctorum* al XXIX aprile. Si consultino il cap. V della II parte n. 168 e sgg., e il cap. XV.

(c) CONFERENCE GIVEN BY
REV. FATHER I. TAURISANO, O.P.

in the University of Turin, May 16th, 1928, and repeated in the University of Siena, June 12th, 1928, now published with the author's kind permission.

S. CATERINA ED IL RITORNO DEL PAPATO A ROMA

Non credo dir cose nuove affermando : che il centro di gravità dell'incivilimento, dopo essersi spostato dall'Asia, con i grandi imperi militari in Egitto e poi lungamente in Grecia trova il suo assetto in Roma, prima nella Roma repubblicana ed imperiale poi definitivamente nella Roma cristiana. Sembra che oggi questo centro si vada spostando, ma noi sappiamo che l'oro colle sue conseguenze politiche e militari à dei poteri migratorii. Quant' oro non è passato dall'Italia ! Il primato dell' oro è tramontato, ma Roma è rimasta il centro di gravità morale e religiosa del mondo. Spostare questo centro, è spostare l'equilibrio di leggi superiori, che non si possono impunemente offendere. Una prova, durissima prova, fu tentata nel 300, che fu il secolo di tutti gli ardimenti, ma le conseguenze furono così micidiali, la lezione così dura da consigliare i dirigenti a non ripetere più la prova. Il trasferimento del Papato in Avignone, rendendo il Papato francese, fu la causa iniziale di quel profondo turbamento politico, religioso e sociale che sconvolse non solo l'Italia ma divise la cristianità, e preparò la defezione del nord d'Europa con le conseguenti terribili guerre di religione. Conosco benissimo tutta la moderna scuola francese che cerca di mettere in nuova luce i Papi d'Avignone, ma la questione è molto più complessa ; essa sorvola sui singoli fatti e le persone per fermarsi sul principio che il Papato deve rimanere nel suo centro naturale, in questa Roma cioè, *onde Cristo è Romano.*

Caterina da Siena vide tutto questo, lo sentì istintivamente come tutti i suoi contemporanei, e forte d'una forza che le veniva dal Cristo, opera e va ad Avignone per strappare definitivamente il Pontefice da quella terra non sua, per ricondurlo a Roma. Il grande fatto storico del ritorno rimase offuscato dal susseguente scisma sì, ma la storia non si ferma ad un fatto conseguente, per quanto grave, ma corre dritta alle leggi regolatrici dell'umanità, come il medico che dopo l'iniezione del siero salvatore non si allarma della necessaria reazione organica, anzi ne gode, poichè è l'indice della sanità che ritorna.

La miopia nella storia, e non solo nella storia, non è stata mai una virtu !

Nel 1376 il nome di Caterina era già universalmente conosciuto ; la sua santità mirabile non era più chiusa nella piccola cerchia delle mura senesi, le sue penitenze, i digiuni lunghissimi, le estasi continue dopo la S. Comunione, le attrazioni potenti che esercitava su tutti quelli che l'avvicinavano amici e nemici, eransi divulgate come onde concentriche in tutta la cristianità. Le lettere di fuoco che Caterina scriveva per portare ai lontani la sua parola e la volontà energica erano lette, commentate, conservate come reliquie e richieste ansiosamente da grandi e da piccoli, piu dai grandi che dai piccoli : in un periodo in pieno dissolvimento l'apparizione di santità doveva commuovere profondamente gli animi che vedevano nel divino l'unica ancora di salvezza. Si aggiunga che la santità di Caterina aveva subito due anni avanti, nel 1374, la prova del fuoco. Poichè tutta la terrificante malvolenza umana, che in quel secolo toccò profondità sconosciute oggi, si abbatè sulla debole fanciulla, ed i superiori del suo Ordine domenicano la chiamarono in giudizio a Firenze nello stupendo Capitolo di S. Maria Novella davanti a tutti i Padri riuniti nella Pentecoste di quell'anno in assemblea internazionale. Lo spirito di Dio si rivelò manifesto davanti a quel supremo consesso di inquisitori, e Caterina potè d'allora in poi, guidata da fr. Raimondo da Capua, discendente di quel Pier delle Vigne che

> tenne . . . ambo le chivai
> del cuor di Frederico

potè cominciare un apostolato unico di donna e predicare la crociata per alleggerire la pressione del sangue in quell'organismo in dissoluzione, volere la pace tra le repubbliche italiane, lavorare per la riforma della Chiesa e specialmente ricondurre il Papa a Roma. Tutte le grandi questioni erano imperniate su quel fulcro ; bisognava assolutamente risolvere quel problema insolubile, poichè Gregorio XI prometteva sempre ma non atteneva mai.

L'occasione non poteva mancare.

Inutile rifare la storia, accenno soltano. Milano con i Visconti, Firenze dal 1371 al 78, fu il centro della rivolta contro la Chiesa. E poichè in guerra di tutto si profitta, cosi tutti i numerosi errori dei legati papali in Italia nell'amministrazione del Patrimonio di S. Pietro sono messi abilmente a profitto, ingigantiti, lumeggiati dal nascente umanesimo che trovò in Coluccio Salutati, cancelliere della republica Fiorentina, un abile manovratore. Bisogna leggere non solo i proclami a stampa, ma quei molti inviti nell'archivio di stato di Firenze, diretti ai Comuni italiani, alle repubbliche toscane, a Roma, Bologna, Perugia, per sentire come sapevano toccare il tema della libertà contro i nuovi barbari che scendevano in Italia considerata terra da conquista. Gregorio XI rimandando di continuo la data di ritorno in Roma aumentò il malcontento generale e la rivolta scoppiò furibonda. Il Pontefice dopo vari tentativi di pace andati falliti per il malvolere fiorentino, finalmente lanciò il 31 maggio 1376 l'interdetto contro Firenze, mettendola al bando della cristianità. Il colpo era terribile. Nella preoccupazione generale per i commerci che fallivano e il danno spirituale susseguente, la parte guelfa di Firenze, che era uno stato nello stato, corse ai ripari e si pensò di mandare ad Avignone Caterina da Siena, per implorare pace. L'intervento della parte guelfa in quel torbido pericolo di storia fiorentina, non studiato dagli storici di S. Caterina, à portato a dei giudizi superficiali e delle conclusioni erronee.

Già Caterina, spinta dal proprio sentimento e anche dalla parte guelfa, aveva ripetutamente scritto a Gregorio XI implorando pace e misericordia. Fece anche di piu, mandando Neri dei Pagliaresi, suo discepolo, e fra Raimondo da Capua, suo direttore, ad Avignone per disporre il Pontefice a miti consigli. E quando sotto la pressione della parte guelfa, del popolo malcontento per l'interdetto e più per lo stringersi delle milizie papali attorno al territorio della republica, Caterina vien chiamata a Firenze per essere mandata ad Avignone, noi ci domandiamo : fu manovra politica di ordine interno o sincero desiderio di pace ? Lo svolgimento del dramma ci dice che fu una manovra politica. Infatti Caterina seguita da 22 discepoli, va in Avignone dove arriva il 18 Giugno, suscitando naturalmente un enorme interesse.

Vedere una Santa, parlare, toccare, assistere ai miracoli di una santa quale . . . quale sport ! Anche una nipote del Papa spinta da curiosita morbosa, volle vedere l'estasi in cui cadeva Caterina dopo la Communione, e per accertarsene, nascostamente, trafisse il piede della santa con uno spillone d'oro !

Alla presenza del Pontefice la vergine domenicana perorò la causa dei ribelli fiorentini, ne ebbe delle lusinghiere promesse. Ma sotto il fiore si nasconde la vipera in agguato ; cosi quando vennero gli ambasciatori, con molto ritardo, e Caterina festosa, andò loro incontro, si sentì dire freddamente : *Chi ti conosce ? noi non abbiamo nessun mandato di trattare con te.*

L'amarezza e lo schianto fu enorme e vedersi sfuggire di mano l'ulivo di pace lungamente sognato, le dettò quella tremenda lettera a Buonaccorso di Lapo, dove bolla a sangue con parole roventi la viltà dei reggitori della republica. La lettera della Santa vale piu di qualunque documento d'archivio, che invano gli studiosi cercheranno, poichè se quei signori pensavano in cuor loro di ingannare così vergognosamente una serva di Dio chiamata nel momento della paura, ebbero almeno il pudore di non lasciare traccia nei loro archivi della loro fellonia.

Ma i Santi hanno la virtu di sapere dimenticare e di sapere aspettare ; l'ulivo non era ancora maturo, e ci vollero altri due anni di passione dolorosa, prima che Caterina potesse dare ai Fiorentini la pace, ciò che fu nel luglio del 1378.

Frattanto i destini del mondo si maturavano in Avignone sotto la possente pressione di Caterina ; la pace con Firenze era un semplice episodio, un'occasione fortunata per lo svolgimento del piano completo ideato e perseguito da quella donna eccezionale con acume profondo e volontà ferrea. Nessun fatto grande, ripeto, si poteva compiere, nè la crociata, nè la pace, nè la riforma della Chiesa senza risolvere il problema centrale : il ritorno del Papato a Roma. Ora che la Provvidenza a messo Caterina a contatto con Gregorio XI, ammalato di volontà, la santa ebbe l'immediata intuizione, sentì che era l'ora di Dio, sentì che non era ambasciatrice dei Fiorentini, ma la voce, la coscienza, il grido della cristianità e specialmente dell'Italia, che non voleva piu un Papato francese, e operò come superna messaggera di pace.

La questione è complessa e grave, bisognava quindi affrontarla con calma e serenità. Un fatto è fuori di discussione : Gregorio XI ritorna a Roma mentre Caterina era in Avignone.

Ora storici e critici si domandano : quale e quanta parte ebbe Caterina in quell'avvenimento ? Le conclusioni sono diametralmente opposte : per gli uni l'intervento della vergine senese fu decisivo, per gli altri fu quasi nulla e quel poco fu enormente esagerato dai discepoli della Santa quali falsari. Alludo al signor Robert Fawtier, di cui molti ànno gia sentito parlare.

Il Fawtier, è bene affermarlo a suo onore, à una preparazione unica in materia, i documenti trovati, le scoperte di scritti preziosi ne ànno fatto un benemerito della letteratura cateriniana. L'appunto grave, gravissimo che bisogna fargli e che ha impostato il suo lavoro sulle fonte cateriniane col preconcetto che i discepoli ànno alterato, anzi deformata e falsificata l'opera della Santa ; e conclude che dalle loro testimonianze lo storico non può prendere nulla o quasi nulla. E il metodo ipercritico, fortunatamente già superato e condannato. Un altro errore fondamentale à commesso il Fawtier quando nell'esame delle fonti cateriniane esclude i documenti personali di Caterina, cioè le lettere, perchè, egli dice, non sono autografe, e poi rimaneggiate dai discepoli e alcune sono apocrife, anzi giunge con una leggerezza imperdonabile ad affermare che quella stupenda lettera dove Caterina con parola e stile personalissimo racconta la decapitazione di Toldo perugino è apocrifa, ed opera di fra Tommaso Caffarini. Tutta la sua critica poi è un'asprezza, un accanimento che sconcerta, e fa sorgere la domanda : perchè tutto questo ?

L'accanimento contro fra Raimondo da Capua e il Caffarini raggiunge un diapason pauroso, specialmente quando si tratta dell'opera politica di Caterina ; quale la pace con Firenze ed il ritorno del Papato in Roma.

Dopo avere concluso a pag. 180 che Caterina non ebbe nessuna ambasceria, pubblica o segreta presso il Papa in Avignone, portando cosi un nuovo colpo alla veridicità di fra Raimondo da Capua, soggiunge :

" Questa constatazione sulla veracità della leggenda maggiore prende una grande importanza quando si vuole studiare un altro intervento della nostra Santa durante il suo soggiorno in Avignone. E' infatti a quest'epoca che Gregorio XI, prendendo la decisione di riportare a Roma la capitale della cristianità, influiva, determinando la crisi del grande scisma con tutte le sue conseguenze, influiva sull'evoluzione storica della Chiesa, dell'Europa ed anche del mondo intiero.

" Ora la *legenda maior*, dà alla nostra Santa una parte importante in questa risoluzione del Papa e ne fa la vera autrice del ritorno del papato in Italia. A dir vero, (aggiunge con sarcasmo), questa bella storia è stata un po' contradetta dalle ricerche degli storici moderni. E' stato dimostrato che Gregorio XI aveva da lungo tempo l'idea di lasciare Avignone, e che il 1 agosto 1375 aveva solennemente annunziato la sua intenzione di partire nella Pasqua del 1376. Malgrado tutto questo si continua ad ammettere la missione importante di Caterina. Ella avrebbe coi suoi propositi e colle sue lettere sostenuto la vacillante volontà del Papa. Nel fatto ella sarebbe stata la causa morale del ritorno a Roma."

A conforto, a documentazione di tutto questo, il Fawtier, dopo aver fatta la rara scoperta che Gregorio non conosceva l'italiano, e che per parlare con Caterina usava come interprete fra Raimondo da Capua ; dopo aver notato che nei racconti degli storici e cronisti contemporanei sul ritorno del Papato, non si accenna a Caterina, dopo aver volutamente trascurate le lettere di Caterina al Papa conchiude : " sembra dunque saggio di non parlare dell'influsso di S. Caterina da Siena nel ritorno del Papato a Roma, influsso che le circostanze rendono inverosimile, e che il silenzio di tutti i documenti contemporanei non ce lo può far accettar senza prova." (Pag. 184.)

Rispondiamo pacatamente : per trattare gli affari anche di somma importanza è necessario conoscere la lingua italiana, come vuole il Fawtier ? Perchè quindi scandalizzarsi e uscire in quell'espressione irriverente : " *è possibile vedere un politico o un legista, quale era Gregorio XI, divenire una marionetta tra le mani di una piccola religiosa di cui non comprendeva nemmeno una parola ?* "

(Pag. 182.) Inoltre : gli storici e i cronisti contemporanei non hanno accennato a Caterina ; bene, ma forse la testimonianza dei discepoli della Santa, testimoni oculari, non ha più valore del silenzio del cronisti preoccupati solo dell'avvenimento da registrare freddamente ? I cronisti ci hanno detto tutto ? Dove è sepolta la storia, io domando : negli archivi o nei camposanti ? La vita tormentata di oggi forse la leggiamo nei giornali ? E' bene notarlo : i fattori morali e spirituali che intervengono nella risoluzione dei grandi problemi sfuggono quasi sempre all'indagine storica.

In ben sedici lettere la Santa parla del ritorno a Roma, sia che scriva a Gregorio XI, ai suoi segretari, o ai Cardinali, insiste con una forze che si fa sempre piu violenta su questo assoluto bisogno di ritornare a Roma : Tutto questo gruppo di lettere non è stato ancora criticamente studiato. Si vedrebbe da un attento esame che tra Gregorio e Caterina vi è stato uno scambio continuo di lettere, di messaggi segreti, direi quasi di una lotta tra la Santa che prepotentemente vuole e Gregorio che oscilla come pendolo e chiede a lei coraggio e forza. Nelle lettere di Caterina appena notiamo degli accenni, dei lampi, poichè di tutto quell'immenso dramma che si svolse ad Avignone dal 1375 al 76 nulla ci è rimasto negli archivi vaticani o francesi, solo degli atti ufficiali che promettevano un ritorno che non avveniva mai e dei rapporti degli ambasciatori.

Tutte le pressioni assillanti, il carattere di Gregorio da parte della Francia, della corte, dei familiari, tutti gli enormi interessi materiali che venivano spezzati con la partenza, gli interessi politici, religiosi, tutto è per sempre sepolto. Fortuna per noi l'Epistolario di Caterina con tanta leggerezza trascurato dal Fawtier !

Ma la verità ha i suoi diritti, e a nessuno è lecito, tanto meno ad un critico, di offenderli. Chi ha deformata la verità non è stato nè fra Raimondo da Capua nè gli altri discepoli, ma è stato il signor Roberto Fawtier. L'accusa è grave, lo so, e la provo.

Mentre da una parte noi ci troviamo di fronte alle lettere di S. Caterina incitanti insistentemente, ardentemente il Pontefice a ritornare a Rcma, dall'altra parte, avvenuto il ritorno, troviamo non solo i cronisti che ignorano l'intervento di Caterina, ma vediamo che i suoi stessi discepoli appena accennano al fatto, anzi cercano di sminuirlo, riducendolo al minimo necessario, fino a farlo dimenticare. Cosi mentre i discepoli svalorizzano l'intervento di Caterina, il Fawtier li accusa formalmente di averlo creato. Dove è la verita ?

Cominciamo dalle Lettere.

Nella lettera 181 a Niccolò di Osimo, segretario di Gregorio XI, scrive : " Pregovi che non allenti il desiderio vostro ne la sollecitudine di pregare il Padre Santo che tosto ne venga e che non indugi più a rizzare l'arme dei fedeli cristiani, la santissima Croce. Non guardate per lo scandalo che ora sia avvenuto (la ribellione dei Fiorentini). Non tema ma virilmente perseveri e tosto mandi ad effetto il santo suo buono proponimento."

Nella lettera 196 a Gregorio XI nella quale implora pace per i figli ribelli, dice : " Oimè, Padre, io muoio di dolore e non posso morire. Venite, venite e non fate più resistenza alla volontà di Dio che vi chiama ; e le affamate pecorelle v'aspettano che veniate a tenere e possedere il luogo del vostro antecessore e campione l'apostolo Pietro. Perchè voi, come Vicario di Cristo, dovete riposarvi nel luogo vostro proprio. Venite dunque, venite, e non piu indugiate ; e confortatevi e non temete d'alcuna cosa che avvenire potesse, perchè Dio sarà con voi ! "

La lettera 206 a Gregorio XI è ancora più forte : " Io vi dico, Padre in Cristo Gesù, che voi veniate tosto come agnello mansueto. Io vi doco : Venite, venite, venite, e non aspettate il tempo, che il tempo non aspetta voi." E più avanti : " Da parte di Cristo Crocifisso vel dico : non vogliate ai consiglieri del demonio che volsero impedire il santo e buono proponimento. Siatemi uomo virile e non timoroso."

Scrivendo a Fr. Raimondo (lettera 211) da lei mandato ad Avignone nel 1376 dice : " Dite a Cristo in terra che non mi faccia piu aspettare. E quando io vedro questo canterò con quello dolce vecchio Simeone : nunc dimittis. . . . "

Importante è la lettera 229 a Gregorio scritta pochi giorni prima di andare ad Avignone : " Padre mio dolce, voi mi dimandate dell'avvenimento vostro, io vi rispondo e dico da parte di Cristo Crocifisso che veniate il piu tosto che potete. Se potete venire, venite prima di Settembre. E non mirate a veruna contradizione che voi aveste, ma come uomo virile e senza alcun timore, venite."

Le lettere scritte a Gregorio XI durante la permanenza ad Avignone sono tutte sul ritorno ed in forma polemica.

Mentre Caterina, sia da lontano che in Avignone, scrive queste possenti lettere al Papa, il Pontefice, in perpetua altalena, un giorno che era alla sua presenza, le domandava : " Cosa ne pensi del viaggio di ritorno a Roma ? " E qui avviene un fatto strano. Quella donna che nelle lettere ci apparisce un angelo ed una divina suscitratrice di energie, di fronte alla persona del Pontefice si tace, si umilia, si scusa e parla solo quando Gregorio XI le impone per ubbidienza, non di darle consiglio ma di fargli conoscere la volonta di Dio. Come spiegare questo ? Umiltà di santa o misteri della natura femminile ? Forse. Caterina, scusandosi ancora, risponde : " Chi meglio di vostra Santità conosce la volontà celeste, voi che faceste voto a Dio di ritornare a Roma ? "

Questa conoscenza del segreto suo voto fece finalmente decidere Gregorio XI al ritorno, e rotti tutti gli indugi, opponendosi energicamente a tutte le pressioni dei Cardinali, della Corte, del Re di Francia, dei parenti, del proprio Padre che buttatosi sulla soglia gli impediva il passaggio, superando la crisi finanziaria che lo tormentava, facendo persino un debito di 80 mila fiorini d'oro, finalmente lasciò Avignone, e dopo un viaggio ostacolato anche dagli elementi ritornò a Roma.

Di fronte a questo fatto capitale che fu il pernio di tutta la storia del papato, di fronte a quest'intervento provvidenziale di Caterina, fra Raimondo da Capua, presente al fatto ed interprete tra lei e il Pontefice, è di una laconicità sconcertante : egli così prolisso quando si tratta della pace tra Firenze e il Pontefice per mezzo di Caterina diviene in questo fatto di una estrema riservatezza : se la cava con tre sole parole : " ipsa eum inducente " : dietro suo consiglio.

Stefano Maconi che fu Generale dei Certosini, anch'egli presente in Avignone che mette una nota personalissima quando racconta le cose viste, dice : " Post haec vero ipse summus Pontifex venit ad urbem romanam, ipsa virgine *sacratissima solummodo confortante, tamen ex divino praecepto, prout apertissime mihi constat.*" Sembra che il Maconi tema chi sa quali alterazioni sull'intervento di Caterina nel ritorno del Papato.

Fra Bartolomeo Dominici, altro discepolo presente in Avignone, ci informa sulla scena voltatasi tra Gregorio XI e Caterina, e si limita a dirci che solo dopo aver la Santa rivelato a Gregorio il suo voto il viaggio fu deciso. Un altro discepolo, il notaio Guidini, che non era presente, nelle sue memorie scrive : *"Andò prima a Vignone, e tanto adoperò che la Corte si partì da Vignone e tornò a Roma."*

Il loquace Fra Tommaso Caffarini, che raccolse tutto ciò che poteva essere onorifico per Caterina, diviene muto come un pesce, solo nel *Supplementum* (cosi sapientemente studiato dalla Signora de Sanctis) ci rivela il fatto svoltosi a Genova, quando Gregorio XI preso di nuovo dai suoi dubbi e sentendosi vacillare, notte tempo va nella casa ove era Caterina per avere un colloquio con Lei, che ne sostiene i propositi e lo sospinge verso Roma. Il fatto il Caffarini, a scanso di equivoci, dice che lo ha saputo da un certo fra Securiano. . . .

Dall'esame sia delle lettere che delle testimonianze ne seguono due conseguenze : la prima e la dimenticanza completa da parte dei discepoli delle lettere di Caterina al Papa ; la seconda una preoccupazione costante nei discepoli di ridurre il fatto dell'intervento di Caterina nella decisione del Pontefice ai minimi termini, ad una semplicissima notizia di cronaca ; nessun elemento che ci possa spingere a sospettare una valorizzazione e tanto meno una falsificazione o deturpazione della verità. Riesce quindi strana l'accusa rivolta dal Fawtier ai discepoli di Caterina, e questo sol perchè non trova i pezzi d'appoggio o di controllo in documenti d'archivio. L'attendibilità di un testo non si ha solo dai pezzi d'appoggio ma da tutti quegli elementi ed esami che la critica storica ha a sua disposizione e che il Fawtier trascura.

La più elementare critica gli imponeva il dovere di conoscere di fronte a quali personalità egli si trovava, se capaci di mentire o alterare anche in buona fede i fatti, metterli nell'ambiente storico in cui vissero, farceli vedere come attori in quel turbinoso periodo storico che avvolse la Chiesa e la società sullo scorcio del secolo XIV, quando la cristianità divisa dallo scisma, parteggiante per Roma o per Avignone aveva bisogno di caretteri, di sacerdoti. I discepoli di Caterina furono degli attori principali di quel dramma, li troviamo tra i più fieri lottatori per la romanità del papato, non avevano quindi bisogno di *creare la leggenda* del ritorno del papato a Roma per opera di Caterina : tanto piu che quella leggenda si opponeva anzi era un ostacolo grave alla realizzazione dell'ideale che animava i discepoli di Caterina : *la sua canonizzazione.*

Ecco la vera causa di quel problema che il Fawtier non ha saputo nè voluto vedere, preoccupato ciecamente dal suo lavoro di demolizione. I demolitori sono i primi a subire gli effetti della polvere solevata dalla macerie.

La chiave di questo problema il Fawtier l'aveva nelle mani, l'ha vista, l'ha esaminata, doveva pubblicarla e l'ha taciuta. *Un critico deve essere innanzi tutto onesto !*

A pagina 30 del suo studio, il Signor Fawtier, esaminando tutte le deposizioni componenti il processo di canonizzazione, di Caterina al N. 19 segna : " *nota supplementare di Tommaso Caffarini priore del Convento di S. Domenico a Venezia, fatta a Venezia il 16 Marzo 1415 e presentata il 20 Luglio 1415.*" Ma si guarda bene dal manifestare ai lettori il contenuto di quella nota supplementare, quando discute quell'argomento. Ora, in quella nota, troviamo la risoluzione del problema che ci interessa. Fra Tommaso Caffarini, che viene di continuo accusato dal Fawtier come uno dei principali demolitori e falsificatori della vera Caterina, quel frate ebbe un immenso amore per la sua santa consorella, e, nell'organizzare il processo di canonizzazione, si accorge che vi erano dei dubbi, delle ombre, offuscanti la figura di Caterina che ostacolavano la sua canonizzazione : la principale era : *di aver consigliato il Pontefice a ritornare a Roma.*

Noi che ci troviamo a distanza di secoli da quel profondo sconvolgimento che turbò la cristianità durante lo scisma d'occidente, in cui due e anche tre pontefici si disputavano la tiara, non possiamo sentire ne comprendere con quanto accanimento da amici e nemici si cercassero le origini dello scisma, come oggi si cercano le origini della guerra ! Naturalmente la causa principale si faceva risalire al ritorno di Gregorio XI, e in conseguenza la figura di Caterina, consigliante il Papa, era additata quale causa efficiente e determinante.

Una serva di Dio, si diceva, che consiglia il ritorno a Rome, da cui ne segue uno scisma, non può essere una santa, poichè quel consiglio non può essere da Dio. *L'avvocato del diavolo* aveva colto nel segno. Lo scandalo nella cristianità era grave.

E che cosa fa il Caffarini, avvocato di Caterina ? In quella lettera sopra citata, scritta nel 1415, mentre più accanito infieriva lo scisma, il buon frate porta quattro ragioni per giustificare l'opera della Santa. Nella prima ricorda la testimonianza di Fra Bartolomeo Dominici con la rivelazione al Papa del suo voto segreto. Quella decisione improvvisa, dice il Caffarini, fece credere a tutti che Caterina avesse spinto il Papa a tornare. Questa era la voce comune nella cristianità. Ma Caterina non persuase il Papa, insiste il Caffarini, ma solo rivelò il voto. Ridotto a queste proporzioni il fatto, il Caffarini nelle altre tre ragioni cerca timidamente di scagionare ancor più Caterina, con esempi presi dall'antico e dal nuovo Testamento circa i mali gravissimi che vennero dal ritorno a Roma, aggiungendo poi che ne vennero anche dei beni, come la pace con Firenze ; e perciò egli conclude, l'accusa che si fa a Caterina che il consiglio dato non era da Dio, è falsa.

Per i discepoli quindi il ritorno a Roma del papato voluto da Lei formava una nube sulla santità della loro Madre, era un grave scoglio per la canonizzazione, un fatto da sorvolare, da tacere per non creare difficoltà ; non un argomento per esaltare la sua opera e far di lei una eroina del papato.

Perchè, domando, il Fawtier ha taciuta quella nota supplementare rivelatrice che aveva nelle mani ? Come si permette in nome della critica non solo di capovolgere i fatti, accusando i discepoli, ma di ingannare il pubblico, che non conoscendo i documenti ha fiducia nella sincerità e nella obbiettività del critico ? Quella nota supplementare del Caffarini ci spiega limpidamente tutta la laconicità usata dai discepoli quando sono costretti a parlare del ritorno a Roma, ci spiega perchè fra Raimondo se la cava con tre sole parole, perche Don Stefano Maconi insiste in quel *tantummodo confortante,* come il Caffarini taccia metodicamente, e ci spiega anche la voluta dimenticanza dei discepoli delle numerose lettere invocanti il ritorno del Papa, cosi come le ha volute dimenticare il Fawtier. Io metterei in stato d'accusa anche i discepoli come testimoni reticenti. Se un rimprovero era dunque da fare ai caterinati era di aver per paura sminuita l'opera di Caterina, mai di averla creata.

I posteri invece sorvolando sulla paura dei discepoli e sulle melanconie degli impercritici dicono e diranno sempre che il papato a Roma è tornato per opera di Caterina.

P. Innocenzo Taurisano, O.P.

APPENDIX III

NOTES AND DOCUMENTATION

1.—Reference to minutiae and to all that is generally accepted in the Saint's life is omitted for economy of space.

2.—The following abbreviations are used throughout these Notes :—

Leg.   The *Leggenda Maggiore* by Raimondo delle Vigne da Capua, Italian translation, Gigli, Vol. I, reprinted in Rome, 1866.

Leg. Min.   Caffarini's Summary of the *Leggenda Maggiore*, or *Leggenda Minore*, Grottanelli, Bologna, 1868.

Lett.   The Letters of Saint Catherine as numbered in Piero Misciattelli's edition, Siena, Libreria Editrice Giuntini Bentivoglio & C., 1922, Six Volumes, Third Edition.

     The translations of the letters are original and in most cases the excerpts given are abridged or condensed.

Mir.   " Miracoli di S. Caterina da Siena," as printed in Appendix I, " Sainte Catherine de Sienne—Essai de Critique des Sources," R. Fawtier, E. De Boccard, Paris, 1921.

Proc.   *Processus*, either as published in Martène et Durand, Vol. VI, or as indicated.

PART I

CHAPTER I

Page 6. Paragraph 1.—*Monna Lapa.* For her shrewish character, cf. Mir. 6 : *Se io ti metto mano ne' capelli, io te ne cavero più di sette*, etc.

Page 14. Paragraph 2.—*The Third Order of St. Dominic.* For a copy of the fourteenth-century rule, see " La Regola del Terzo Ordine," by P. Misciattelli, in *Studi Cateriniani*, Anno III, No. 1-2. Compare this with the last version of the Rule approved in Rome, 1926, published by the Collegio Angelico.

CHAPTER II

Page 19. Paragraph 2.—*Catherine's explanation of ecstasy :* Dialogo, Cap. LXXIX, Gigli, Vol. III, p. 100.

Page 21. Paragraph 2.—*Temptations.* Cf. Interior Castle of St. Teresa, Dalton, London (Baker), 1893, pp. 129-131.

Page 26. Paragraph 2.—*Catherine resumes family life :* That the mere odour of food must have been insupportable is shown by Leg. I, Ch. VI, 2 : " *non potea senza nocumento del corpo ne pur sopportarne l'odore.*"

257

Chapter III

Page 28. Paragraph 1. *Lisa Columbini*, wife of Catherine's *half-brother :* for interesting details of Catherine's family see Fawtier, *op. cit.*, pp. 133, 134.

Page 29. Paragraph 2.—*Catherine's almsgiving*. Cf. " The Early Italian Poets," translated by D. G. Rossetti, London, Dent, 1908. Sonnets of Folgore da San Geminiano, February, p. 79 ; December, p. 84, Dedication, p. 85.

Page 32. Paragraph 2.—*The Misericordia*. In Catherine's day, this hospital was on the site of the present Galleria delle Belle Arti.

Page 33. Paragraph 2.—Ecclesiastical affairs. Cf. *History of the Popes*, Pastor, London, Kegan Paul, Vol. I, Book I.

Chapter IV

Page 47. Paragraph 1.—*Catherine's sayings*. Cf. Letts. Nos. 193, 258, 211, 144, and Dialogo, Cap. CXXXVIII.

Page 48. Paragraph 2.—*Catherine's first letters*. Cf. Leg. Min. Grottanelli, Notes, p. 211 and Lett. No. 225.

Page 49. Paragraph 1.—*Neri di Landoccio*. Letts. Nos. 99, 25, 29, 44 and 69

Page 50.—*Patience and sense of the value of time*. Cf. Letts. Nos. 13 and 110.

Page 54. Paragraph 2.—*Fra Simone*. Cf. Dep. Fra Simone da Cortona, Proc. Bib. Cas. Rome. MS. 2668 and *Lettere dei Discepoli*, No. XV (Misciattelli, Vol. VI).

Page 56. Paragraph 2.—*Ser Cristofano*. The best idea of this personage may be had from his own " Memorie," Ed. C. Milanesi in Arch. Stor. It., Seria I, Vol. IV, pp. 25-47. Cf. Lett. No. 43.

Page 59. Paragraph 3.—*William Flete*, cf. Lett. No. 77.

Page 60. Paragraph 2.—*Mamma*. Cf. Lettere de' Discepoli, Misciattelli, Vol. VI and Leg. Min. Grottanelli, Notes, p. 234.

Chapter V

Page 65.—*Work for the Crusade*. Lett. No. 66.

Page 67. Paragraph 2.—*Letters to the Cardinal d'Estaing and to Marmoutier* Nos. 7 and 109.

Page 69. Paragraph 2.—*Letter to the Visconti*, No. 28.

Chapter VI

Page 75. Paragraph 2.—*Plague in Siena*, Ensamples, Heywood, p. 82.

Page 79. Paragraph 2.—Catherine's first letter to Gregory is not extant.

Page 80. Paragraph 1.—*Work for the Crusade in Pisa*, Letts. Nos. 133, 138, 143, 145.

Page 81. Paragraph 1.—*Letter to John Hawkwood*, No. 140. For an account of this personage, see *Giovanni Acuto*, by Temple-Leader and Marcotti, Florence, 1889.

Page 81.   Paragraph 3.—*El Bianco.*   See his Laudi Spirituali, No. 72 (Lucca, Bini, 1851).   Lett. No. 92.

Page 84.   Paragraph 2.—*Letter about Niccolò di Toldo,* No. 273.   Cf. Appendix II (a), Page 222.

CHAPTER VII

Page 87.   Paragraph 1.—*The Tuscan League.*   See A. Gherardi, *La Guerra dei Fiorentini con Papa Gregorio XI.*   In Archivio Storico Italiano, Seria III, Vol. V, VI, VII, VIII.

Page 89.   Paragraph 2.—*Pisa again.*   Lett. No. 139.

Page 91.   Paragraph 2.—*Second letter to Gregory XI.*   No. 185.

Page 93.—*Third letter to Gregory,* No. 196.   Also Letter No. 171 to Soderini.

Page 94.   Paragraph 3.—*Abbot of Marmoutier.*   For details of his release from Perugia, see *Giovanni Acuto, op. cit.,* p. 81.

Page 95.   Paragraph 2.—*Delle Vigne goes to Avignon.*   Lett. No. 206.

Page 97.   Paragraph 3.—*Neri goes to Avignon.*   Letts. Nos. 211, 226, 228 and 218.

Page 99.   Paragraph 3.—*Catherine offers Florence her services.*   Lett. No. 207, Lett. No. 229.

CHAPTER VIII

Page 102.   Paragraph 1.—Dr. Fawtier (*op. cit.* p. 182) paints a different portrait of Gregory XI : " . . . *dont tout le monde s'accorde à reconnaître la ferme volonté.*"   Cf. Appendix III and Capecelatro, *Storia di S. Caterina da Siena,* Libro Terzo.

Page 103.   Paragraph 2.—*Letter to the Eight of War.*   No. 230.

Page 106.—*Letter to Di Lapo.*   No. 234.

Page 107.   Paragraph 2.—*Louis d'Anjou.*   Cf. Valois, *La France et le Grand Schisme,* Vol. I, p. 145.   Letts. Nos. 238, 235.

Page 109.   Paragraph 3.—*Seventh, eight and ninth letters to Gregory,* Nos. 231, 233, 239.

Page 111.   Paragraph 2.—*Gregory leaves Avignon.*   Capecelatro, *op cit.,* Libro Quinto.

Readers familiar with the sources will notice that we have omitted the information that Catherine revealed to Gregory her knowledge of a secret vow he had taken to restore the Holy See to Rome.   It is related by Bartolomeo Dominici in his Deposition (*Proc.,* col. 1325) that Gregory questioned Catherine about his return to Rome and she answered : " It is not meet that a wretched little woman should give advice to the Sovereign Pontiff."   The Pope insisted : " I do not ask you for advice, but to tell me the will of God in this matter."   As she still made excuses, he charged her on her obedience to say if she knew the will of God in the affair. Whereupon Catherine bowed her head, saying : " Who knoweth this better than your Holiness, who vowed to God that you would do this thing."   Gregory was so impressed by her knowledge of his secret vow, that this conversation put an end to his irresolution.   This episode was omitted because of the excessive difficulty of welding it into the text in such wise as to make it coherent.   Already by letter, and in no unmistakable terms, Catherine had told Gregory five times what the will of God was in the matter of restoring the Holy See to Rome. They had even arrived at discussing the month of departure *before* she arrived in Avignon. Why then Gregory should ask her such a question at that stage is a mystery. More mysterious still is Catherine's attitude, utterly out of line with all our knowledge of her. On no other occasion in her life did she think herself unqualified to advise the Pope. Father Taurisano wonders if the episode can be explained by the mysteries of feminine nature! (See Appendix [II], c.) But Catherine always exhibited masculine force of mind, and none of that freakish irrationality usually attributed to women. Besides, the Pope's share in the conversation is just as puzzling. The present writer's conviction is that Bartolomeo Dominici (with all the great respect due to him) unconsciously coloured this conversation—another instance of the disciples' bewilderment in face of the attacks on Catherine as having provoked the schism. It is well to remember also that Bartolomeo Dominici's testimony is the only evidence controlled by his colleagues. Caffarini rectified it once and Maconi on another occasion. (Cf. Fawtier, *op. cit.*, p. 37 and p. 185, N. 1.) Everything considered, it seemed preferable to stress the material reasons for the transfer of the Holy See, stressed by Catherine herself in her letters to Gregory.

Page 115. Paragraph 1.—*Letter to Monna Lapa*, No. 240.

Page 115. Paragraph 2.—*Letter to Monna Maconi*, No. 267.

Page 115. Paragraph 3.—*Pisa*. Cf. *Lettere dei Discepoli*, No. V.

Page 116. Paragraph 2.—*Stefano's letters to Neri*. *Lettere dei Discepoli*, Nos. V, VI.

Page 117. Paragraph 2.—*Gregory in Rome*. Cf. Lett. No. 231.

CHAPTER IX

Page 119. Paragraph 1.—*Malavolti*. Lett. No. 45.

Page 120. Paragraph 2.—*Cesena*. Cf. Gherardi, *op. cit.*, and *Giovanni Acuto*, *op. cit.*, p. 95.

Page 121. Paragraph 2.—*Letter to Gregory*, No. 270.

Page 121. Paragraph 3.—*The Salimbeni tangle*. Cf. *S. Caterina da Siena ed i Salimbeni*, Eugenio Lazzareschi, Rome, 1927.

Page 123. Paragraph 2.—*Letter to Monna Lapa*, No. 117 ; to friends in Siena, No. 118.

Page 124. Paragraph 2.—*Letter to the Government of Siena*, No. 123.

Page 125. Paragraph 2.—*Letter about slanders*, No. 122.

Page 125. Paragraph 3.—*Second letter to the Government of Siena*, No. 121.

Page 126. Paragraph 3.—*Letter to Gregory*, No. 285.

Page 127. Paragraph 3.—*Last extant letter to Gregory*, No. 255 ; to Delle Vigne, No. 267.

Page 129. Paragraph 1.—*Monna Tolomei*. Lett. No. 120.

Page 130. Paragraph 1.—" *That Other*," *Lettere dei Discepoli*, Nos. 7, 8. Cf. Lett. No. 192 to Neri. There are various speculations as to the identity of that other, cf. Gardner, *Saint Catherine of Siena*, pp. 218-221.

Page 131. Paragraph 3.—*Letter to Alessa*. Lett. No. 119.

Page 133. Paragraph 1.—*Admonishing*. Cf. Gherardi, *op. cit.*, p. 120, Vol. V.

Page 134. Paragraph 1.—*Death of Gregory.* One still occasionally reads the statement that Gregory, on his deathbed, solemnly warned his cardinals against the alleged revelations of women, this being interpreted to mean Saint Catherine and Gregory therefore finally repented having followed her advice. The historian, Gerson, is supposed to be responsible for the statement. Cf. Capecelatro, *op. cit.*, Libro Sesto, for a refutation of the authenticity of this passage and a long discussion of the whole point. Dr. Fawtier (*op. cit.*, p. 183), quoting from a later edition of Gerson than that used by Cardinal Capecelatro, accepts the authenticity of the statement, but, despite his admiration for Gerson, denies its credibility. It is anyhow against the facts : Gregory was irresolute, but certainly not to the point of folly, as this account of his death would imply. Also, whatever the estrangement between him and Catherine may have been, they were reconciled some months before his death. Cf. Letter No. 272, in which Catherine tells Delle Vigne she has been consoled by a letter from the *dolce babbo.* Further, Gregory had sent Catherine to Florence, where she was loyally working for him at the moment of his death.

Page 135. Paragraph 1.—*Urban VI.* Cf. Capecelatro, *op. cit.*, Libro Ottavo, for a discussion of the various accounts of this pontiff.

Page 135. Paragraph 2.—*Hope of peace.* Letts. Nos. 227 and 277.

Page 136. Paragraph 1.—*Revolt in Florence.* Cf. Capponi's account in *Tumulto de' Ciompi*, pp. 234-242.

Page 137. Paragraph 1.—Lett. No. 295.

Page 137. Paragraph 3.—*Letter to Urban.* No. 291.

Page 138. Paragraph 1.—*Letter to Sano di Maco*, No. 303.

Page 139. Paragraph 1.—*Farewell to Florence*, Lett. No. 12. (Vol. VI, M.)

Page 139. Paragraph 2.—*Bad news from Rome.* The history of the Schism fused into this biography is based on *La France et le Grand Schisme d'Occident*, par Noel Valois, Paris (Picard & Fils), 1896, 4 Vols. He is the single historian of the Schism who endeavours consistently to reconcile Urbanist and Clementine evidence, thus approaching a true version of what occurred.

CHAPTER X

Page 140. Paragraph 1.—*The Conclave of* 1378. Cf. Capecelatro, *op. cit.*, Libro Ottavo. Pastor, Vol. I, p. 117. Valois, Vol. I, pp. 8-55. For an interesting discussion of the cardinals' measure of fear *before* the Conclave, see pp. 14-19.

Page 141. Paragraph 3.—*Tebaldeschi.* Cf. Valois, Vol. I, pp. 53 and 62.

Page 142. Paragraph 2.—*Urban's reforming zeal.* Valois, Vol. I, pp. 67-72.

Page 143. Paragraph 1.—*Prior of Gorgona's letter. Lett. dei Discepoli*, No. 3 and Letts. No. 302 and 291.

Page 144. Paragraph 2.—*Letters to the Cardinal de Luna*, Nos. 284 and 293.

Page 145. Paragraph 4.—*Schism.* Cf. Valois, Vol. I, pp. 74-80.

Page 146. Paragraph 2.—*Letter to the Count of Fondi*, No. 313.

To the Three Italian Cardinals, No. 310. The date of this letter is generally assigned to after Catherine's arrival in Rome. It has been quoted before her departure from Siena in the present work for the sake of greater coherence and because the text is substantially the same as that of Letter No. 312, to the Queen of Naples, which was certainly written in October.

Page 148. Paragraph 1.—*Letter to Urban*, No. 305.

Page 148. Paragraph 2.—*Election of rival Pope.* Letter No. 306. Cf Valois, Vol. 1, p. 80, pp. 97-101 and pp. 107-108.

Page 149. Paragraph 3.—*The Dialogue.* The assertion that Catherine dictated the book in four days is often ridiculed, but it is not an impossibility. Cf. Dep. F. Malavolti, Lazzareschi, *op. cit.*, for description of her method of dictating. Cf. *Memorie di Ser Cristofano*, p. 37. Quotations are from Cap. LXIV and Cap. III.

Page 152. Paragraph 4.—*Clement is crowned.* Valois, Vol. I, pp. 80-82. For the false prophecies pullulating out of the schism, see Pastor, Vol. I, p. 151. Cf. the conclusion of Valois (Vol. I, p. 82) : " La solution du grand problème posé au XIVe siècle échappe au jugement de l'histoire," with Pastor's (Vol. I, p. 120) : " It cannot, indeed, be denied that the election of Urban VI was canonically valid " ; and Valois, Vol. IV, pp. 502, 503 : " Les pères de Constance n'avaient point cherché a débrouiller le problème ardu posé en 1378 . . . Cette neutralité de l'Englise devait longtemps durer. On peut même dire qu'elle dure encore : car la question n'a jamais été tranchée dogmatiquement. Tout au plus s'est-il établi en faveur de la légitimité des papes de Rome une tradition que les investigations de l'histoire tendent à confirmer."

Page 153. Paragraph 2.—*Failure of Crusade through Schism.* Lett. No. 340. Cf. Leg. II, Ch. X, 12, 13.

Page 154. Paragraph 3.—*Failure of Church reform.* Cf. Pastor, Vol. I, p. 141. Lett. No. 109.

Page 155. Paragraph 3.—*Catherine blamed for Schism.* Cf. Taurisano in Appendix III (b) and (c). See also the brilliant article on the *Processus* by Signora Emilia De Sanctis Rosmini in " Studi Cateriniani," Anno III, N. 3, 1926, p. 93. This article has been reprinted and amplified in " Letture Cateriniane della R. Università di Siena," Libreria Editrice Senese, Siena, 8th August, 1928, pp. 265-309 ; see particularly p. 291 with reference to this point. The testimonies of Mino di Vanni and Caffarini, taken in conjunction, are of the greatest interest as affording some insight into *contemporary* opinion regarding the Schism and the Saint's work. Cf. Piero Misciattelli : (Studi Cateriniani, Anno III, N. 1-2, " La Romanità di S. Caterina," p. 19) :

> " La vera tragedia di Caterina, tragedia spirituale che i suoi storici non hanno avvertita, si generò dal fatto che il ritorno a Roma del Pontefice, da Lei invocato ed in gran parte determinato, cui seguì la nomina al Sommo Soglio di un italiano, fu la causa del grande scisma religioso nella Chiesa. Ella ebbe subito la coscienza del danno immenso che il trionfo politico da Lei ottenuto minacciava a le anime, e si accinse alla difesa dell'unità romana della Chiesa, cioè del Pastore Italiano, con l'impeto disperato della Sua passione."

Cf. also Taurisano, Appendix [II] (b) and (c).

PART II

CHAPTER I

Page 159.—*Course of Schism.* Cf. Valois, Vol. II, p. 9 and pp. 65, 66.

Page 160. Paragraph 1.—*Asks for written order to go to Rome.* The letter in question has not been preserved.

Page 160. Paragraph 2.—*Preparing for Rome.* Lett. No. 13, Vol. VI, Misciattelli.

Page 162. Paragraph 2.—*Lando di Francesco's report.* Lett. dei Discepoli, No. 10.

Page 162. Paragraph 3.—*The position in Rome.* Valois, Vol. I, pp. 158-163. Cf. p. 169.

Page 163. Paragraph 2.—*Raimondo's embassy to France.* Charles V had already secretly declared for Clement. Cf. Valois, Vol. I, p. 112.

Page 164. Paragraph 2.—*Embassy to Queen of Naples.* Cf. St. Bridget of Sweden, Steele, London, Washbourne, 1909. Letts. Nos. 312, 317.

Page 165. Paragraph 3.—*Raimondo leaves Rome.* Cf. Valois, Vol. I, p. 124.

Page 166. Paragraph 3.—*Sketch of Urban.* Cf. Pastor, Vol. I, pp. 136, 137. Valois, Vol. I, pp. 34, 35 and Vol. II, pp. 112-118 and 151-157.

Page 167.—*Future course of Schism.* For Catherine's prophetical spirit in connection with this, see Leg. II, Chap. X, 10 : " Questo e un giuoco di fanciulli," etc.

CHAPTER II

Page 168. Paragraph 2.—*Report of Lando di Francesco.* Quoted by Fawtier, *op. cit.*, p. 56, N. 1. For Urban's Bull to the Prior of Gorgona, see Gigli, Vol. II, p. 366.

Page 169. Paragraph 2.—Letts. Nos. 323, 326, 327, 322.

Page 171. Paragraph 2.—Lett. No. 330.

Page 171. Paragraph 3.—Lett. No. 324.

Page 171. Paragraph 4.—Lett. No. 329.

Page 171. Paragraph 5.—Cf. Lettera di ser Barduccio a suor Caterina Petriboni. Gigli, Vol. I.

Page 172. Paragraph 1.—*Raimondo's failure.* Cf. Valois, Vol. I, p. 124.

Page 172. Paragraph 2.—*Raimondo's second embassy.* Cf. Valois, Vol. I, pp. 312, 313.

Page 173. Paragraph 2.—Lett. No. 344.

Page 174. Paragraph 2.—*Abbot of Sant' Antimo.* Lett. No. 344 and cf. Lett. No. 121.

Page 174. Paragraph 3.—*William Flete.* Memorie di Ser Cristofano, p. 34. Flete's behaviour is sometimes defended by saying he was working for Urban by his letters to England, which inspired the *Rationes Anglicorum*, etc. This, however, is very doubtful. Cf. Fawtier, *op. cit.*, pp. 59-66.

Page 175. Paragraph 2.—Lett. No. 328.

Page 176. Paragraph 2.—*Don John of the Cells.* Cf. Pastor, Vol. I, pp. 145 and 151, N. Lett. No. 27, Sorio.

Page 176. Paragraph 3.—Lett. No. 332. Cf. *Lettere dei Discepoli,* Nos. 12, 13, 14.

Page 177. Paragraph 1.—Lett. No. 344.

CHAPTER III

Page 179. Paragraph 1.—*Alberigo da Barbiano.* Lett. No. 347. Valois, Vol. I, p. 169.

Page 180. Paragraph 2.—*Castel Sant' Angelo and Marino.* Valois, Vol. I, pp. 164 and 169-172.

Page 180. Paragraph 3.—*Clement's movements.* Valois, I, pp. 165-174. Cf. Pastor, Vol. I, pp, 132, 133.

Page 181. Paragraph 3.—Lett. No. 349.

Page 182. Paragraph 1.—Letts. Nos. 349, 348.

Page 182. Paragraph 3.—Cf. Capecelatro, *op. cit.*, Libro Nono. Valois, Vol. I, p. 178.

Page 183. Paragraph 2, *et seq.*—Letts. Nos. 310, 350, 311, 367, 321, 368, 337, 339, 357, 372, 334, 338, 341, 345, 352, 353, 354, 356, 360, 361, 336, 340, and No. 16, Vol. VI, etc.

N.B.—For the chronology of Catherine's political letters we have accepted that established by the Baroness von Seckendorff in *Die kirchen-politische Taetigkeit der hl. Katharina von Siena unter Papst Gregor XI,* Berlin, 1917. This work is reviewed in "Studi Cateriniani," An. 1, N. 3, by Eugenio Dupre Theseider, who gives a useful table of the chronology resulting from the researches of the Baroness von Seckendorff. Occasionally, however, for the coherence of the story, the strict chronological order of the letters is not adhered to ; as, for instance, in the above paragraph, which contains reference to the letter to the Three Italian Cardinals, previously quoted more fully in Part I, Chapter X, p. 146.

Page 185. Paragraph 3.—Lett. No. 362. Cf. Valois, I, p. 178. Letts. Nos. 364 and 370.

Page 188. Paragraph 2.—Lett. No. 369 and Lett. No. VIII, Vol. VI.

Page 189. Paragraph 1.—Lett. No. 370.

CHAPTER IV

Page 190. Paragraph 1.—*Lettere dei Discepoli,* Misciattelli, Vol. VI, Nos. 11, 12, 13, 14.

Page 191. Paragraph 2.—Ibidem, Nos. 15, 16.

Page 193.—*Catherine's mystical experiences.* Lett. No. 373.

Page 201.—*Death of Catherine.* Lettera da ser Barduccio a suor Caterina.

CHAPTER V

Page 205. Paragraph 4.—*Ser Cristofano.* Cf. his Memorie, frequently cited.

Page 205. Paragraph 5.—*Lettere dei Discepoli,* No. 46.

Page 207.—*Lettere dei Discepoli,* Nos. 19, 21, 23, 24, 25, 27, 32, 34, 35, 36, 42.

CHAPTER VI

Page 208.—Cf. Bibliography I. See *Lettere dei Discepoli,* Nos. 29, 30, 31, 37, 43 and 44. All information about the International Society for Catherine Studies may be had from the Secretary, Donna Francesca Curci-Sofio, Piazza Umberto I, Siena.

INDEX